PRIVATE MORTGAGE INVESTING

How to Earn 12% or More on
Your Savings, Investments, IRA
Accounts, and Personal Equity:

A Complete Resource Guide with 100s of Hints,
Tips, & Secrets From Experts Who Do It Every Day

REVISED 2nd EDITION

By Martha Maeda, Teri B. Clark,
and Matthew Stewart Tabacchi,
Certified Mortgage Consultant

rivate Mortgage Investing: How to Earn 12% or More on Your Savings, Investments, IRA Accounts, and Personal Equity: *A Complete Resource Guide with 100s of Hints, Tips, & Secrets From Experts Who Do It Every Day REVISED 2nd EDITION*

Copyright © 2011 by Atlantic Publishing Group, Inc.
1405 SW 6th Ave. • Ocala, Florida 34471 • 800-814-1132 • 352-622-1875–Fax
Web site: www.atlantic-pub.com • E-mail: sales@atlantic-pub.com
SAN Number: 268-1250

Maeda, Martha, 1953-
  Private mortgage investing : how to earn 12% or more on your savings, investments, IRA accounts and personal equity : a complete resource guide with 100s of hints, tips & secrets from experts who do it every day / by Martha Maeda, Teri B. Clark and Matthew Stewart Tabacchi. -- Rev. 2nd ed.
    p. cm.
  Includes bibliographical references and index.
  ISBN-13: 978-1-60138-274-0 (alk. paper)
  ISBN-10: 1-60138-274-X (alk. paper)
  1. Mortgage loans--United States. 2. Real estate investment--United States. 3. Real property--United States--Finance. 4. Investments--United States. I. Clark, Teri B. II. Tabacchi, Matthew Stewart. III. Title.
  HG2040.5.U5M325 2010
  332.63'2440973--dc22

                                        2008027226

PROJECT MANAGER: Melissa Peterson • mpeterson@atlantic-pub.com
EDITOR: Brad Goldbach • PROOFREADER: Brett Daly • brett.daly1@gmail.com
COVER DESIGN: Jackie Miller • millerjackiej@gmail.com

Printed on Recycled Paper

Printed in the United States

We recently lost our beloved pet "Bear," who was not only our best and dearest friend but also the "Vice President of Sunshine" here at Atlantic Publishing. He did not receive a salary but worked tirelessly 24 hours a day to please his parents.

Bear was a rescue dog that turned around and showered myself, my wife, Sherri, his grandparents Jean, Bob, and Nancy, and every person and animal he met (maybe not rabbits) with friendship and love. He made a lot of people smile every day.

We wanted you to know that a portion of the profits of this book will be donated to The Humane Society of the United States. *–Douglas & Sherri Brown*

The human-animal bond is as old as human history. We cherish our animal companions for their unconditional affection and acceptance. We feel a thrill when we glimpse wild creatures in their natural habitat or in our own backyard.

Unfortunately, the human-animal bond has at times been weakened. Humans have exploited some animal species to the point of extinction.

The Humane Society of the United States makes a difference in the lives of animals here at home and worldwide. The HSUS is dedicated to creating a world where our relationship with animals is guided by compassion. We seek a truly humane society in which animals are respected for their intrinsic value, and where the human-animal bond is strong.

Want to help animals? We have plenty of suggestions. Adopt a pet from a local shelter, join The Humane Society and be a part of our work to help companion animals and wildlife. You will be funding our educational, legislative, investigative and outreach projects in the U.S. and across the globe.

Or perhaps you'd like to make a memorial donation in honor of a pet, friend or relative? You can through our Kindred Spirits program. And if you'd like to contribute in a more structured way, our Planned Giving Office has suggestions about estate planning, annuities, and even gifts of stock that avoid capital gains taxes.

Maybe you have land that you would like to preserve as a lasting habitat for wildlife. Our Wildlife Land Trust can help you. Perhaps the land you want to share is a backyard— that's enough. Our Urban Wildlife Sanctuary Program will show you how to create a habitat for your wild neighbors.

So you see, it's easy to help animals. And The HSUS is here to help.

THE HUMANE SOCIETY
OF THE UNITED STATES.

2100 L Street NW • Washington, DC 20037 • 202-452-1100
www.hsus.org

Table of Contents

CHAPTER 2:
Private Mortgages—What is in it for You?   33

CHAPTER 3:
Why Borrowers Seek Private Mortgages 47

CHAPTER 4:
Evaluating a Loan Opportunity 57

CHAPTER 5:
Mortgages, Interest Rates, and Fees 71

CHAPTER 6:
Ways to Invest   93

CHAPTER 7:
Getting the Most from Your IRA   105

CHAPTER 8:
Selling Mortgages and Notes   125

CHAPTER 9:
Finding Potential Borrowers   133

CHAPTER 10:
Verifying Property Information   143

CHAPTER 11:
Insuring Your Investment   153

CHAPTER 12:
More Safety Measures for the Private Lender   159

CHAPTER 13:
Bookkeeping and Taxes   171

Conclusion   185

Appendix A: Sample Real Estate Forms   189

Appendix B: Calculations   241

Foreword

Did you just say I could be earning three, four, or five times the interest I am currently getting with my pathetic savings account? Where do I sign up?

It is rough out there right now. I think we are all aware that the economy has had more ups, downs, and turns than a rickety roller coaster, and we are all just hanging on, trying not to lose our lunch. It is also true that money is no longer growing on trees in the form of home equity, but we still need a way to maximize and grow what we have. And although there is no "get-rich-quick" scheme I would ever recommend or endorse, the idea of private mortgage investing for the average person is something most people have not considered — but they should. Here is why.

You may have some immediate reservations when you hear the words "private mortgage investing," especially if you do not even really know what the phrase means. "Private mortgage investing" means that a person who is interested in buying a home obtains the loan from an individual — like yourself — rather than a bank. In the business, we call it "hard money," a term you may be more familiar with.

If you think about it, you have probably been giving out hard money loans most of your life. Have you ever slapped a 20 in your kid's hand after 10 minutes of weeping and whining that he will pay you back? That is essentially a hard money loan. In real estate, the stakes are a bit higher, and there may be a few pieces of paper that need reviewing and signing, but otherwise, it is really all one in the same.

We have gotten past the initial intimidation factor of unfamiliar terms; now, let's address the issue that you are not a real estate professional and do not intend on becoming one anytime soon. Not to worry. No experience in real estate is necessary to invest in private mortgages. You do not have to be a real estate agent, broker, mortgage lender, or any of the sort to be a private mortgage investor. In fact, most private mortgage investors work in fields completely unrelated to real estate. You can be a postal worker, a teacher, a preacher, or even a student with some fat pockets. The only tools you need are a little money to invest, some attention to detail, and the desire to grow your bank account.

Private mortgage investing is a common sense way to invest your money because a house is tangible and will always have value, as opposed to company stock which can dissolve right along with the company. We really have no idea what company executives are doing up there in those fancy high rises and whether they are going to make good decisions that will make your stock go up or down.

The bottom line is that few places give you a 12 percent return on your investment. The stock market is sluggish and unpredictable. If you pick the wrong company or do not diversify your money, you could end up in big trouble. Other types of funds can ultimately throw you back into the stock market and leave you with paltry single-digit growth, if that. In this economic climate, we need to get a bit more creative with our money to make it flourish, and *Private Mortgage Investing* shows you how. Learn about private mortgage investing step by step with easy-to-read case studies, examples, and dozens of relevant websites. After reading this book and following the simple key items to make your investing decisions, you will see how simple and lucrative private mortgage investing can be.

As a 20-year veteran of the real estate industry, I have worked in almost every facet of the business, including mortgage lending, loan servicing, loss mitigation, home sales, and property management. I have been a private mortgage investor and used private mortgage funds for many of my real estate investments because it is quick, simple, and relatively hassle free.

One thing I have learned throughout the years is this industry is not going anywhere, and regardless of the economic climate, you can always make money in real estate. People will always buy and sell houses, and they will always need money to borrow; therefore, there will always be a need for people or institutions to lend. As banks continue to tighten their belts and criteria for lending, the individual private mortgage investor will develop as a key component in the future of home ownership and investment. Use this book as a stepping stone to become more familiar with the industry and the concept of private mortgage investing. Challenge yourself to step out into new territory. It can be rewarding, both personally and financially, to learn something new. The rewards you reap can secure a better future for you and the ones you love. Not to mention, imagine how interesting you will sound at the next family gathering when you casually chat about the latest private mortgage investment deal you just closed. Go for it!

Mia Melle

Broker and president of West Coast Property Specialists, Inc. (WCPS, Inc.)

WCPS, Inc. is a cradle-to-grave real estate brokerage developed to meet the needs of the residential real estate investors. WCPS, Inc. acts as an umbrella for a family of companies, each designed to meet a specific need. Renttoday.us is an online rental portal and property management firm; FixD Construction specializes in the rehabilitation and repair of residential investment homes, and Bale Investments, Inc. handles the sale and acquisition of investment property, as well as facilitates private mortgage investment transactions.

*More information can be found at **www.wcpsinc.com** and **www.renttoday.us.***

Introduction: Say Hello To Private Mortgage Investing!

Congratulations! With the purchase of this book, you are taking the first step into the world of private mortgage investing. Not only will you learn how to earn double-digit interest on your hard-earned money, but you will also learn how to invest it virtually risk free.

Are you:

New to investing? *Chapter 1 compares investment alternatives and guides you in your first foray into the world of private mortgage investing.*

Interested in diversifying? In the pages that follow, you will find many reasons to include private mortgages in your portfolio.

An experienced real estate pro? Read on and discover how to enjoy safe, lucrative investing in the area you know and love without tying up your money for decades.

Tired of trusting stockbrokers and fund managers with your money? This book shows you how to "be the bank" and take control of your own investing destiny.

This book takes the mystery out of getting started in private mortgage investing. Its pages are crammed with practical information, websites, product recommendations, and case studies of people just like you who began investing in private mortgages and never looked back. You will find out exactly what you need to do and when to do it to maximize your earnings and minimize your worries. For example, you will learn:

- What sets private mortgage investing apart from other types of investments.

- Exactly what private mortgages are and how to configure them to help you meet your personal investing objectives.

- The reasons so many good borrowers want to use private lenders instead of banks.

- Five criteria you must consider before you make a mortgage loan.

- Proven ways to protect yourself against loss.

- How to make interest, fees, points, and the magic of compounding work over time for you.

- The pros and cons of going at it alone or partnering with other investors.

- Why you should consider making private mortgage loans from your IRA.

- How to make quick cash through buying and selling mortgages and notes.

Whether you are a brand-new investor just learning the ropes or a seasoned veteran with a diversified portfolio and years of experience under your belt, this book will change your attitude toward investing. Say hello to a little-understood investment vehicle that offers a high rate of return with relatively little risk.

Chapter 1: Investing in Real Estate

This book is about private mortgage investing — a real estate investment opportunity with the potential to earn steady double-digit interest rates. Real estate is often overlooked as an investment option. Many investors are unaware that another investment vehicle exists besides stocks, bonds, mutual funds, exchange traded funds (ETFs), certificates of deposit (CDs), and money market accounts. The return on these investments, after adjusting for inflation, averages between 4 and 7 percent. Private mortgages realize returns considerably higher than this and have the additional advantage of being backed by real property.

Private mortgages offer stable returns and fit well within a portfolio of stocks, bonds, and real estate. Because they have little correlation to the ups and downs of the stock market, adding them to a portfolio will make the returns of the portfolio more consistent. At times when stocks bring in lower, or even negative, returns, private mortgage investments will continue to perform consistently. An examination of typical returns from other investment vehicles will demonstrate why you should include private mortgages in your portfolio.

INVESTING BASICS

Investing is a way of putting your money to work to increase your wealth. When you make an investment, you purchase an asset and hold it for a time frame. During that period, you expect your investment to either earn a steady rate of interest or increase in value so you can sell it for a substantial profit. You choose not to spend your money today so you will have a larger amount to spend in the future, perhaps for your children's college expenses or for your own retirement.

Many factors determine how much your investment earns, including fluctuations in the stock market, changes in interest rates, and rising inflation that can diminish the spending power of your money over time. All of these factors represent risks your investment will not perform as expected. To be a successful investor, you must learn to evaluate these risks and compensate for them.

Today, more Americans than ever have become investors. Employers in the United States are rapidly phasing out defined-benefit pension plans that guarantee an annual pension after retirement. They are being replaced with defined-contribution plans, such as 401(k) plans, that make individual employees responsible for investing their own savings and making their own investment decisions. In 2009, more than 46 million U.S. households had tax-advantaged Individual Retirement Arrangements (IRAs). Most individuals can no longer rely on the expertise of a professional pension-fund manager to assure their financial futures. They must make their own choices about how and where to invest so their savings grow enough to meet their financial goals and provide for a comfortable retirement. Private mortgage investing is an effective vehicle for managing wealth and getting the most out of your investment portfolio.

CHOOSING YOUR INVESTMENT VEHICLE

Several factors determine which investment vehicle is best for you, including the level of your annual income, your tax status, your current financial needs, your long-term plans, and the amount of money available to you for investment.

How much do you need to get started?

How much money do you have to invest? Will you be making small, regular contributions to your investment account, or are you looking for a good way to invest a nest egg or an inheritance? Some stock brokerages allow you to open an investment account with as little as $100, and you can begin investing in a 401(k) by contributing a small deduction from each paycheck. The U.S. Treasury sells EE Savings Bonds in amounts starting at $25. You will need several thousand dollars to begin purchasing bonds, and some hedge funds and mutual funds require a minimum investment of $25,000.

You cannot start investing in private mortgages with $100, but you can get started with much less than what is required by many traditional vehicles. Many states have a minimum net worth requirement for private mortgage investors, and some states limit the number of private loans you can make without becoming a licensed lender. Your broker will know the requirements for your state; in Florida, you must have a net worth of at least $250,000. Your net worth is the value of all your assets, including property, cash, stocks and bonds, and bank accounts, minus any debts or liabilities. Every time an investor gives money to a broker to lend out, the investor must also submit a letter certifying that he or she has a net worth of at least $250,000, accompanied by audited financial statements or other supporting documentation.

When do you need your money?

Some investments allow you to withdraw money throughout the investment process, while others require you to wait until the investment has reached full maturity. Before putting your money into a long-term investment, always consider how tying up your funds will affect you. If you have to sell an investment prematurely to meet a pressing financial need, you will not realize the expected return and may even lose money.

Accessibility, or liquidity, refers to the ease and frequency with which you can withdraw money from your investment. For many investment opportunities, the longer you are willing to hold the investment, the higher the interest rate. This means that if you want your money to be accessible, you often have to settle for a lower interest rate.

This is not true of private mortgage investments. When you invest in private mortgages, you are typically investing your money for a period of six months to two years. Despite the short term of your investment, you will earn an interest rate of more than 10 percent.

Growing capital versus earning income

What do you want your money to do for you while invested? Are you hoping to supplement your income, or do you want to build your capital by reinvesting it? When you choose to invest in private mortgages, you can do either. For instance, if you have loaned out $60,000 at 12 percent, you will have interest payments of $600 a month ($7,200 in annual interest, divided by 12 months). You can withdraw that money for your living expenses or put it into another investment.

Do not rely on private mortgage investing as a sole source of income.

Private mortgage investing is a vehicle for increasing wealth, but experienced investors emphasize that you should not rely on it to generate income for your daily living expenses. If your borrower goes into default, your monthly interest payments will suddenly stop coming. It may take several months to foreclose on the property, recover your capital, and reinvest it in another income-producing loan. If receiving a regular monthly income is your top priority, fixed-income investments, such as municipal bonds or annuities, are a better choice.

How much interest would you like to earn?

Market factors determine the return on most investment opportunities. Interest is controlled by money market rates, fixed for the entire length of the investment, or determined by a bank. Private mortgage interest rates are determined, in large part, by you. You should follow certain guidelines, but in the end, the mortgagor decides whether to accept the interest rate you offer or look elsewhere for a loan.

The typical interest rate for a direct private mortgage ranges from 10 to 16 percent. This range depends upon many factors, including the length of the loan, the purpose for the loan, the creditworthiness of the borrower, and your exit strategy.

The interest rate can be either fixed or floating. A fixed rate remains the same throughout the life of the loan. A floating rate is partially linked to market interest rates and fluctuates when those rates go up or down. When you choose a fixed rate, you risk locking in a low interest rate if the market rate goes up during the life of the loan. Since most private mortgage loans are for two years or less, this risk is not as great as if you bought a 10- or 20-year bond. If you choose a floating rate, it is often set so there is a floor, allowing you to raise your rates if the prime rate goes up and protecting you from loss if the prime goes down.

A LOOK AT TRADITIONAL INVESTMENT OPTIONS

Every investment option has advantages and disadvantages that determine whether it is appropriate for your circumstances and financial goals. These are the most common ones, with the advantages and disadvantages of each:

Savings account

A savings account is a bank account in which you deposit money for the purpose of accumulating funds over time. Only the owner can withdraw funds. The bank pays interest on the account and may require holding the funds for a certain time before being withdrawn.

- **Pros:** Savings accounts can be used as collateral and are insured by the FDIC for up to $100,000. Money is easily accessible, and interest is paid monthly. You can start a savings account with any amount of money.

- **Cons:** Interest rates are low, often less than 0.5 percent today. Interest is subject to federal and state income taxes.

Money market account

A money market account is a bank account that pays a slightly higher interest rate than savings accounts, competitive with the money market fund's interest rate. In exchange, you must maintain a high minimum balance, and there is a restriction on the number of monthly transactions.

- **Pros:** Interest on money market accounts is slightly higher than that of savings accounts, which at the time of printing in early 2011 was about 1.5 percent. The FDIC insures money market accounts offered by banks. Money is easily accessible and liquid.

- **Cons:** There are penalties, which vary depending on the bank you use, for not maintaining the minimum balance. Interest rates are still quite low and are subject to change. Interest income is subject to federal and state income taxes.

Money market fund

A money market fund is an open-ended mutual fund that invests in short-term debt. Shares sell for a fixed price of $1 each, but the interest rate fluctuates.

- **Pros:** There are no penalties for withdrawal, making the account very accessible. Interest is calculated daily instead of monthly.

- **Cons:** There is no FDIC guarantee on your money. Interest rates vary according to the market. Interest income is subject to state and federal income taxes. You have to deposit a minimum amount to get started.

Certificate of deposit (CD)

A CD is a debt instrument offered by banks that pays interest on funds deposited for a specific amount of time.

- **Pros:** You can determine if you wish to grow your capital investment by reinvesting the interest, or you can take the interest as quarterly payments. Your investment is federally insured.

- **Cons:** CDs require that you keep your money invested for a specific time. You get penalized for early withdrawal, and your interest earnings are subject to federal and state income taxes.

U.S. Savings Bond, Series EE

Series EE U.S. Savings Bonds are sold by the U.S. Treasury, through banks and participating employers, and online at **www.treasurydirect.gov**. The paper bonds are sold at half their face value, and you can redeem them for face value at maturity. Electronic bonds are sold at face value and pay a fixed interest rate, added to the bond monthly and compounded semiannually.

- **Pros:** Your investment is guaranteed. There are no fees associated with buying these bonds. They are very liquid, and there are no penalties for redeeming them before maturity. Interest earnings are exempt from state income taxes and, if used for tuition, are also exempt from federal taxes.

- **Cons:** This is a very long-term investment, and interest is reduced if redeemed early. If you hold a bond longer than 18 years, it stops paying interest.

Municipal bond

Municipal bonds are issued by state, local, and city governments to fund their projects and operations. They are backed by taxpayer dollars and pay a fixed interest rate, returning the principal at maturity.

- **Pros:** This investment is relatively safe. Two major credit rating agencies, Moody's and Standard & Poor's, rate the creditworthiness of municipal bonds. Interest from municipal bonds is exempt from federal income tax. Expect a return on this investment of 7 to 8 percent.

- **Cons:** Because the interest rate is fixed, you may earn more or less than the return on other investments. If market interest rates rise during the duration of the bond, you will be locked into the lower fixed-interest rate. You could also lose the opportunity to profit from a stock market boom because your money is tied up in bonds. Some municipal bonds are callable, meaning that your principal can be repaid to you prematurely, depriving you of interest income and obliging you to seek a new investment.

Federal agency bond

Federal agency bonds are issued by organizations and corporations sponsored by the U.S. government, such as Sallie Mae, Ginnie Mae, Fannie Mae, and Freddie Mac, and the Federal Home Loan Banks. Federal agency securities are implicitly guaranteed; in the case of Ginnie Mae, they are backed by the full faith and credit of the United States.

- **Pros:** This is a very low-risk investment with returns of about 7 percent. You can pick bonds with maturities from one to 40 years. They are exempt from state and local taxes.

- **Cons:** You typically need at least $5,000 to get started. The interest earned is subject to federal income taxes.

U.S. Treasury Bill, note, or bond

These are debt obligations issued by the U.S. government. They are backed by its full faith and credit and are considered one of the safest investments in the world. U.S. Treasury Bills have a maturity of one year or less. U.S. Treasury Notes have maturities of one to ten years. U.S. Treasury Bonds have maturities of 10 to 30 years. All Treasury securities are issued with a minimum face value of $100 and in subsequent increments of $100. Income from U.S. Treasury debt is exempt from state and local taxes. The yield on a treasury bond is determined by a monthly auction in which large investors, such as banks and pension funds, bid on the interest rate they want to receive. An individual investor can purchase Treasury bonds through TreasuryDirect with a non-competitive bid — the buyer accepts whatever interest rate is decided at the auction — or through a bank or broker with a competitive bid — the buyer specifies the interest rate he or she will accept.

- **Pros:** These investment vehicles are guaranteed by the government and are considered risk free. The interest is exempt from state and local taxes. U.S. government securities can be easily bought and sold on the market.

- **Cons:** The earned interest is subject to federal income taxes. When purchasing bills, you must send your money without knowing the exact price until the auction ends. For notes and bonds, you will not know the price until after competitive bidding at auction.

Corporate bond

Corporations issue corporate bonds to raise money for expansion of their businesses. A corporate bond represents a legal business debt obligation. The issuer contracts to repay the principal by a certain date and to make regular interest payments.

- **Pros:** Corporate bonds are a relatively safe investment because Moody's and Standard & Poor's rate their creditworthiness. They typically return 6 to 8 percent. Different bonds issued by the same company may have different credit ratings depending on the current financial status of the company and the purpose for which the bonds are issued. Some corporate bonds are insured, meaning that the insurance company will repay your capital if the corporation fails to do so.

- **Cons:** Corporate bonds are issued with maturities ranging from two to 30 years. The company can redeem some bonds before the maturity date, depriving you unexpectedly of interest income and forcing you to seek another investment. As interest rates go up, bond yields go down. All interest earnings are subject to federal and state income taxes. Some corporate bonds might become difficult to sell if the financial status of the company declines.

Mutual fund

A mutual fund pools investors' money and invests it in various stocks, bonds, money market instruments, and commodities, according to a stated set of financial objectives. The value of mutual fund shares rises and falls with the value the fund's underlying investments.

- **Pros:** A small outlay can get you into mutual fund investing. The fees associated with trading in the stock market are smaller when you use a fund than when you trade independently. You can choose a mutual fund that meets your needs from more than 9,000 offered by banks, brokerages, financial institutions, and mutual fund companies.

- **Cons:** There is no guarantee you will not lose your principal because the value of mutual fund shares goes up and down. Interest and earnings are subject to federal and state income taxes. Mutual funds charge trading and management fees that can eat into your returns.

Corporate stock

Shares of stock in public corporations can be bought and sold on the stock exchanges. You can profit from ownership of corporate stock in two ways. You make a profit when the value of a company's shares increases, and you sell them for more than you paid for them. Some companies pay quarterly dividends to stockholders from their earnings as an incentive to own company stock when the company's growth has stabilized.

- **Pros:** You can start investing in corporate stocks with very little money. Some brokerages allow you to open an investment account with as little as $25. Corporate stocks have no maturity date, and you can hold them indefinitely as long as the company remains in business.

- **Cons:** Corporate stocks can be risky, and determining which ones will make a lot of money is difficult. Brokers charge commissions and trading fees when you buy and sell stocks. Dividends, if paid, are subject to federal and state income taxes. Stock prices may fall, and you may lose money. Additionally, you will lose your principal if the company in which you invested goes bankrupt.

Private mortgage investing

A portfolio combining a selection of these investment vehicles will earn 3.2 percent to 6 percent, when adjusted for inflation. If you invest $500,000, that gives you a return of between $1,300 and $2,500 a month.

That same $500,000 invested in private mortgages would yield interest of between

10 and 16 percent, and depending upon the loan, the yield could be as high as 25 percent. For this example, we will use an interest rate of 12 percent. That would give you $5,000 a month to live on. If you only have $250,000 to invest, you are still earning double what you would earn with a traditional $500,000 portfolio.

Not many investments can dependably generate such strong returns, and few other investments are backed with an asset like real estate to provide protection against loss.

- **Pros:** Privately held mortgages provide a high return on investment (ROI). If you sell an investment property, the IRS allows you to defer paying capital gains taxes if you purchase a similar property within 45 days to replace it. This is known as a "like-kind exchange" or "1031 exchange," for Section 1031 of the U.S. Internal Revenue Service Code. If a borrower defaults on a private mortgage, you will acquire the property for approximately 60 percent of its value and can sell it for a profit.

- **Cons:** You are obligated to hold the mortgage for the time specified in the contract. If a better investment opportunity arises in the meantime, you cannot take advantage of it because your money will be tied up. To get started, you have to make a relatively large initial investment — typically at least $5,000. You are responsible for choosing a reliable borrower or broker and confirming that the details of the loan contract are accurate.

One of the advantages of private mortgage investing is it brings in a high return on investment. Below is an example of an initial investment held over 5 years, 10 years, and 20 years:

5 YEARS (COMPOUNDED)			
Amount	7%	15%	Additional Earnings at 15%
$10,000	$14,176	$21,071	$6,895
$25,000	$35,440	$52,679	$17,239
$50,000	$70,881	$105,359	$34,478
$100,000	$141,762	$210,718	$68,956

10 YEARS (COMPOUNDED)			
Amount	7%	15%	Additional Earnings at 15%
$10,000	$20,096	$44,402	$24,036
$25,000	$50,241	$111,005	$60,764
$50,000	$100,483	$222,010	$121,527
$100,000	$200,966	$444,021	$243,055

20 YEARS (COMPOUNDED)			
Amount	7%	15%	Additional Earnings at 15%
$10,000	$40,387	$197,155	$156,768
$25,000	$100,968	$492,887	$391,919
$50,000	$201,937	$985,774	$783,837
$100,000	$403,837	$1,971,549	$1,567,712

As you can see, if you invest $10,000 for 20 years, the difference between investing that money at an annual rate of 7 percent and an annual rate of 15 percent is $156,768.

The advantages of private mortgage loans compared to other types of investments are higher rates of return and the security of having the loan backed by real estate property that can be sold to recoup losses. Private mortgage investing is not appropriate for everyone, though. Before you can begin investing in private mortgages, you must have at least $5,000 investment capital available for one or two years. You cannot make regular monthly contributions as you can with a mutual fund, IRA, or savings account. Though a mutual fund, 401(k), or managed investment account demands minimal attention once you select your initial portfolio, private mortgage investing requires you to be directly involved with a reliable broker or to spend time researching potential borrowers and properties. *The following chapter will help you understand how private mortgages are structured and the process of private mortgage investing.*

Chapter 2:
Private Mortgages—
What is in it for You?

After you grasp the potential of high-yield mortgage investing, the investment returns available from banks and other lending institutions will seem paltry by comparison. High returns on investment do not necessarily mean high risk. If you know what you are doing and use common sense, mortgage investments can be safer than government bonds. This chapter is an overview of the basic elements of private mortgage investing.

WHAT IS A PRIVATE MORTGAGE NOTE?

A private mortgage is similar to a bank mortgage, except that an individual rather than a financial institution or a government agency, such as Fannie Mae or Freddie Mac, provides the money for the loan. The property used as collateral, not the borrower's credit score, determines the interest rates and amount of a private mortgage loan.

Private mortgage loans are relatively safe because they are backed by the real estate property purchased with the loan. To further protect your principal, the amounts loaned are only 65 to 70 percent of the appraised value of the property. For construction loans or lots, the typical loan is 55 percent of the appraised value. If the loan goes into default, you, as the lender, can start foreclosure proceedings and acquire the property for 65 to 70 percent of its value. Then, you can sell the property for a substantial gain or earn monthly income by renting it out to a tenant. Because you acquire the property for only a fraction of its value, you can price it for less than similar properties on the market to ensure a quick sale.

When you invest in a private mortgage, you can set the interest rate based on the market rate for similar mortgages, the purpose of the loan, and the condition of the property. In most cases, first mortgages, or first liens, yield about 12 to 14 percent. Second liens, or loans in which the property used as collateral is already mortgaged, yield about 16 to 18 percent because you are taking a greater risk — if the borrower defaults and the property is sold in foreclosure, you will receive only what remains after the first mortgage is paid off. You will typically get six points more than the current prime rate, or the lowest interest rate available from banks, offered to their most credit-worthy customers.

Private mortgage investment loans are usually short term in length. They typically range from one to three years; although, some investors in this book suggest that private mortgage loans can be made for shorter periods of time, such as six months. These loans are usually interest-only loans and amortized over 30 years, with a balloon payment and prepayment penalty. The length of the loan can affect the interest rates borrowers are charged. Loans made for a very short term can charge incredibly high interest rates and might violate your state's usury laws, which are state laws that specify the maximum legal interest rate at which loans can be made. Investors should be familiar with the usury laws in their state and know how a loan's terms affect interest rates.

PRIVATE MORTGAGE INVESTING VERSUS RENTAL INCOME

Suppose you buy a house and rent it to tenants for $1,000 a month. If the house cost $100,000, you get a return on investment of 12 percent. This sounds like a good investment, but the reality is more complicated. When you borrow money to rent a house and rent it out, a sizable portion of the monthly income goes to the mortgage payment, including the interest you are paying for the loan. You are building equity in the property but at a very slow rate. In addition, you must pay for maintenance of the property and property taxes. Every time a toilet leaks or a hot water heater fails, part of your rental income is eaten up. When a tenant moves out, you must clean, paint, and make repairs to prepare the property for the next tenant. You could lose several months' rent if you do not find a new tenant right away. You might also have to pay legal costs if a tenant does not pay the rent and has to be evicted. As a landlord, you must either deal with tenants all the time or pay a management company to do it for you. In contrast, the job of the bank that holds the mortgage on your rental property seems much easier — it simply collects your mortgage payment every month. The bank makes money while you do the work.

If you would like to act as the bank, that is what private mortgage investing is all about. You receive the monthly payments, and the borrower does everything else.

You are the bank

A real estate loan transaction proceeds something like this:

1. A potential buyer finds a piece of property.

2. The buyer goes to the local bank to apply for a loan. If he or she qualifies, the loan is approved.

3. After approval, the ownership of that property transfers to him or her.

4. The previous owner gets paid from money out of the loan.

5. The new homeowner begins making mortgage payments to the bank.

In a private mortgage transaction, the property is bought not with money borrowed from a bank but with money borrowed from an individual — you. You become the bank, and you make money from the transaction.

The mortgage note you hold is fully collateralized by income-producing real estate. A typical private mortgage loan has a duration of one year and provides a monthly income of interest-only payments. At the end of the year, your initial principal is returned to you.

MORTGAGE VERSUS DEED OF TRUST

When a person borrows money, the lending institution or individual typically requires the borrower to sign a promissory note agreeing to pay the lender back according to specific terms. This note can be a mortgage or a deed of trust, depending on the laws of the state in which the transaction takes place.

In title-theory states, a mortgage is used. The lender holds the title, a legal document establishing ownership of the property, and it transfers to the borrower when the loan is paid in full.

A mortgage is also used in lien-theory states. The difference is that the borrower holds the title, but a lien, or legal claim entitling the lender to claim the property, is charged against the property. The lien is removed when the property is paid off.

Some states are deed-of-trust states. A deed of trust is similar to a mortgage, but the title is held by a third-party trustee and is given to the borrower when the loan is paid in full.

In California, a deed of trust, or trust deed, is used to tie the mortgage note to the property and create a lien. The note is not recorded — just the deed of trust.

MORTGAGE AND DEED-OF-TRUST STATES

State	Mortgage	Deed of Trust	State	Mortgage	Deed of Trust
Alabama	•	•	Montana		•
Alaska		•	Nebraska		•
Arizona	•	•	Nevada		•
Arkansas	•	•	New Hampshire		•
California		•	New Jersey	•	
Colorado		•	New Mexico		•
Connecticut	•		New York	•	
Delaware	•		North Carolina		•
District of Columbia		•	North Dakota	•	
Florida	•		Ohio	•	
Georgia		•	Oklahoma	•	
Hawaii		•	Oregon		•
Idaho		•	Pennsylvania	•	
Illinois		•	Rhode Island		•
Indiana	•		South Carolina	•	
Iowa	•		South Dakota	•	•
Kansas	•		Tennessee		•
Kentucky	•	•	Texas		•
Louisiana	•		Utah		•

State	Mortgage	Deed of Trust	State	Mortgage	Deed of Trust
Maine		•	Vermont	•	
Maryland	•	•	Virgin Islands	•	
Massachusetts		•	Virginia		•
Michigan	•	•	Washington		•
Minnesota		•	West Virginia		•
Mississippi		•	Wisconsin	•	
Missouri		•	Wyoming		•

RECORDING THE LOAN

You should record all mortgages and deeds of trust with the county clerk of court in which the real property is located. If you are recording a deed or a mortgage, you must take the proper steps to ensure the documents meet all the legal requirements for recording. Errors and omissions are common; the county clerks reject more than 30 percent of all deeds and return them for correction. Although the title company is responsible for ensuring the accuracy of a mortgage or deed of trust, you should verify these basic points when recording a deed of trust or mortgage:

- Every deed must contain the names and physical addresses of the purchaser and the seller. Post office boxes are not acceptable.

- The deed must contain a complete description of the property, including the state, county, township, and village in which the property is located.

- The document must be signed and properly acknowledged by a notary public — notarized.

- If a deed incorporates exhibits, such as surveys, photos, or blueprints, you must include these with the deed at the time of recording.

A "perfected" deed or mortgage is one for which the creditor has secured the proper documentation necessary to make it valid. A mortgage is perfected when you record a deed of trust or mortgage with the county recorder. Your deed is considered complete when it has been signed, sealed, and delivered.

The law does not require the recording of a deed for the transfer from the seller to the buyer to take place. However, failing to record deeds of trust can cause private lenders to lose their money. To protect yourself from future claims on the title, you should record the deed. You should do this simultaneously with the closing or as soon after the close of escrow as possible.

To record a deed yourself, you need only to take the deed to the appropriate recording office in your area. The recorder will then index and transcribe the deed in the public records, and anyone can see it.

Once the deed is recorded, it has been given "constructive notice." Constructive notice means that anyone can learn about the deed by making an inquiry. Unrecorded deeds, while valid between the grantor and grantee, do not give constructive notice to the public.

For example, suppose you lend someone $100,000 to buy a piece of property. The deed is notarized and ready to be recorded, but you forget about it, and the deed simply sits on your desk. Several months later, another lender comes along and lends money to the very same borrower for the very same piece of property. This lender, too, gets a deed in recordable form and heads straight to the clerk's office.

Now, the borrower skips out on both of you, and you both go in to foreclose on the property. Here is the problem: The first lender — you — never recorded the deed. So who owns the lot? The answer is the second lender, who had no knowledge of the previous sale of the property but won the race to the courthouse.

This example demonstrates why it is critical to promptly record every property deed or any document affecting real estate titles. The deed becomes part of the property's chain of title. If anyone looks up your property, your name would show up as the official owner.

An authorized person, such as a judge or notary public, must acknowledge the document. Documents not witnessed by a notary public are usually not recordable. The acknowledgment of a notary public verifies the identity of the person signing the document but does not make any statement or guarantee as to the validity of the document itself.

In California, whenever a deed is recorded, the buyer must also file a Preliminary Change of Ownership Report (PCOR). The assessor uses these reports to determine which properties are exempt from property tax.

In most states, you must pay a transfer tax when a deed is recorded. Depending on your area, the amount of the tax will vary but is based on a rate per $1,000.

For example, it may be $1.10 per $1,000 of the value or the consideration or price paid for the property. The borrower typically pays the transfer taxes.

Creating the note yourself

You can create the note yourself or use a mortgage broker. If you decide that you want to create the note yourself, you will need to find a borrower yourself.

Borrowers of private mortgage loans can be of two types: individual homeowners or professional real estate investors. Lending to professional real estate investors tends to be safer than lending to individual homeowners because they have experience and can show they have used and repaid private mortgage loans in the past. Professional investors use the property to generate income and can pay you out of the rent money, or they plan to sell the property quickly after making improvements. Individual homeowners, on the other hand, use the house as a residence and have to come up with the money for monthly payments from their salaries or other personal income — a much riskier investment.

Next, you have to do your due diligence. Due diligence is a legal term meaning that you do everything a reasonable person would do to research a potential loan and verify it is a good investment. For private mortgage lenders, due diligence involves finding out everything you can about the property used as collateral and determining whether a particular borrower is going to cooperate well with you.

Hire a real estate attorney to draw up the note or deed of trust for you. These documents are legal contracts and should be written to favor you — the lender — and not the borrower. Never use the borrower's attorney to draw up a note or deed of trust or let the borrower's attorney change the note in any way. The borrower might insert a clause that, under certain circumstances, would allow him or her to declare a breach of contract and avoid paying back your principal. If the contract does not require the borrower to purchase insurance for the property, a fire or flood could wipe out your investment, or you could be held liable for accidents or injuries that occur on the property.

Many states require the lender and borrower to appear before a judge to determine the validity of a foreclosure and decide how the money is to be distributed after the property is sold. This process, known as judicial foreclosure, is time consuming and costly. In states with non-judicial foreclosure, the lender can proceed with the foreclosure without going to court as long as certain guidelines set forth by state law are followed. It is safer to lend money in non-judicial states because you can begin foreclosure on a property as soon as one payment is missed. This prevents you from losing too much interest income or having the property deteriorate while legal ownership is determined.

The following states have non-judicial foreclosure:

- Alabama
- Alaska
- Arkansas
- California
- Colorado
- District of Columbia
- Georgia
- Hawaii
- Idaho
- Massachusetts
- Michigan
- Minnesota
- Mississippi
- Missouri
- Nevada
- New Hampshire
- North Carolina
- Oregon
- Rhode Island
- South Dakota
- Tennessee
- Texas
- Virginia
- Washington
- West Virginia
- Wyoming

Using a mortgage broker

Using a private mortgage broker instead of doing it yourself can save you time — and time is money. Mortgage brokers are sought out by potential borrowers and often offer a selection of investment opportunities that would not be available to you as an individual. The mortgage broker finds a borrower for you, determines the parameters of the loan, and handles all the legal work.

Mortgage brokers tend to be borrower-friendly rather than investor-friendly, creating deals that favor the borrower. If you decide to use a mortgage broker, find one who considers the investors rather than the borrowers as his or her clients. A broker with this attitude will be much more diligent about researching both the borrower's background and the condition of the property used as collateral for the loan. A good broker imposes strict requirements on borrowers and does not allow a lender to be deceived into lending money for a poorly organized or overvalued business proposition.

The borrower, not the lender, is the one who pays the mortgage broker. The borrower pays fees to the broker to initiate the loan and find an investor.

A good private mortgage broker will strongly encourage the borrower to make payments on time for 12 months because this benefits the borrower, the lender, and the broker. If the borrower makes regular payments for 12 months, the broker can demonstrate a good mortgage history for 12 months and help the borrower straighten out his or her credit. Then, the broker can help the borrower find a new loan with a lower interest rate. The broker benefits by getting a commission for arranging the new loan. The investor benefits because his or her money is returned and can be invested again, and he or she will get another point — a point is a one percent commission paid to the lender — to initiate a new loan.

Loan-Servicing Companies

For some, dealing with the collection of monthly payments from a borrower seems like too much trouble. If you want to try private investing but also maintain a distance from its day-to-day responsibilities, you can use a loan-servicing company.

Once a broker sets up the loan, he or she has nothing more to do with it. The borrower sends a monthly check directly to the investor. If you prefer, you can have a loan-servicing company act as the middleman. Loan-servicing companies offer some or all of the following services:

- Filing and updating loan documents and ensuring all required documents are present.

- Sending out welcome letters to new borrowers.

- Mailing or e-mailing monthly billing statements to each borrower and providing payment coupons if needed.

- Collecting monthly principal and interest payments, along with any applicable taxes, insurance, and other escrow payments.

- Posting payments to a borrower's account and applying the correct amounts to principal, interest, late charges, and escrows.

- Preparing and sending out reminder notices, late notices, and delinquency notices and enforcing collection procedures for late payments.

- Preparing, filing, and mailing the annual IRS Form 1098: Mortgage Interest Statements to borrowers and providing them with copies of their reports.

The typical cost of loan servicing is 1 percent of your portfolio. A good loan-servicing company will send you a check every month and a report similar to the reports you receive on other types of investments. Many loan-servicing companies just service loans but some service and collect. If your loan servicing company does not do collections, you will have to use a real estate attorney to handle delinquent payments.

Here is an example: Suppose Jack has $50,000 to invest. He gives it to the broker, who lends it to John. Every month, John sends a payment to Jack. Jack decides he does not want to deal with the responsibility of collecting the payments and keeping the records so he hires a loan-servicing company to act as an intermediary. John begins sending a check to the loan-servicing company, payable to the servicing company. The servicing company keeps up with the loan, passes on the payments to Jack, and charges Jack a fee.

 Licensed brokers cannot service loans.

If your broker is licensed, then he or she cannot service your loans. It is illegal to do both. It is not illegal if your broker is also a lender.

From the lender's perspective, investing in mortgages is quite beneficial. The lender gets a high rate of interest on a short-term investment with very little risk. *The next chapter explains how the borrower benefits from a private loan.*

CASE STUDY: INTERVIEW WITH A MORTGAGE BROKER

Matt Tabacch
President and licensed real estate broker
Allstate Mortgage of Florida Loans
& Investments, Inc.
809 NE 25th Ave. * Ocala, FL 34470
Phone: 352-351-0200
Fax: 352-351-4557

What exactly does a mortgage broker do?

People come to me — a mortgage broker — looking for money. I turn around and find them the money from people looking to invest. I connect the match together. These investors can be private individuals who lend money, as well as banks and other institutions. When someone comes in for a loan, we first try to get him or her a loan through the bank. If a bank cannot do it, we turn around and try to do a private mortgage. I guess you could call me the go-between.

Why do private investors use a mortgage broker?

Private investors use brokers because we have the borrowers to give them, and we have the license to do it. As a private investor, you might be able to find a borrower or two on your own, but as a mortgage broker, I can find several. And, you do not have all the work involved. You can loan out one or two mortgages without a license, but if you want to do many, you will be considered a lender and will need to get a license. How much can you do without a license? The law is very gray. My advice is to always use a broker.

How safe do you think private mortgage investing is? Have you ever had problems?

Out of 2,000 private mortgages I have brokered, we have never had an issue. I know of brokers who have problems, but they are not following safe practices. They are too busy chasing the money and making unwise investments.

Do you worry about clients not paying on time?

No, I never worry. In fact, you make more money when they do not pay you on time. That is what late fees are for. When you do a loan for somebody, the interest keeps coming, and after ten days, you get a late fee, and that is repeated for every ten days the payment is late. We enter these at such a low loan-to-value ratio (LTV), and it is such a harsh penalty for these guys that they want to pay on time.

Do you have any recommendations for someone just starting in private mortgage investing?

I recommend driving by every piece of property you lend money out on. Just by driving by, you will know if the property is a $100,000 house or a $200,000 house. You can see the neighborhood. Once you have a good relationship of trust with your broker, you do not have to do it with every piece of property, but I would still do spot checks.

- Find a team that consists of a good broker, accountant, and appraiser. It is also smart to have a real estate attorney.

- Start small, and see how you feel about it.

Doing what I do is pretty complicated because every deal is so different. There are basic guidelines, but there is a lot of gut instinct involved.

Do you have any good stories about real people who have begun private mortgage investing?

My mother and father owned a little rental store in Pittsburgh, Pennsylvania, and wanted to move to Florida to be with the grandkids and us. They are in their late 50s and have been self-employed their whole lives. They are just simple, hard-working, blue-collar people with a bit of property.

About five years ago, I started investing their money — they gave me $50,000 to invest. That is what they had in the bank. They started making $500 a month in interest. Because of the type of interest they make every month, they could sell all of their property, retire, move to Florida, and live off the interest. Their money is getting ready to double.

They now have three of their best friends from Pennsylvania involved and have all moved to Florida. They enjoyed it so much that both have become part-time brokers with me.

CASE STUDY: THE ROLE OF PRIVATE MORTGAGES

Carey Pott, Founder
January Financial
26080 Getty Drive, Suite A
Laguna Niguel, CA 92677
Phone: 949-373-5472
Fax: 949-257-0586
E-mail: carey@januaryfinancial.com
Website: www.januaryfinancial.com

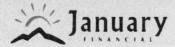

January Financial formed in 2005 to serve the needs of its valued clients in the residential and commercial lending areas. It operates on a "referral-only" basis, meaning the majority of its business comes from referrals from clients, business partners, friends, and family. January Financial guarantees you will have an outstanding experience each time you do business there, from beginning to end.

Do people use private mortgages as their sole source of income? Is it beneficial?

In my experience, people very rarely use private mortgages as a sole source of income. Normally, the investors who supply capital for private mortgages are financially savvy individuals and have fully diversified their investment capital.

I would say the only time I have seen individuals using private mortgages as their only source of income is when they have acquired a large amount of property over their lives, are nearing retirement age, and are utilizing private mortgages as a way to trade equity for income. These people lend money for properties they are selling, not to anyone who walks in off the street.

What is the best story you have heard while helping someone with a private mortgage?

I worked with a borrower who saved her house from foreclosure, replaced a broken-down car, and flew back to Colombia to visit her sick grandmother. This woman had horrible credit scores and did not qualify for a conventional mortgage, but she had lots of equity in her home. I paired her with a group of investors who replaced the existing mortgage and gave her enough cash to accomplish her goals when every bank said no.

How many people use their private mortgages wisely? What ways are there to prevent people from misusing them?

I cannot recall a single instance when one of my borrowers used his or her private mortgage unwisely. The private mortgages are set up to ensure the borrower can make the payments in the short term, while making it sufficiently uncomfortable that he or she has an incentive to refinance out of the private mortgage as soon as possible. This benefits both the borrower and the investor. The borrowers have a short-term solution to their problems and get their financial lives back on track. The investors get their capital back to invest in another venture, most likely another private mortgage.

In my opinion, the best way to prevent private mortgages from being used unwisely is to structure them correctly right from the beginning — a payment that is bearable, but not comfortable, and no prepayment penalty. This ensures the borrower has incentive to refinance after fixing his or her problem and returns the investment capital to the investor.

Do you think that private mortgages are a good source of investment income? Why?

As long as the loan-to-value ratio is kept sufficiently low — less than 65 percent, rarely more than 70 percent — the investor's capital is protected. Even if the borrower ceases to make his or her payments, the investor is all but guaranteed to get his or her money back. Additionally, private mortgages can provide much higher rates than are available in the security or money markets with very little additional risk. Couple this with the fact that if private mortgage lending is done ethically, it allows investors to solve problems for people who the conventional banks cannot help.

Chapter 3:
Why Borrowers Seek
Private Mortgages

The previous chapter demonstrated how private mortgage investing benefits the lender but not how it benefits the borrower. If a borrower must pay high interest rates and points, why go to a private investor instead of a bank? A borrower may not get a conventional loan for many reasons. Banks require a borrower to have a good credit history and a certain credit score. The borrower must also demonstrate that he or she receives regular monthly income from employment or investments. Many prospective borrowers cannot meet all the conditions set by the banks. Below are the ten most common reasons why borrowers seek private loans:

TIME IS A FACTOR

It takes at least six weeks for the approval of a traditional loan. Sometimes, the borrower cannot wait that long. For instance, a borrower may be waiting for a conventional loan, but the closing date for the purchase of a property is earlier than the date when the loan will get approved. In this case, the borrower may get a "bridge loan," a temporary loan until the conventional loan is available, with a private lender. He or she can then close on the deal and wait for the bank to provide a permanent loan without worrying about deadlines.

Time might be a factor if a borrower purchases a vacant property, intending to develop it and use it for another purpose. Banks would prefer to loan the money after the property has been converted and fully rented out — not before.

Payment for a property sold at a foreclosure auction is due within a few days.

A real estate investor may not have time to obtain a bank loan for a foreclosed property that is clearly a good business deal.

It takes so long for conventional loans to get approved because the bank must locate and examine the borrower's credit history, tax returns, and financial statements before approving a loan. Banks also need to know about all other property owned by a borrower. It takes time to gather all this information, have appraisals done, and get the approval of bank officials. A private mortgage lender does not have to go through a lengthy process to get official approval and can make a decision quickly. Because the private loan is for only 65 to 70 percent of the value of the property and is backed by the property rather than the borrower's creditworthiness, a private lender does not need to investigate the borrower's financial history as thoroughly.

THE BORROWER NEEDS PRIVACY

There are times when a borrower may not wish to have all his or her financial information in the hands of a banking institution. For instance, if the borrower is going through a divorce or business separation, that information could be used against him or her. Perhaps the borrower has not yet filed income taxes for the year or does not have all the financial statements required by a traditional lender.

Any of these situations would prevent the borrower from getting a conventional loan. If the property is producing income and the borrower has a good track record, none of these things should keep you from loaning money as a private lender. Your only concern is whether the borrower has income to make the monthly payments.

PRIVATE MORTGAGES ARE EASIER

Private mortgages are relatively easy to do; it requires less paperwork. A borrower does not have to find all the past years' paperwork, bank statements, tax forms, payment receipts, and other documents that must be submitted with an application for a bank loan. A private mortgage also costs less because the borrower does not have to get the expensive appraisals and surveys required by the bank.

THE AMOUNT MAY BE MORE THAN THE BANK WILL LEND

It is possible that a borrower will get more money from a private lender than he or she can get from an institutional mortgage lender. Institutions calculate the amount they are willing to lend as a percentage of either the cost of the property or its appraised value — whichever is lower. If someone finds a good deal and gets a piece of property at a bargain price, the bank is going to lend an amount of money based on that low price rather than on the true value of the property.

A private lender, though, always bases the loan on the appraised value of the property. This way, the borrower is not penalized for finding a good deal.

BAD CREDIT

Sometimes the borrower cannot get a traditional loan because his or her credit score or debt-to-income ratio is too low. He or she may not meet all the qualifications for a bank to make the loan.

Because private mortgage lenders are mainly concerned with the appraised value of the property, credit is not often an obstacle. The main factors in a private loan are whether the property produces or can produce enough income to pay the note and whether the value of the property will more than cover the note. If these two conditions are met, then the borrower's credit is not an issue.

FORECLOSURE

If someone is delinquent with his or her mortgage payments and at risk of foreclosure, sometimes a private mortgage investor can help. Suppose a homeowner has a $200,000 home and owes just $70,000 but is behind on his payments. You might decide to give that homeowner a second chance and lend him $80,000. The borrower can then pay off the bank and start making payments to you. Keep in mind that the loan-to-value (LTV) ratio in this case is just 40 percent: the $80,000 loan equals only 40 percent of the $200,000 value of the house. Even if the borrower goes into foreclosure again, you will get your money back out of the deal.

SELF-EMPLOYMENT

If you are or ever have been self-employed, you know that getting a loan is much tougher for you than it is for your corporate-employed counterpart. You have to produce numerous financial statements and prove to the bank you are financially sound. Self-employed people often seek private mortgages because they simply do not have the financial background to meet a bank's criteria for creditworthiness. This is especially true for someone with a new business who has been self-employed for less than five years. Financial statements for the initial years of a business start-up might show small or even negative earnings as the owner invests in equipment and builds a client base, even if the business now brings in a steady income.

None of this will matter to you as a private mortgage investor. Your only concern is the value of the property used as collateral.

A SHORT-TERM LOAN IS NEEDED

A short-term loan is one that matures in one to five years. To get a short-term loan from a bank, a borrower is often required to have a larger down payment and much better financial standing than for longer-term loans. A real estate investor looking for a two- to three-year loan is often better off looking for a private lender.

An example of a short-term loan is a construction loan that pays for the costs of building a home or commercial building. A borrower who uses a private mortgage construction loan can easily qualify for a regular mortgage loan once the building is complete. In the meantime, the private mortgage loan bridges the gap.

COMMERCIAL PROPERTY

At a traditional lending institution, the criteria for borrowing money to buy, improve, or construct buildings on a commercial property are strict. The borrower's instinct that the property is a good investment is not enough — the bank wants cold, hard facts about the property, including appraisals, historical details, income projections, and information about comparable business properties. The borrower must also have a substantial amount of capital to invest in the commercial enterprise. A local real estate developer might have a good business plan and confidence that he or she will succeed but may not qualify for a bank loan. In situations like this, many real estate investors turn to private mortgages.

THE PROPERTY ITSELF MAY BE IN QUESTION

Some properties just do not meet the criteria for a bank loan.

For example, an old, historic house might be partially renovated. The house is owned free and clear and is worth $200,000. The owner needs $75,000 to finish the renovations. Most banks will not loan this money because the house is in an unfinished state and cannot easily be sold. A private mortgage investor who sees that the renovations are feasible and will increase the value of the home would offer a loan.

Another type of property that often does not qualify for a traditional bank loan is a mobile home. For example, the owner of a doublewide mobile home on 10 acres of land that is worth $250,000 wants to borrow $50,000 — a 20 percent LTV. In order to meet bank criteria for a mobile home equity loan, the home must have been built after 1977, must comply with Housing and Urban Development standards, must meet minimum size and square footage requirements, must be livable and have skirting. Most banks refuse these loans because the current foreclosure rate for mobile homes greatly exceed the foreclosure rate for regular homes, making the risk too high. A private mortgage investor would make the loan, knowing that the borrower would not want to lose $200,000 by defaulting and that the mobile home and land could be sold for a very competitive price if the borrower did default.

IS PRIVATE MORTGAGE INVESTING SAFE?

The money you invest in private mortgages is guaranteed. For every $100,000 you invest, you will make between $1,000 and $1,200 per month in interest. Someone who has invested $500,000 has the potential to make close to $6,000 per month.

Fraud presents the only way you can lose money in private mortgage investing. Fraud occurs when a borrower or an appraiser misrepresents the value of the property serving as collateral for the loan. The main criterion for a private loan is the loan-to-value ratio — the lender will lend an amount equal to only a percentage of the value of the property. If you lend out $50,000 on a home the borrower says is worth $100,000 when the home is really only worth $30,000, you will lose $20,000 if you have to foreclose on the property.

Before making a loan, you must first do your own research on the property to protect your investment. This research includes:

- An appraisal.

- A title search.

- A proper LTV ratio. *See Chapter 4 for more information on this topic.*

Have the appraisal done by an independent appraiser you know to be reliable. If the borrower tells you the property is worth $100,000 and the appraisal comes back with the same number, you can be fairly confident that is the true value of the house. There are other ways to verify the value of the house. You can go to SearchSystems.net (**http://publicrecords.searchsystems.net**) and search for property records for your state. Most county property appraisers have websites. For example, if you go the website for the Marion County Property Appraiser (**www.pa.marion.fl.us**) and type in the address of the property, you can see an appraisal like the one below. It shows the appraised value of the land and the building for taxation purposes. Appraisals for taxation are slightly lower than the current market value of a property — or if prices have dropped dramatically during the last few months, the property tax appraisal could be higher.

41551-000-00

```
                                    MARION COUNTY
41551-000-00 Alt Key:1031109    ** Property Information **  Map It!  As of  10/07/05
-----------------------------------------------------------------------------------
WELLS ROGER K & MARIAN L         TAXES/ASSESSMENTS:      $1,622.30    M.S.T.U.
13369 SE HIGHWAY 484             LOCATION:               MAP: 218 D2    PC: 01
BELLEVIEW FL                     013369 SE HWY 484           IMAGES Mill Grp 9001
                                 344205827 SEE LETTER IN HX FILE       .60 Acres
-----------------------------------------------------------------------------------

                       **       Current Values        **

Property Values: Land Just Val        7,498
               : Buildings           80,268
               : Miscellaneous       14,551
               : Total Just         102,317
               : Total Assessd       86,704    Amendment 10 Impact    -15,613
               : Exemptions         -25,000    Ex Codes: 01
               : Total Taxable       61,704
-----------------------------------------------------------------------------------
```

** History of Assessed Values **

Year	Land	Building	Misc Impr	Just	Assessed	Exemption	Taxable
2005 1	7,498	80,268	14,774	102,540	84,179	25,000	59,179 TN
2004 1	6,504	73,546	12,395	92,445	81,728	25,000	56,728 TN
2003 1	6,079	70,813	12,565	89,457	79,027	25,000	54,027 TN

** Property Transfer History **

(Official Records Transfer) Book Page	Date	Instrument	Code	Qualified/ Unqualified		Vacant/ Improved	Price
3827/1968	09/04	07 WARRANTY	7 PORTIONUND INT	U		I	100
3383/0283	03/03	05 QUIT CL	0		U	I	100
3383/0280	03/03	07 WARRANTY	0		U	I	100
2127/0441	04/95	07 WARRANTY	2 V-SALES VERIFI	Q	QUALIFIED	I	88500
2093/1229	09/94	71 DTH CER	0		U	I	100
2095/1961	12/91	74 PROBATE	0		U	I	100

** Property Description **

```
01  -  SEC 12 TWP 17 RGE 22
02  -  BEG AT PT ON W BDY OF E 1/2 OF NW 1/4 N 00-02-52 W
03  -  634.5 FT FROM SW COR OF E 1/2 OF NW 1/4 TH
04  -  N 00-02-52 W 210 FT TO SELY ROW OF SR 484 BEING ON
05  -  A CURVE AND BEGINNING 30 FT FORM THE RADIAL TO THE
06  -  CENTERLINE OF SAID ROD, TH NELY AL ROW LINE CURVE
07  -  A CHORD BEARING OF N 48-58-40 E 150 FT TH S 42-19-53 E
08  -  RADIAL TO ROW LINE CURVE 143.79 FT TH S 00-02-52 E
09  -  201.98 FT TH S 89-57-08 W 210 FT TO POB LESS ANY PART OF
10  -  PROPERTY THAT LIES WITHIN FOLLOWING DESCRIPTION:
11  -  FROM SW COR OF NW 1/4 OF SEC 12 RUN N 89-42-17 E 1340.54 FT
12  -  TH N 00-16-03 E 708.19 FT FOR POB TH N 00-16-03 E 138.55 FT
13  -  TO POINT ON EXZISTING ROW LINE OF CTY RD 484 S ROW LINE
14  -  BEING A NONTANGENT CURVE CONCAVE NW'LY RAD OF 3849.55 FT TH
15  -  FROM TANGENT BEARING OF N 50-13-02 E RUN NE'LY 148.69 FT
16  -  ALONG ARC OF CURVE & EXISTING ROW LINE CHORD BEARING OF
17  -  N 49-06-38 E THRU CENTRAL ANGLE OF 02-12-47 TO POINT ON
18  -  E'LY BDRY OF PARCEL OF LAND BEING DESC IN OR BK 2127/PG 441
19  -  TH S 41-47-06 E 147.12 FT TH S 00-25-32 W 21.84 FT ALONG
20  -  E'LY BDRY TO POINT ON AFORESAID LINE BEING PARALLEL WITH
21  -  & 100 FT SE'LY OF CTY RD 484 TH S 63-40-48 W 235.31 FT
22  -  ALONG SAID PARALLEL LINE TO POB
```

** Land Data **

LN	Use	Front	Depth	Zone	C	Notes	Units	Type	Rate	Dph	Loc	Shp	Phy	Just Val
01	0100			A1		IRREGULAR	.60	AC	4500.00	100	100	215	110	6,386
02	9990			A1		CR484	150.00	UT	7.41	100	100	100	100	1,112
Neighborhood	9400	17/22	& 17/23 W of Hwy 441				Total Land	-	Class					6,386
Mkt: 10 70							Total Land	-	Just					7,498

** Building Characteristics **

```
Building 01 of 02
--------------------------------------------------------------------------------
FGR01=U29R23D29L23.U3
RES02=L50U26R20U20R30D46.
FOP03=D1R1D3L21U4R20.U26
FOP04=R23U6L23D6.U20
EPA05=R21U18L10U20L25U3L20D10L10D31R44.
```

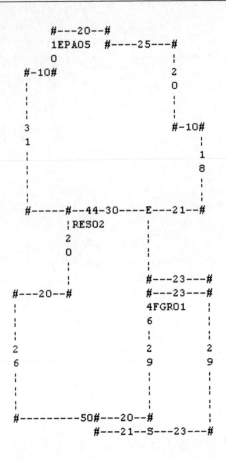

```
                              #---20--#
                              1EPA05  #----25---#
                              0                :
                          #-10#                2
                          :                    0
                          :                    :
                          :                    :
                          3                #-10#
                          1                    :
                          :                    1
                          :                    8
                          :                    :
                          :                    :
                          #-----#--44-30----E---21--#
                          :RES02                :
                          2                     :
                          0                     :
                          :                     :
                          :                 #---23---#
              #---20--#                     #---23---#
              :                             4FGR01   :
              :                             6        :
              :                             :        :
              2                             2        2
              6                             9        9
              :                             :        :
              :                             :        :
              #--------50#---20--#          :        :
                        #---21--S---23---#
```

Improvement Type 1F SFR   - 01 FAMILY RESID
Effective Age   3 10-14 YRS   Obsolesence: Functional 0%
Condition   6 GOOD   Year Built   1965   Locational 0%
Quality Grade   500   Architecture   0 STANDARD SFR
Inspected on 09/02/03 by 174-SCOTT ANDERSON   Base Perimeter   192

| (Section) | | | Nbr | Year | Attic | /- Basement Data -/ | | Ground |
Type	ID	/- Exterior Walls -/	Stories	Bilt	Finish	% Area	% Finish	Flr Area
FGR	01	29 VINYL SIDING	1.00	1965	N	0	0	667 SF
RES	02	29 VINYL SIDING	1.00	1965	N	0	0	1,900 SF
FOP	03	01 NO EXTERIOR	1.00	1965	N	0	0	83 SF
FOP	04	01 NO EXTERIOR	1.00	1980	N	0	0	138 SF
EPA	05	01 NO EXTERIOR	1.00	1985	N	0	0	2,260 SF

Roof Type   10 GABLE   Floor Finish 24 CARPET   Bedrooms 3 Kitchen   Y
Roof Cover 08 FBRGLASS SHNGL Wall Finish 16 DRYWALL-PAINT 4FixBath 0 Dishwasher Y
Heat Type1 22 DUCTED FHA   Heat Source1 10 ELECTRIC   3FixBath 2 Disposal   Y
      Type2 00   Source2 00   2FixBath 0 Compactor N
Foundation   7 BLK PERIMETER   Fireplaces   1   Xfixture 2 Intercom   N
A/C   Y   Vacuum   N

                    ** Building Characteristics   **

Building 02 of 02

APTO1=L30U16R30D16.
PTOO2=R13U16L13D16.

```
#--------------------30--------------------#--------13--------#
| APT01                                     | PT002            |
|                                           |                  |
|                                           |                  |
|                                           |                  |
|                                           |                  |
|                                           |                  |
|                                           |                  |
1                                           1                  1
6                                           6                  6
|                                           |                  |
|                                           |                  |
|                                           |                  |
|                                           |                  |
|                                           |                  |
|                                           |                  |
|                                           |                  |
#--------------------30--------------------E--------13--------#
```

```
Improvement Type 1F SFR    - 01 FAMILY RESID
Effective Age    3 10-14 YRS                        Obsolesence: Functional  0%
Condition        5 AVERAGE          Year Built  1980            Locational  0%
Quality Grade   200                 Architecture   0 STANDARD SFR
Inspected on 09/02/03 by 174-SCOTT ANDERSON                Base Perimeter   92
```

```
(Section)                        Nbr   Year Attic /- Basement Data -/   Ground
Type  ID  /- Exterior Walls -/ Stories Bilt Finish % Area  % Finish    Flr Area
APT   01   20 MH ALUM SIDING    1.00   1980  N       0        0          480 SF
PTO   02   01 NO EXTERIOR       1.00   1980  N       0        0          208 SF
```

```
Roof Type  02 FLAT WOOD STR  Floor Finish 24 CARPET        Bedrooms  1 Kitchen     Y
Roof Cover 17 KOOL SEAL/MTL  Wall  Finish 16 DRYWALL-PAINT 4FixBath  0 Dishwasher N
Heat Type1 22 DUCTED FHA     Heat Source1 06 GAS           3FixBath  1 Disposal   N
     Type2 00                     Source2 00               2FixBath  0 Compactor  N
Foundation  7 BLK PERIMETER  Fireplaces   0               Xfixture  2 Intercom   N
A/C         N                                                          Vacuum     N
```

** Miscellaneous Improvements **

```
Type              Number Units/Type  Life    EYB  Grade Length Width  Just Value
256   WELL   1-5 BTH     1.00 UT      99     2003    2                     1,200
190   SEPTIC 1-5 BTH     1.00 UT      99     1965    2                       730
190   SEPTIC 1-5 BTH     1.00 UT      99     1980    1                       460
226   RES SWIM POOL    648.00 SF      20     1984    5   36.0  18.0        5,876
099   DECK             444.00 SF      50     1984    1                       711
UDS   SCRN PORCH-UNF   380.00 SF      40     1980    1   20.0  19.0        1,197
UDU   UTILITY-UNFINS   120.00 SF      40     1980    1   12.0  10.0          441
159   PAV CONCRETE    2582.00 SF      20     1980    3                     1,756
UDC   CARPORT-UNFIN    420.00 SF      40     1993    2   20.0  21.0        1,942
114   FENCE BOARD      128.00 LF      10     1993    4                       238
                              Total Just Value as of 10/20/03            14,551
```

```
              **  Appraiser Notes              **

  01  -  COULD NOT DO A COMPLETE REVIEW
  -----------------------------------------------------------------------

                 **  Planning and Building  **
                    County Permit search

     Permit       Permit  Date    Date    Construction Description
     Number       Amount  Issued  Complete
  01 M041073       2,315   04/03   04/03   WELL PUMP ELECTRIC          -
  02 M120194         450   12/03   06/04   ABANDON WELL                -
  -----------------------------------------------------------------------

                  **  Cost/Market Summary  **

  Buildings  R.C.N.     100,203 03/28/01  Bldg  Reproduction   Amount of    R.C.N. Less
  Total Depreciatio     -19,935           Nbr   Cost New    Depreciation   Depreciation
  Bldg - Just Value      80,268           01      85,251        16,197         69,054
  Misc - Just Value      14,551 10/20/03  02      14,952         3,738         11,214
  Land - Just Value       7,498 05/18/05
  Total  Just Value     102,317
```

Every county has a system for assigning identification numbers, called parcel ID property has already been used as collateral for a loan, your claim will be secondary to the first mortgage in case of default, and you might not be able to recover any of your money. Second mortgage loans are not a good investment unless you have some assurance that the borrower will not default.

Finally, keep your LTV ratio at no more than 65 percent of the property's value. That way, even if the value of the property was somewhat overstated, you will still make a profit if the borrower defaults on the loan, and you have to sell the property.

There are many reasons why a responsible borrower might want to take out a private mortgage and pay higher interest rates than on a conventional loan. The arrangement benefits both borrower and lender: The lender gets a good return on his or her investment, and the borrower gets a mortgage he or she could not obtain through a bank. There are, however, some circumstances in which it would not be wise to lend your money, even when the borrower seems sound and responsible and able to repay the loan. *The following chapter will help you determine whether a particular opportunity is right for you.*

Chapter 4: Evaluating a Loan Opportunity

An important difference between conventional bank loans and private mortgage loans is that the interest rate and amount of a private loan are determined by the value of the property used to secure the loan, not by the borrower's credit score. When evaluating an investment opportunity, a private mortgage lender considers several factors: the loan-to-value ratio, the type of property used as collateral, the potential of the property to produce income, the way in which the loan will eventually be paid off, and whether the borrower has had previous experience with private mortgages.

LOAN-TO-VALUE RATIO (LTV)

The most important consideration — the one that the deal really hinges on — is the loan-to-value ratio (LTV). This is a simple calculation of the loan amount as a percentage of the value of a property.

Loan amount

Property value

For instance, if you loan $63,000 on a $100,000 piece of property, the LTV is 63 percent. If you loan out $56,000 on a $96,500 piece of property, the LTV would be $56,000 divided by $96,500, or 58 percent.

Private mortgage lenders typically seek an LTV that is:

- Up to 55 percent for undeveloped or raw property.

- Up to 65 percent for commercial properties, such as shopping centers and office complexes.

- Up to 70 percent for residential properties, such as houses, duplexes, and apartment complexes.

These are merely guidelines. You should combine the LTV with other criteria to determine whether to make the loan. If the market for that type of property is slow or if the property is in less than optimal condition, you might only want to loan 55 percent on a commercial property or even on a residential property. A low LTV value is an incentive for the borrower to pay back the loan and avoid default because if you foreclose, you will get the property for a fraction of its value. The borrower will lose whatever equity he or she has in the property and will still be responsible to pay back any other loans associated with the property. The borrower will want to make sure that you do not foreclose.

A low LTV also guarantees that you will recover your capital if the property goes into foreclosure. Suppose you loan $50,000 on a house worth $100,000, an LTV of 50 percent. If the borrower defaults and you foreclose, you will acquire a $100,000 house for only $50,000. You can then sell it for a very competitive $75,000. Even if the housing market is slow, you will find a buyer quickly because of the low price. When the house sells, you will recover your original $50,000 plus an additional profit of $25,000. If your LTV had been higher — for example, if you had loaned $75,000 on the $100,000 house — you would not have as much freedom to lower the price in order to make a fast sale.

As you become more experienced with real estate investors and property, you will develop an instinct for situations in which you should lower the LTV ratio.

When Do You Lower the LTV Ratio?

Matt Tabacchi, president of Allstate Mortgage of Florida Loans & Investments, Inc., offers the following tips for evaluating an LTV ratio:

- *I drive by the piece of property and determine how much I want to lend. There are some basic guidelines, but there is also a lot of gut feeling involved. What is your sense of the person? How do you feel about the property?*

- If someone has a well-maintained piece of property, it is a very good looking piece of property, and the person needs 67 percent, then I may do it. On the other hand, if the property is run down, in bad shape, and in a poor location, then I might only loan 40 to 50 percent. A lot of it is gut feeling. The more you do it, the better your instinct is about these things.

- You can literally stay at 65 percent and not go wrong, even if the property is not in top shape. You can get 65 percent out of a piece of property regardless of its condition.

- The other concern is to be sure that you are loaning 65 percent of the real value of the property and not some inflated value. Be careful in an inflated market. If somebody paid $100,000 for a piece of property six months ago and now asks to borrow $150,000 because the house is now worth $300,000, that should raise a red flag. The probability that its value appreciated that much in six months is pretty small.

- Any time someone has owned a house for less than a year, you want to find out what they paid for it, and you also want to see why its value appreciated so much. Was the house totally remodeled? Was it inherited or bought cheaply from a relative? Or is the house just not worth that much money? There may be legitimate reasons why it appreciated so quickly, but you need to check it out. A realtor and an appraiser will give you the true value of a house.

 Find a real estate appraiser or a real estate agent who you can trust.

Find yourself a real estate appraiser or a real estate agent who you can trust in the area where you are going to lend. Ask your real estate professional what he or she thinks is the value of a house. This person should work for you and for the seller of the property. The real estate professional can bill you for his or her services, and you can charge the borrower.

TYPE OF PROPERTY

If the borrower defaults on a loan, you suddenly become the owner of the property. Interest payments stop, and you become responsible for property maintenance and taxes. You will lose money if cannot sell the property quickly or for a large profit. The type of property used as collateral affects your ability to dispose of it quickly in case of a default. If the market for that type of property is strong in the area where it is located or if you have expertise in selling or managing that type of property, you might be more willing to risk your money on the loan.

- **Single-family dwellings:** These often take up to a year to sell. Unless you can rent them out while you attempt to sell them, you risk losing money. Not only will you not receive a monthly interest check, but your capital will also be tied up, and you cannot use it for another investment.

- **Single-use buildings:** Some buildings can only be used for one purpose. For instance, a building built specifically for an oil-changing company can only be used by other oil-changing businesses. It is not easy to sell a specialized building quickly, and finding a suitable renter will also be difficult.

- **Multi-tenant, multi-use buildings:** Office buildings typically sell quickly, especially if you are selling below market value to simply recover your capital. Additionally, an office building with existing tenants can produce income while you attempt to sell, helping you to retain the monthly payments you had counted on in the original deal.

CASH FLOW OR INCOME POTENTIAL OF THE PROPERTY

If the borrower plans to generate income by renting out the property or operating a business on the premises, your investment will be more secure. Ideally, as the lender you would like to see the property producing enough income to pay for the note, as well as all the expenses. To get an idea of how much income might be earned from the property, look at the borrower's cash flow from other properties and businesses. Lending money when there is no apparent cash flow is risky.

If you believe the borrower can come up with the monthly interest payments without generating income from the property, you can be less concerned about this factor. A borrower who buys the property as a residence will have to raise money for payments through employment or some other source of personal income.

EXIT STRATEGY

Private loans are short-term loans. Therefore, it is essential to know the borrower's exit strategy — how the borrower plans to repay the loan at the end of the term. Once you know the plan, you have to decide if it is a good one. If the exit strategy is too risky, you might determine that you do not want a part of the deal, or you might decide to ask for higher interest rates or a lower LTV or both.

There are many ways that a borrower can "exit" the private mortgage that you hold:

1. **Sell the property before the note is due.** Many real estate investors buy a bargain-priced house or building, renovate and repair it, and sell it again within a few months, before the mortgage comes due. This is a good strategy for a single-family dwelling as long as the note is at least a year in length. It is also likely to succeed if the building is an office complex or other type of real estate property in demand in the local market.

2. **Finance through a traditional lender.** At the end of the term, the borrower will obtain a traditional mortgage with a lower interest rate and use the money to repay you. By making timely payments on your loan for at least 12 months, the borrower establishes a good credit record and can qualify for a lower interest rate from a bank. This is a good exit strategy as long as the borrower's credit is good enough to get a traditional loan and the condition of the property is such that a bank will accept it as collateral.

3. **Obtain a blanket mortgage on all properties owned.** A real estate investor might own several rental properties or other real estate properties under development. A borrower might also own several personal properties, such as a residence, vacation home, and business property. To pay off your loan, the borrower could obtain a "blanket mortgage" from a bank, using all of the properties combined as collateral. The success of this strategy will depend upon the borrower's credit record and the properties involved.

4. **Borrow equity from another property.** A borrower who owns another real estate property could take out an equity loan, such as a home equity loan, on that property and use the money to pay off your loan. The home equity loan will have a lower interest rate. This is a good exit strategy as long as the equity in the other property is sufficient to cover the mortgage. You should also feel comfortable that the borrower will use that equity toward your loan and not for something else.

5. **Find a partner for investment purposes.** Once he or she has begun developing a property, a real estate investor could seek one or more partners to invest in the next phase of a business project and use the investment to pay off your loan. The success of this strategy will depend on the nature of the business, the type and condition of the property, and the likelihood that others will want to become equity investors in that property.

6. **Self-amortize the exit.** A self-amortization exit involves full repayment of the loan from the property cash flow. Each month, the borrower sets aside part of the money generated by the property to pay back the capital. This strategy is uncommon because most property cannot produce enough income to repay the loan in full during the one- to three-year duration of the loan.

These are the most common exit strategies, but there are many other possibilities. There is not one right exit strategy. Success depends upon the borrower, the nature of the property, the purpose of the loan, and the soundness of the borrower's business plan. You, as the lender, must decide if a particular strategy is feasible and whether it suits your own investment goals. You should know the planned exit strategy before you lend the borrower money.

BORROWER'S EXPERIENCE

The final factor in determining whether to make a loan is the borrower's experience. Has the borrower used a private mortgage loan before? How successful have the borrower's previous ventures been? If you are dealing with a borrower who has a long list of successful real estate ventures, you will feel more secure loaning him or her the money.

On the other hand, new real estate investors taking on huge renovation projects might be at risk of failing. You should determine if they have the right experience; if they have worked in real estate; if they know the construction industry; if they have the necessary licenses and permits; if they can obtain materials and hire subcontractors in a timely manner; and if they have acted in the capacity of a landlord. Evaluate whether a potential borrower has the talents and skills to successfully carry out the proposed project.

An experienced borrower has practical, hands-on knowledge of the proposed project. You feel confident that he or she knows how to renovate a building and sell it quickly. You perceive that he or she has a clear exit strategy and will purchase property that will make a profit. The interest rate on your loan should be inversely proportional to the borrower's abilities and experience. If you have confidence in the borrower, you can provide the maximum loan amount at the minimum interest rate. If you do not feel entirely confident in the borrower's experience but still plan to go ahead with the loan, you can provide a smaller loan with a much higher interest rate.

By looking at all of these factors as a whole, you can set your interest rate and determine the LTV. High marks in all the categories indicate high LTVs. Uncertainty about any of these factors should result in higher interest rates and lower LTVs. When you have doubts about a borrower, you should only consider making the loan if you would like to own the property yourself. If the borrower defaults, would you be happy to acquire that property? If the answer is yes, then it might be worth the risk.

CREDIT SCORES AND WHAT THEY MEAN

Though the borrower's credit rating is not really a consideration in a private mortgage loan, you may find yourself looking at the borrower's credit score when you evaluate his or her abilities and experience. You should understand how a credit score is calculated and what the number means to you as a private mortgage investor.

A credit score is simply a number calculated using the borrower's credit history. The borrower is assigned points based on information in his or her credit report. These points are compared to those of other similar consumers and help the lending agency quantify the risk of loaning money to this particular person or entity.

Based on the credit score, the lending agency predicts how likely the borrower is to repay money. The higher the score, which can range from 300 to 900, the more likely a borrower will repay. Knowing this, traditional bankers gladly accept borrowers with high numbers; accept borrowers with mediocre numbers if they can charge enough points and higher interest rates to compensate for the additional risk; and reject prospective borrowers with low numbers.

The score most commonly used by lenders is known as a FICO score for the Fair Isaac Corporation that developed it. Although the exact formula for determining a score is not public knowledge, this is an approximate breakdown of how the score is determined:

- 35 percent — Payment History. This includes late payments, collection payments, bankruptcies, and so forth. The more recent these events, the more they lower the score.

- 30 percent — Outstanding Debt. This includes any debt: car loans, mortgages, and unsecured debt, such as credit cards.

- 15 percent — Length of Credit History. This looks at how long a person has used credit. People with no previous credit history get a lower credit rating.

- 10 percent — Number of Inquiries on the Credit Report. Too many inquiries makes it appear that the borrower is in some kind of financial trouble or is getting too heavily in debt.

- 10 percent — Types of Credit Held. How much debt is secured? How much is unsecured? What are the loans for?

In the context of private mortgage lending, the payment history is the most relevant factor. A borrower who is late with other payments might also be late with yours. But, do not jump to conclusions. Late payments, bankruptcies, and judgments can occur for a number of reasons. If the borrower's income is not sufficient to meet his or her expenses, you will be affected. In many cases, financial problems are due to specific circumstances, such as a recent divorce, unpaid medical bills resulting from an accident or illness, or a recent layoff. A bankruptcy resulting from a divorce is reported on a credit report in the same way as a bankruptcy resulting from irresponsible spending. When you find a bankruptcy or other negative information on a prospective borrower's credit report, ask for an explanation before refusing the loan. A borrower who has resolved a one-time financial crisis is still a good prospect if he or she is back on a sound financial footing and if the property used as collateral for the loan is valuable.

Too much outstanding debt has a negative effect on a credit score and may discourage you from lending. Like late payments, outstanding debt may be readily explainable. *In Chapter 6, you will learn you can find money for investment purposes by taking an equity loan on your home.* "Borrowing" from a credit card at 6 percent and loaning out the money at 15 percent can also be a good strategy. Either strategy could show up unfavorably on your credit report as outstanding debt, even when you are financially sound. Many real estate investors show too much outstanding debt on their credit reports at any given time because they are in the business of buying and selling real estate. This does not make them poor candidates for loans; having experience investing in real estate actually makes them better candidates for you.

A credit score that is low because the person has not had credit for a certain length of time hinders those who have chosen to live without credit or young people who have yet to establish a credit record. None of these circumstances directly affect the criteria you will use to determine if you wish to loan money to a borrower. At worst, someone just beginning to establish credit may be inexperienced. If the other criteria for lending are met, this should not be an obstacle.

Borrowers who deal in real estate, buy and sell cars, or have any other reason to obtain several loans a year will find that their credit scores go down — even if they are making their payments on time. Each time these people apply for a loan, their credit reports are checked, and those inquiries are recorded in their credit reports. Too many inquiries, according to the lending industry, make someone a bad credit risk. In reality, they may have a legitimate reason for the number of inquiries.

The final component of the FICO score is the type of credit held. Since the mortgage loan you are going to provide will be secured by collateral, it really does not matter what types of loans your borrower has open. You are more concerned about the value of the property than with the borrower and with the borrower's experience rather than with his or her credit score.

The previous chapters have explained that private mortgage loans generate wealth primarily by earning interest, and have reviewed the factors you should consider when deciding whether to make a loan. *The next chapter will discuss the different types of mortgages, their interest structures, and other vehicles you can use when structuring your loan to provide you with even more return on your investment.*

CASE STUDY: WHY I LIKE PRIVATE MORTGAGE INVESTING

Bob
Private mortgage investor

I was in the stock market. In fact, I lost money in the market. It was always up and down and up and down. Because I have my own business, I just did not have time to keep up with the market. It was too difficult to assess, which is why I got into private mortgages almost 20 years ago.

At first, I had most of my money in real property. I put any extra into private mortgages. It has been really beneficial for me. I have never had a foreclosure, and I keep my loan-to-value ratio at 65 to 70 percent. This makes things safe and keeps me covered in case of a real estate market fluctuation. The rates I earn and the ease of keeping up with the trends are a whole lot better than the stock market.

You do have to keep up with real estate market trends. In my area, the real estate market has gone crazy in the last few years — I would even say ridiculous. For me, this just means that I have to be careful when evaluating my loan-to-value ratio. For instance, if I am trying to keep my LTV at 65 percent, I want to make sure I loan 65 percent of the real value of the home and not some inflated value. Sometimes, I see a home appraised at $200,000, and I know that it is not really worth much more than $100,000. If I gave 65 percent based on the $200,000 appraisal, I would actually be handing the borrower more money than the home was really worth.

I am very concerned about the appraisal. You do not want to get ahead of the appraisal. You can see the general prices in a Multiple Listing System (MLS), and in a couple of weeks, they will jump up. That does not mean, however, that a property will sell at that price. Be careful that you are not looking at inflated appraisals. You need to watch it. For instance, I have a home that I could easily get appraised for what the other homes in the neighborhood sell for. My home, though, does not have a pool and is smaller than the average home in the area. It should not be appraised that high, but it would be. This is why you need to really look at the property and the properties around it.

Luckily, I have never had to foreclose. The idea does concern me some-what, but I know that my attorney can handle it with minimal effort on my part. In fact, most good mortgage brokers can also help you take care of it. It is not the worst thing that can happen as long as your LTV is good.

People have asked me whether I inspect all the properties that I lend on. My answer is "Yes, times five." You have got to do it. There are so many dishonest people out there. If you do not know your broker, you may find some fraudulent practices going on. For instance, you might be told of a $100,000 house, and you plan to loan $50,000 on it. You look it up on the computer, and it looks great. However, if you were given the wrong legal description, you will be looking at the wrong house. The cor-rect legal description would show a trailer in a trailer park. That is a far cry from a single-family home on an acre lot. This will not happen if you go and have a look. Always be sure that what you see physically is the same piece of property you sign for. Do not let anyone bait and switch.

Other things can occur, too. For instance, I was going to loan out on a $200,000 piece of property. I went out to the address, and it looked pretty good, but something did not seem right with the legal description. Then, I realized what was going on. The piece of property was behind the one on the road, and you could not even see it from the road. That makes a big difference in the value of that property. The mortgage broker had not been out to the property, and the person needing the loan had glossed over the fact that there was no frontage. Avoid all of this by do-ing your homework.

I think that private mortgage investing is the best way to invest. You can take a million and put it out at 12 percent, and I guarantee you can make $120,000 a year. In fact, I think it would be just fine to invest everything you own this way.

The only problem I see is the tax rate. If the money you have invested is not in an IRA, then you can count on being taxed at 30 to 38 percent. It is different with developments. With developments and projects, you can get Uncle Sam to give you tax cuts but not with private mortgage The only problem I see is the tax rate. If the money you have invested is not in an IRA, then you can count on getting taxed at 30 to 38 percent.

It is different with developments. With developments and projects, you can get Uncle Sam to give you tax cuts but not with private mortgage investing. That seems unfair to me, since I am taking all the risk. But, it is the only problem I see with investing everything this way, and, honestly, even with the taxes, you still make a heck of a lot more than normal investment vehicles. Also, getting a good accountant is really wise. They help you pay the least amount of taxes but keep you totally legal. You will know what I mean if you are ever audited.

I follow my own advice and invest everything this way. I use my IRA by going through Trust Administration Services in California. I made 7 to 8 percent, and I now make 12 to 14 percent. Plus, I do not have any concerns because I have control of what I invest in. I keep my LTV to 65 percent, and if I have to foreclose, then I have to foreclose. I would just turn it over to a lawyer, and it is done. The only issue I have with using my IRA is that I have to have the payments sent directly to the trustee in California. I really like seeing the payments and recording them instead of someone else doing it for me. If there is a problem, I may not know about it for ten days or so, but that is the only drawback I see.

I also think that leveraging your home is a great idea. You are going to get at least 5 percent in your pocket on money simply sitting in your home. It is taxable income, but so is stock market income. And, there is no long-term capital gain in a mortgage.

I am a firm believer in finding the right people for your team. For instance, it is really important to find a good broker, especially if you are new to real estate investing. The best way to find a good broker is by word of mouth. A broker can find out all the information you need to know about the property, and this keeps you from doing all the research yourself. Now, even with a good broker, I still inspect the property, but I do not have to do all of the legwork. By the time the broker brings a deal to me, I know all I really have to do is go take a look.

Here is my word of caution: Do not deal with individuals. Individuals do not need a license, and, therefore, do not need to follow any particular guidelines. If a broker is out there without a license, you are much more likely to find yourself getting into fraudulent deals.

As I said earlier, a good accountant is necessary. They keep you straight at the end of the year, and a good real estate lawyer is essential. I do not use them often, but when I have a question, I want to know they have the answer. Remember, you want to speak to a real estate lawyer, not a divorce lawyer.

Here are a few other tips:

1. Escrow is something I have considered, but it is more of a pain than it is worth to me. Some people feel better about it as a safety precaution. I guess I would rather contact the borrower when it is due.

2. If you are going to partner with someone, make sure they are trustworthy. There are several people with whom I would partner. There are several others, however, I would not touch with a 10-foot pole.

3. It is better to get started with any amount you have to invest, instead of leaving that money sitting in the bank earning a measly 2 to 4 percent.

4. Always write in prepayment penalties. I typically go for 4 to 5 percent. This keeps me from having to move my money around as much.

It is like this: If you want to know about Hondas, you certainly would not ask those questions at a Chevrolet dealer. The same holds true about private mortgage investing. Find those who know what they are doing.

Chapter 5: Mortgages, Interest Rates, and Fees

The first chapters of this book explained the general concepts of private mortgage investing. Borrowers who cannot obtain traditional bank loans are willing to pay higher interest rates for short-term loans that help them accomplish their personal or business objectives. Many of these borrowers are experienced real estate investors or developers who have successful business models and want to invest in income-producing properties. Private mortgage lending is primarily concerned with the value of the property used as collateral for a loan, rather than with the borrower's credit score. Private mortgage investments are relatively safe because they are backed by real estate properties that can be sold in case of default to recoup your capital and even make a profit. Private mortgage brokers can help by matching lenders with appropriate borrowers and investment opportunities and by facilitating many aspects of the loan process. Success depends on accurately evaluating the real estate property, the experience of the borrower, the business opportunity, and the borrower's plan for quickly repaying your loan.

Now, you are ready to learn exactly how private mortgage loans are structured. This chapter discusses the types of mortgage contracts you can use.

FIXED-RATE VERSUS ADJUSTABLE-RATE MORTGAGES

Private mortgage widely uses two types of mortgages: fixed-rate mortgages and adjustable-rate mortgages.

Fixed-rate mortgages

Fixed-rate mortgages are the most common type of mortgage available. A fixed-rate mortgage gives the borrower an unchanging interest rate for the entire life of the loan. For instance, if you determine that you will loan $100,000 at 12 percent for 3 years, then you will know exactly what your interest earnings will be each month over the life of the loan.

A fixed-rate mortgage allows you to always know exactly how much you will earn, and works well if you believe market interest rates are about to fall because you will lock in the current, higher interest rate. If market interest rates increase, you will be committed to a lower rate for the term of the loan, meaning your money will not earn as much as it could — a situation known as opportunity cost.

Chapter 14 explains how to determine what interest rate you will charge. The higher the risk you take, the higher the interest rate.

Adjustable-rate mortgages (ARMs)

In an ARM, the interest rate is adjusted based on the changing market rates and economic trends. As a private mortgage lender, you might decide to offer this type of loan if you believe interest rates will rise during the term of the loan so you will not get stuck with a lower interest rate.

While negotiating an ARM, you will want to put a "floor" on your interest rate, meaning the interest rate will not go below a certain limit. For instance, if you start with a 12 percent loan, you can state the conditions for increasing the interest rate, while also specifying the rate will never drop below 12 percent.

ARMs are adjusted according to the terms of the loan. For short-term loans, you will want a shorter-term ARM. For instance, a three-month ARM will adjust interest rates every three months, while a three-year ARM will only adjust rates every three years. If you only offer a five-year loan, you do not want to create an ARM that only has the opportunity to adjust one time. You would want to adjust the interest rate to match market interest rates at least every six months.

The interest rate for an ARM is normally the market interest rate for one-year Treasury bills, CDs, the prime rate, or another index, plus a specified number of additional percentage points. You will specify the index in the contract and then adjust your interest rate accordingly. Suppose you lend at ten points above the current interest rate for $100,000 CDs. If these rates go up two points, then the interest rate you charge the borrower will go up two points the next time an adjustment is made.

CONSTRUCTION LOANS

A construction loan is a short-term, nonpermanent loan to finance the cost of a construction project. Most construction loans last six to nine months but may last longer, depending on the complexity of the project. These loans are interest-only loans, meaning the borrower just makes monthly interest payments instead of paying down the loan amount. The lender gets his or her entire investment back when the home sells or when the builder gets a conventional loan.

As a lender, the best way to ensure the safety of your investment is to only lend out 50 percent of the current value of the project. For instance, if the lot were worth $30,000, you would advance only $15,000 to the builder. You can structure the mortgage so a certain amount of money is put in an escrow account. The builder is allowed to take out a certain amount, known as a draw, each time the project advances to a specific stage. When the home is completed, you will have loaned out only 50 percent of the value of the completed home.

Many private investors like dealing with construction loans because:

- The bookkeeping is simple because you only deal with interest payments.

- You work with a business, as opposed to an individual. Normally, businesses will follow through on commitments. You can assess the risks involved based on the business's past performance.

- The loan is short and the capital, along with the interest earned, can be recovered and put into another project quickly.

Builders like to deal with private lenders who can get the money to them quickly instead of banks that may take weeks to approve a loan. Builders often want to get started on a construction project without delay so they can finish it as quickly as possible, sell or lease the property, and pay off their contractors and financial obligations. Many banks are reluctant to give a mortgage loan for a property that has not been constructed yet or are willing to loan only an amount equal to the appraised value of the vacant lot.

The risk of a construction loan is that if the builder defaults on the loan, you will be left with an unfinished house or building. To get your investment out of the property, you will have to finish the construction yourself and be involved in its sale. For those not experienced with the construction aspect of real estate, this can seem daunting.

Lending for construction purposes can be a good way to build up the amount of capital you have to invest in other projects. For instance, if you loan out $50,000 for construction at 14 percent for nine months, you get the following payments:

MONTH	PRINCIPAL LOANED	PAYMENT
1	$12,500	$583.33
2	$12,500	$583.33
3	$20,000	$583.33
4	$25,000	$583.33
5	$25,000	$583.33
6	$30,000	$583.33
7	$35,000	$583.33
8	$45,000	$583.33
9	$50,000	$583.33

This earns you $5,250 in nine months. After nine months, you will have $55,250 to lend to a new borrower. If you had put the same money into a regular loan for three years, you would not have the capital to reinvest as quickly.

CASE STUDY: CONSTRUCTION LOANS RARELY RESULT IN DELINQUENCIES

Matt Tabacchi, President and licensed real estate broker
Allstate Mortgage of Florida
Loans & Investments, Inc.
809 NE 25th Ave.* Ocala, FL 34470
Phone: 352-351-0200
Fax: 352-351-4557
E-mail: info@allstateocala.com
Website: www.allstateocala.com

Most people building a house feel very excited from day one to the end because they cannot wait to get into their new house. The only time I had delinquencies on construction loans was when I loaned money directly to an inexperienced owner/builder who wanted to build his or her own house. That person usually does not know what he or she is doing. People think they can build this house for $100,000 when it takes $150,000. They run into all kinds of things they did not foresee because they do not do it every day.

When you do a construction loan, you want to make sure a builder is involved. During that construction period, you get the interest on all the money starting day one. So, if you lend a guy $100,000 to build a house, you put $100,000 into the attorney's office's escrow account or title office's escrow account, and you just release money as it goes. You get interest for the whole thing, even if they only take $20,000 now. You get interest on everything until the house is complete.

Construction loans are a little bit more work. When you have a construction loan, you have to look at the progress. The builder will give you a draw schedule — say five draws. You give him the first draw, and it is the clearing of the lot, the cement slab, the well, and a couple of other things.

When he comes in for draw No. 2, he needs to have paid receipts for what was done on draw No. 1. When he comes to get draw No. 3, he has to give paid receipts for draw No. 2 — the frame, the truss, etc. — so you know he is truly making progress.

I also recommend that you have your appraiser inspect the property. The cost of this inspection passes on to the borrower. The appraiser is licensed to inspect these situations and has insurance that will help cover you if a fraudulent matter occurs.

You are building a brand-new house, and you are loaning at such a low LTV that by the time the house is complete, you are at a great LTV, and it is a brand-new, easily marketable house.

Here is an example: If you lend on a singlewide out in the middle of the forest on 5 acres, there are only so many people who will want to live out there if your borrower defaults. If you are building a brand-new house and the borrower defaults, there are many people who will want that brand-new house.

If the borrower defaults, it does not mean you will have the same builder finish the house. The process does not have to slow down at all. You are paying the builder. You are still going to continue and have the builder finish the house. It is not a lot of work for you. Then, you foreclose and have a new house you can sell for a great profit.

FIRST AND SECOND MORTGAGES

A first mortgage is the one registered first against the property. This mortgage takes priority over all other loans using that property as collateral and must be paid first in the event of sale or default. A second mortgage is a second loan using the same piece of property as collateral. If the homeowner is forced into foreclosure, the second mortgage holder will receive no proceeds from the sale of the home until the first mortgage has been completely repaid.

What does this mean to you if you choose to make a loan for a second mortgage? Here is an example.

You loaned $10,000 on the second mortgage of a $100,000 house. The borrower has a first mortgage of $80,000. If the borrower stops making payments on the first mortgage, the house will go into foreclosure, and either the court or the trustee, depending upon the state, will sell the house.

Assume that the house sells at auction for only $60,000. The first mortgage will be paid off first. Since there is nothing extra, the holder of the second mortgage will get nothing.

First mortgages are relatively safe because if you loan 65 percent or less of the value of the property, you will surely recover your capital if the borrower defaults. Second mortgages are a much greater risk because you may not get anything if the borrower defaults. This does not mean you should never make a loan for a second mortgage, but you should use caution. To compensate for the greater risk, you can do two things: Increase the interest rate and loan only a fraction of what the property is worth. As risk increases, the need to protect your investment increases. You should never make a second mortgage loan unless you are confident the borrower will not default. For example, if the owner of a thriving shopping center wants to get a short-term second mortgage to construct an additional store on the property, you can be reasonably certain the loan will be paid back because the business is successful and the new addition will increase its income. On the other hand, offering a second mortgage to the owner of a struggling, half-empty shopping center to refurbish the property in hopes of attracting new tenants is very risky.

AMORTIZATION TABLES

An installment loan is one repaid in regular installments according to a payment schedule. An amortization table is a document showing exactly how much the borrower pays each month for the privilege of borrowing. It gives the payment required on each specified date and a breakdown showing how much of the payment constitutes interest and how much constitutes repayment of principal.

An installment loan has four important components:

1. The *principal,* or amount financed.

2. The *interest rate,* or rate you charge for the use of the money.

3. The *term,* or amount of time for repayment.

4. The *monthly payment,* which is determined by the first three items.

The interest rate determines how much you earn each month on the unpaid balance of the loan. The interest rate is specified in terms of an annual percentage rate or APR. To get the monthly percentage rate, divide the APR by 12.

For example, you loan $100,000 at 15 percent APR. At the end of the first month, you would earn $1,250 in interest alone. If the borrower only paid the cost of interest each month, he or she would pay you $1,250 for life.

Most loan structures require a payoff in a specific number of years. To accomplish this, the monthly payment must be greater than the monthly interest cost so each month, part of the payment goes toward the principal of the loan. As the principal reduces, the monthly interest cost also reduces. When the payment is the same fixed amount each month, more and more of the payment applies toward the principal of the loan.

To continue the example above: If, instead of $1,250, the borrower paid $1,500 the first month, $1,250 would go toward the interest, and $250 would go toward the principal. The balance of the loan for the second month would be $99,750.

So, the interest owed for the second month is $1,246.87. Therefore, the second payment of $1,500 contains $1,246.87 in interest with $253.13 going toward the principal.

Loans can be structured in many different ways. You can apply an amortization table to unconventional, as well as conventional loans. In all cases, it will show for each payment the amount going toward interest and the amount going toward principal. Now, take a look at an actual amortization table. Here are the specifics for this table:

$100,000 principal – 15-year term – 10 percent interest rate

1	2	3	4	5	6
Year	Outstanding Loan Amount	Payment	Interest	Repayment of Principal	Remaining Balance
2000	$100,000	$13,147	$10,000	$3,147	$96,853
2001	$96,853	$13,147	$9,685	$3,462	$93,391
2002	$93,391	$13,147	$9,339	$3,808	$89,583
2003	$89,583	$13,147	$8,958	$4,189	$85,395
2004	$85,395	$13,147	$8,539	$4,608	$80,787

2005	$80,787	$13,147	$8,079	$5,068	$75,719
2006	$75,719	$13,147	$7,572	$5,575	$70,144
2007	$70,144	$13,147	$7,014	$6,133	$64,011
2008	$64,011	$13,147	$6,401	$6,746	$57,265
2009	$57,265	$13,147	$5,727	$7,420	$49,845
2010	$49,845	$13,147	$4,984	$8,163	$41,682
2011	$41,682	$13,147	$4,168	$8,979	$32,704
2012	$32,704	$13,147	$3,270	$9,877	$22,827
2013	$22,827	$13,147	$2,283	$10,864	$11,963
2014	$11,963	$13,147	$1,196	$11,951	$12

The table has the following six columns:

Column 1 — the year of the loan. Since this example is for a 15-year loan, this column shows the numbers 1 through 15.

Column 2 — the outstanding loan amount. In the first year, the borrower owes the entire $100,000. In the last year, he or she will owe $0.

Column 3 — the payment, which is determined by using a financial calculator.

Column 4 — the interest paid. This is based on the interest rate of 10 percent multiplied by the outstanding loan amount in Column 2.

Column 5 — the repayment of principal, which is the difference between the payment in Column 3 and the interest in Column 4.

Column 6 – the remaining balance. This is the difference between the outstanding loan amount and the repayment of principal. Numbers are rounded in this column.

See Appendix A for an example of a 30-year amortization schedule.

SIMPLE INTEREST VERSUS COMPOUND INTEREST

Simple interest is calculated on the original principal only. Accumulated interest from prior periods is not used in calculations for the following periods. Simple interest is normally used for a single period of less than a year, such as 30 or 60 days.

Compound interest is calculated each period on the original principal plus all interest accumulated during past periods. Although the interest may be stated as a yearly rate, the compounding periods can be yearly, semiannually, quarterly, or even continuously.

You can think of compound interest as a series of back-to-back simple interest contracts. The interest earned in each period is added to the principal of the previous period to become the principal for the next period.

This table below shows the results of making a one-time investment of $10,000 for 30 years using 12 percent simple interest and 12 percent interest compounded yearly and quarterly.

Type of Interest	Principal Plus Interest Earned
Simple	$46,000.00
Compounded Yearly	$299,599.22
Compounded Quarterly	$347,109.87

Using an annual compounding method, the amount of interest earned in the first year is added to the principal at the end of the year. During the second year, interest is earned on the total and added to the principal at the end of the year and so on for each year of the loan.

When interest is compounded quarterly, the interest earned in the first quarter is added to the principal balance at the end of the quarter. An important point to remember is that the interest earned is a quarter of the annual interest.

With monthly compounding, the interest earned in the first month — $\frac{1}{12}$ of the annual interest — is added to the balance at the end of the first month.

The calculation is the same for daily compounding. The amount of interest earned each day — $\frac{1}{365}$ — is added to the principal balance.

There is even continuous compounding, which compounds every hour.

To see how these different compounding techniques would affect a loan, here is a $10,000 loan at 15 percent over five years:

Compounded	Future Value
Yearly	$20,113.57
Quarterly	$20,881.52
Monthly	$21,071.81
Daily	$21,166.74
Continuously	$21,169.86

All other things being equal, compound interest has a larger effect as the time period increases and as the interest rate increases. *If you want to learn how to calculate both simple and compound interest, the formulas are provided in Appendix B.*

Besides the actual repayment of principal and the payment of interest, there are other ways to make money on the lending process.

PREPAYMENT PENALTIES

By the time you decide to loan money to a real estate investor, you have invested a lot of time and effort into the process. If you negotiate a three-year term for a loan, you do not expect to go through this process again for this capital for another three years. But, there are times when the borrower decides to pay off the loan early. In order to compensate you for this inconvenience, you can establish prepayment penalties when you draw up the note.

In most cases, a prepayment penalty is a fee charged to a borrower who pays off a loan before it is due. Prepayment penalties may also be assessed when excessive portions of the loan's principal balance — 20 percent or more — are paid in a single year.

Banks calculate a prepayment penalty as six months worth of interest payments on 80 percent of the balance owed on the mortgage. Most private mortgage investors charge 1 to 2 percent of the initial loan amount, but prepayment penalties can be as high as 5 percent. The creditworthiness of a borrower might not deter you from loaning money, but it will help you determine things like interest rates and penalties. If you are concerned about the borrower's credit, you will want to have higher prepayment penalties along with higher interest rates.

POINTS ON THE BEGINNING OF THE NOTE

When a borrower obtains a mortgage, he or she will incur mortgage fees and costs associated with completing the mortgage. One of those costs is a "loan origination fee." The loan origination fee, a percentage of the loan amount, is often expressed as "points."

Each point is equal to 1 percent of the loan amount. For example, one point on a $150,000 loan would be $1,500. One-and-a-half points on the same loan amount would be $2,250. This payment is usually made in cash at settlement. If the loan origination fee were one point, the borrower would pay $1,500 in cash on the day he or she signs the loan contract.

As a lender, you can charge as many points as you want, but you need to be careful to keep the loan from becoming usurious, meaning you are charging too much, and it is illegal. *For more information on usury, see Chapter 13.*

POINTS ON THE END OF THE NOTE

You can also add points to the end of the note. This would be the same as the loan origination fee mentioned above, except that the fee, either in full or in part, would be deferred until the end of the loan. If your borrower needs more money to carry out the project for which he or she is getting the loan, you might consider deferring any points until the end of the loan. You might also decide to ask payment of one point at the beginning and two at the end.

Deferring points to the end of the loan.

Deferring points to the end of the loan is a way to let the client get more money up front. This does not benefit you, the lender, and will only work if it does not matter to you if you get money now or at the end of the term. Borrowers often have difficulty understanding the deferment process or that you are doing them a favor.

KEEP YOUR FUNDS FULLY INVESTED

It is important to keep your funds fully invested. Assume you have $30,000 in an account earning 5 percent interest, compounded yearly. In five years, you would end up with $8,288.45 in interest.

Now, assume you find an investor in need of $27,000 for that five-year period. You decide to give him or her a loan at 15 percent interest. You would have $3,000 still left in your account earning 5 percent interest, and you would have $27,000 earning 15 percent. All interest earned from the loan would be deposited into the interest-bearing account on a yearly basis. At the end of five years, you would have:

- $20,250 from the simple interest earned on the loan at 15 percent.

- $2,936.10 in compounded interest on the $3,000, plus $4,050 interest earned on the annual interest payments from the loan.

This is a total of $23,186.10 in interest earned.

Finally, assume you lend out the entire $30,000 at 15 percent, and on a yearly basis, put the interest into an account bearing 5 percent:

- $22,500 from the simple interest earned on the loan at 15 percent.

- $2,365.34 from the yearly compounded interest on the $4,500 earned yearly on the loan.

This is a total of $24,865.34 in interest earned.

You can see that loaning out the full $30,000 instead of just $27,000 increases your earnings over the five-year period by $1,679.24.

So, how do you go about putting all of your money to work? Go back to the borrower who wants to borrow $27,000 at 15 percent. If the factors are all in your favor and the loan-to-value ratio is less than 70 percent, you can offer the borrower an extra $3,000. He or she may have only asked for $27,000 but may very well be able to use the $30,000 and take you up on the offer. In this way, you have just earned at least an extra $1,600 with no extra effort on your part.

CASE STUDY: START INVESTING WHILE YOU ARE YOUNG

April
Private mortgage investor

Not everyone waits until they start thinking about retirement to invest. Here is what April, age 18, has to say about private mortgage investing:

I saw my dad and my aunt and uncle making great interest rates with private mortgage investing. I could not wait until I was 18 so I could do it, too. Before I was 18, I worked for my family's business and did some baby-sitting, among other things. Then, when I graduated from high school, most people gave me money. By the time I was 18, I had almost $10,000 saved.

I did not save all of my money — I do like to spend. But, I have had a savings account since I was 10 years old. I was never very impressed with my money just sitting in the bank. In fact, it was a big deal if my interest was more than a dollar. Trust me, it is much better with private mortgage investing.

Right now, I am doing a $10,000 loan deal with a broker. My dad helped me get to the $10,000 mark. Apparently, brokers get these small loans all the time. Instead of earning just 2 percent in a savings account, I am earning 14 percent. That is a big deal. My 18th birthday was in August, and I got my first check in October. If I had kept my $10,000 in a savings account at 2 percent, I would have earned $200 by the time I turned 19.

Instead, I invested in a private mortgage and will earn $1,400. The loan I am doing is for about five years. That means I will have $17,000 to invest by the time I am 23.

I have decided to save all of my interest, and when I get all of my principal back, I will reinvest. It is the smart thing to do at my age. If I can keep doing this every five years and add the interest I earned, I will have more than $2 million by the time I am 68. Just imagine what it will be if I start adding other funds.

Especially for someone young like me, I think it is very important to find a broker you can trust. At my age, I am not very knowledgeable about property values or investing so trusting a broker is essential. I am learning, though, and I want to learn more as I go along. I am already learning how to keep track of my monthly earnings. I simply copy the check each month and put that information, along with a breakdown of the principal and the interest, into a folder.

I am glad I started early. The feeling of getting a big check every month is fantastic, and it is much better than chuckling over a dollar's worth of interest.

LATE FEES AND FORECLOSURE: HOW IT WORKS

Another way to earn extra money is by foreclosing on a loan. Because you have invested no more than 70 percent of the value of the property, if it goes to foreclosure, you will have the opportunity to sell it for closer to full value and increase your profits. This is one reason you want to be sure you have accurate appraisals.

Here is a quick look at how foreclosures work.

Foreclosure is a process that allows you, the lender, to recover the amount owed on a defaulted loan by selling or taking ownership — repossession — of the property securing the loan. The foreclosure process begins when a borrower/owner defaults on loan payments, and the lender files a public default notice. The foreclosure process can end in one of four ways:

1. The borrower/owner pays off the default amount to reinstate the loan

during a grace period determined by state laws. This grace period is also known as pre-foreclosure.

2. The borrower/owner sells the property to a third party during pre-foreclosure. The sale allows the borrower/owner to pay off the loan and avoid having a foreclosure on his or her credit history.

3. A third party buys the property at a public auction at the end of pre-foreclosure.

4. The lender takes ownership of the property, usually with the intent to resell. The lender can take ownership through an agreement with the borrower/owner during pre-foreclosure or by buying back the property at the public auction. These are also known as bank-owned properties.

Mortgage notes carry a grace period; a 15-day grace period is normal, but some are as short as ten days. Many people "play the float," or delay through most of the grace period before making a payment, and no one, including the lender, considers this a problem. The day after the grace period ends, you can start charging a late fee. The late fee is usually a percentage of the principal balance; 3 percent is normal. Once 30 days have passed since the payment was due, the borrower is in default. At this point, you can add collection costs, extra charges to cover the expense of hiring someone to pursue collection of the debt, to the late fees.

Laws regarding mortgage default and foreclosure differ from state to state so in any foreclosure proceeding, you should understand your state's rules and have a good attorney.

If the borrower is unable or unwilling to negotiate a payment plan with you, you will begin the foreclosure process. Now, in addition to late fees and collection fees, you will also charge the borrower legal fees. If the foreclosure proceedings go to court and the court decides in your favor, the borrower will pay all legal fees. Even if it settled out of court, you can still charge legal fees.

First, you must order a foreclosure search that reveals all the debts related to the property, such as mechanics' liens, equity loans, utility-company liens, and tax liens. Someone will have to pay all these debts so you include them with the amount still due under the original mortgage.

Next, you file a lis pendens, or notice of default, depending on the state you are in, with the state court. This legal procedure announces publicly that a creditor — you — is foreclosing on a debtor — the borrower. You will also serve the borrower with a copy of the complaint in the action, and if the borrower does not successfully contest it, then the court will appoint a referee, who is a neutral third party in charge of the sale of the property.

The referee will give notice of the sale of the property, according to the requirements of state law. This means publishing a classified advertisement in a newspaper, normally in the local papers and in the largest and closest metropolitan daily newspaper, posting a notice in the courthouse, or both. The advertisement might give the date of the auction on which the property will be sold, or a separate advertisement might announce the date.

The law in most states gives the homeowner several opportunities to stop the foreclosure, right up to the minute that the auctioneer's gavel comes down, and sometimes even afterward. In some states, there is a period after the foreclosure during which the homeowner can redeem the property, known as the right of redemption.

At the auction, you will offer the property subject to a minimum bid, or upset price. If nobody submits a bid at least as high as the upset price, then you will withdraw the property and attempt to sell it through other means.

CASE STUDY: FORECLOSURE IN FLORIDA

Matt Tabacchi, President and licensed real estate broker
Allstate Mortgage of Florida Loans & Investments, Inc.
809 NE 25th Ave. * Ocala, FL 34470
Phone: 352-351-0200
Fax: 352-351-4557
E-mail: info@allstateocala.com
Website: www.allstateocala.com

I lend Jack money, and he does not pay me by the tenth of the month. At this point, I charge him a late fee. I give him a call or send him a letter. If 30 days go by and he does not respond, I take his file with all the disclosures down to a local real estate attorney and ask them to process the loan for foreclosure proceedings.

The attorney will then send a demand letter to the client saying he or she is required to pay off the loan within 30 days. If not, the attorney will proceed with the foreclosure.

Once we get to that point, 99 percent of the time, the borrower can refinance and pay us back. Since we only loaned 65 percent, they will often find someone. They do not want to lose their house.

If they do not pay off, you proceed with the foreclosure. That process will take a little bit of time to get through all of the proceedings. You do not have to do anything; the attorney does it all.

Now, it is time for the foreclosure sale. Say your balance was $50,000 plus the attorney fees of $3,000, and your interest and late charges are another $2,000. That is $55,000. When the house goes to auction at the courthouse, the attorney will not sell it for less than $55,000. Because we want that cushion, we stay within 65 percent LTV.

Foreclosure works differently in different states. Check with your local mortgage broker to understand the laws of your state.

FORECLOSURE IN NORTH CAROLINA

The borrower has fallen behind on payments. You, as the lender, send out at least one, and maybe two or three, demands for payment. Once you believe the borrower either cannot or will not pay the mortgage, you start the foreclosure process. In North Carolina, this is a court proceeding.

First, you send a letter saying you are exercising your right to accelerate the mortgage, meaning you are declaring the entire mortgage due. This is a necessary step in North Carolina before proceeding to foreclosure. At this point, you can refuse to accept any partial payments. If you do accept partial payments, you may waive your right to proceed with foreclosure.

Next, you serve the borrower with a Notice of Foreclosure Hearing. This hearing gives you permission to sell the real property. As the lender, all you have to do is prove the borrower is behind on the payments.

Once you get the go-ahead to put the real property up for sale, your foreclosing attorney will post and publish a Notice of Sale. Someone must serve a copy of the notice to the borrower at least 20 days in advance of the sale.

The sale is then conducted in a public place, normally the county courthouse, during courthouse operating hours. Anyone interested in buying the property comes to the sale and bids on the property. This highest bidder gets the property unless you determine the amount does not cover your investment. If this is the case, you have the option of using other methods to sell the property.

If the process concludes at auction, the highest bidder must then pay a deposit in the amount of 10 percent of the bid price at the end of the auction.

After the auction, there is a ten-day waiting period, called the upset bid period, during which the borrower is given a chance to pay off the entire mortgage, which almost never happens. Other people are then given a chance to post higher bids for the property. In most cases, no higher bids are posted. Assuming this is the case, the sale is considered final at the end of the ten-day upset bid period.

Once the sale is final, the highest bidder pays the rest of the bid price and receives a deed that conveys title to the property from the foreclosing attorney.

The money received from the highest bidder is first applied to pay any outstanding property taxes, and then it is applied toward the debt owed to you. If for any reason the sale price does not cover all outstanding debts, a deficiency judgment can be issued requiring the borrower to pay the difference.

FORECLOSURE IN UTAH

The foreclosure process in Utah normally begins when the borrower becomes delinquent. The term delinquent is loosely defined and depends upon the terms of the note or the type of loan. But normally, delinquency is considered to be three months in arrears, at which point the foreclosure process begins.

To begin the process, you appoint a trustee to record a notice of default with the county recorder of the county in which the property is located. From the date of the recording of the notice of default, the borrower has three months to reinstate or pay off the loan.

If the loan is not reinstated during that period, then you set a foreclosure sale date, send a notice of sale to the borrower, and post the notice on the property. Additionally, you post the notice at the county recorder's office and publish it in a newspaper with general circulation in the county.

The sale is held at the county courthouse and is conducted by either your trustee or an attorney representing your trustee. You set the opening bid on the property. If no one presents a bid higher than the opening bid, the attorney conducting the foreclosure sale purchases the property on your behalf. Otherwise, the property is sold to the highest bidder.

The highest bidder must present $5,000 to the trustee or attorney and remit the balance by noon the following day.

FORECLOSURE IN COLORADO

In Colorado, a loan may be considered in default after only 30 days. Once a loan is in default, foreclosure action can begin.

To begin foreclosure, you hire a foreclosure attorney. At this point, to stop the foreclosure, the borrower must pay all the back payments, late fees, and foreclosure costs. If done, this "cures" the loan. The borrower's right to cure the loan ends 15 days before the auction.

The foreclosure attorney prepares and files the documents with the public trustee's office for the county in which the property is located. When the public trustee receives the foreclosure documents from the lender's attorneys, the trustee schedules a public auction of the property 45 to 60 days in the future.

Your attorney must then schedule a Rule 120 Hearing to take place before the auction date. The judge may cancel this hearing if the borrower does not officially respond when given notice. The hearing legally establishes whether the lender has the right to foreclose on the property and sell it at the public auction.

Once the property sells, the borrower has a 75-day redemption period. During this time, the borrower can still get the property back by paying off the bid, fees, taxes, insurance, and interest to the public trustee's office.

The beginning of this section explained how you could earn extra money when your borrower becomes delinquent by charging additional late fees and collection fees. If the borrower is ultimately unable to pay off the loan, you can go through with the foreclosure and sell the property to recover your capital. If you have followed the principles of private mortgage discussed earlier in this book, you have loaned no more than 60 percent of the market value of the property, and you have made certain the property is desirable and in good condition so you can sell it easily. If so, you will probably make a profit in addition to recovering your capital.

Because foreclosure is handled differently from state to state, it is very difficult to predict what circumstances you might encounter during foreclosure proceedings. Familiarize yourself with the laws of your state, and if you decide to foreclose on a property, hire an experienced real estate attorney to help you. You can add the legal fees to the amount that must be paid off by selling the property.

As a private lender, you can directly loan money to a real estate investor, homebuyer, or developer. You can also pool your money with that of other investors to make larger loans or set up an investment fund to manage your loan investments and the proceeds from them. *The following chapter discusses several ways to structure private mortgage lending.*

Chapter 6:
Ways to Invest

A private mortgage investor can hold a loan personally, in a partnership with other investors, or in a self-directed IRA. This chapter describes the advantages and disadvantages of each arrangement.

HOLDING THE NOTE PERSONALLY

This is the simplest way to hold a note. If you live in a state that uses mortgages, you are named as the note holder. In states where a deed of trust is used, you are listed as the beneficiary. *See Chapter 2 for an explanation of the difference between a mortgage and a deed of trust.*

When you hold the note personally, you are in charge. You take on all the profit and all the risk. Any taxes and capital gains are your responsibility, and any losses are incurred by you alone. The advantage is that you make all the decisions concerning the loan. You determine a loan amount or interest rate based on your own judgment rather than the consensus of a group of investors.

Using your equity

When you hold the note personally, you must fund the entire loan yourself. If you own a home, you can use the equity in your home to find money for investing. Your equity is the percentage of the property that you own outright. If you bought a $150,000 house, your equity is the amount you put down when you purchased plus any principal you have paid on your mortgage. If your home has increased in value since you bought it by a certain percentage, you have that much more equity. When your mortgage is fully paid, your equity is 100 percent.

Unless you sell your house, you cannot spend your equity. Rather than leaving equity sitting in a structure, you could consider taking out a home-equity loan, a loan that uses your equity as collateral. Because real estate is perceived as a very stable investment, banks and finance companies often given favorable interest rates on home-equity loans. Often you can also get a tax deduction for the interest you pay on a home-equity loan. Consult your tax adviser regarding the deductibility of interest.

Private mortgages can earn far more interest than you pay for the equity loan. For instance, you could earn 16 percent interest on a private mortgage loan of $50,000 and only have to pay 7 percent to your bank, meaning your equity earns you 9 percent instead of sitting idly in your home.

Equity line and second mortgage

What is the difference between a home-equity line of credit and a second mortgage? The terminology is often confusing. A second mortgage is any loan that involves a second lien on the property. Confusion started when second mortgages began to be structured as lines of credit and became known as home-equity loans or home-equity lines of credit (HELOCs). These loans are adjustable-rate mortgages.

If you own your house free and clear and you want a line of credit secured by a mortgage, that loan is a HELOC, even though it is a first mortgage. Similarly, if you use a HELOC to refinance your first mortgage, the HELOC becomes a first mortgage. Otherwise, HELOCs are considered second mortgages. You can use a HELOC to get the money to invest in a private mortgage loan.

SHARING A LOAN

Just like other types of investments, a group can hold private mortgages jointly. Instead of one person investing all the money, several people pool their money to make investments. Although you can do this simply by gathering together some friends, family, or investors, it is often in your best interest to form a legal partnership or a corporation. Consult your accountant to determine which option works best for you.

Hold the note through a partnership

For many people, getting started in private mortgages is a big leap and one they do not feel ready to fund on their own. They may also feel concerned about taking on all the liability and responsibility associated with sole ownership of a private mortgage loan. In this situation, a partnership offers a good alternative.

Limited partners invest in a company but are not involved in the management of the business. Each partner is responsible only to the extent of his or her investment in the partnership for any liabilities incurred by the partnership. A general partner is fully responsible for all liabilities incurred by the partnership. Limited partners assume only limited liability and receive special tax privileges. Both general and limited partners are taxed at their personal rates on their shares of taxable income from the business. The limited partnership itself is not taxed, meaning the income from investments is not taxed, but instead is divided among the partners who are then taxed.

A limited partnership is like a corporation in many respects. It allows individuals to invest in the business while limiting their liability to the amount of their investment or as agreed in the limited-partnership agreement. If there is no partnership agreement, the income, losses, and gains are allocated in proportion to the partnership interests of each partner. Partners can agree among themselves how income, losses, and gains are to be divided among the partners. The partners then report the amounts allocated on their own income tax returns and pay tax accordingly.

You can either form your own limited partnership or join one already functioning as an investment partnership set up to invest in private notes. Forming your own company will be a difficult endeavor, and you will need the help of a good lawyer. If you decide to join an existing limited partnership, you will have the benefit of experienced management and will avoid losing money while learning the ropes.

Holding the note through a limited partnership limits your liability but has some disadvantages. When working with a limited partnership, you do not have full control. If you believe an investment is a good proposition but the others in the partnership do not agree, the deal will not be made. You should evaluate your prospective partners carefully before entering into an agreement to work with them. Are they financially strong? Are they trustworthy? Do they comprehend when an investment makes sense and when it does not? Just because these "partners" are friends or family members, the answers to these questions are not an automatic "yes."

Once you have determined that you and your partners have similar investment goals and your partners are trustworthy, you must evaluate the proposed mortgage deal. What kind of return on investment can you expect and over what period of time? Does it sound too good to be true? Is the risk level acceptable to you? Do you have an exit strategy if you want to get out of the partnership? How long will this investment require you be in the partnership?

Partnerships seem to work best when all sides have some experience, similar investment goals, are not dependent on the income to live, and have taken time to plan out a good partnership structure.

In a partnership, you should have an agreement describing how decisions will be made. Will there be managing partners? How will deadlocks be resolved? The best way to develop a consistent approach to your investments is by drafting a written real estate partnership agreement with the help of an attorney. Be sure to have a partnership attorney separate from your own personal attorney. If any disputes or issues arise, you will want your own attorney to review the documents.

You should also consider how will you stay abreast of the investments and what kind of meeting schedule or reporting schedule you will have.

Checklist for partnership agreement

Use this checklist to organize your partnership agreement and make sure you have covered all the important points:

1. The purpose for the company's formation and the company's goals.

2. Partnership allocations.

3. Capital investment or initial contributions.

4. Value of the investments.

5. Determine the legal ownership entity: corporation, LLC, LLP.

6. The partnership's management strategy.

7. How and when to make partnership decisions.

8. How and when to make the decision to sell the investment or buy more.

9. The decision process for when to increase rent or other charges.

10. Do you need a managing partner to manage your investments?

11. Who is the managing partner?

    a. What is the term of office of the managing partner?

    b. Under what circumstances might the manager be removed from his or her position?

    c. What kind of authority does the manager have?

    d. What kind of power does the manager have and what actions will he or she be able to take?

    e. How much compensation will the manager receive?

    f. Will the manager be allowed to delegate responsibilities?

    g. Will the manager have the authority to convey the ownership of property?

    h. The standard of care: what an average managing partner in similar circumstances would be expected to do.

    i. Restrictions on the authority of the manager.

    j. How the managing partner will make reparation to the other partners if his or her actions cause any harm to them.

    k. What is the extent of the managing partner's duty of loyalty to the partnership?

12. Taxes:

    a. Who gets tax benefits?

    b. In which proportions?

    c. Who prepares the Schedule K-1 (IRS Form 1065: Partner's Share of Income, Deductions, Credits, etc.) and by what date?

    d. How are accounting costs shared?

13. What happens when a cash shortfall occurs?

14. What happens when one or more partners fail to pay contributions?

15. Loans by members.

16. Meetings: Where and how often will they be held?

17. Quorum: How many partners must be present for voting and making decisions?

18. How will profits and losses be allocated?

19. What kind of liability insurance will the partnership have?

20. Directors' insurance: Will the directors be insured against liability?

21. Life insurance and how the cost of the insurance is to be funded. Life insurance is needed so if a partner dies, the other partners will have the funds needed to purchase his or her share of the business from the heirs.

22. Liquidating distributions if and when the company dissolves.

23. Books and records:

    a.   Accounting period.

    b.   Fiscal year.

    c.   Banking.

    d.   Monthly reporting.

    e.   Tax returns.

    f.   Location of books and reports.

24. What will take place upon the death or incompetence of a member?

    a.   Transfer by means of a will.

    b.   Transfer to a permitted transferee.

    c.   Limited or unlimited power of appointment.

    d.   Sale of share to a partner and right of first refusal.

    e.   Estate-planning transfers: Review life insurance arrangements so a partner's share will go to a single person, such as a spouse, rather than divided among multiple heirs.

25. How will disputes be resolved?

    a.   Mediation — impartial third party guiding the disputants to arrive at a solution.

    b.   Arbitration — impartial third party resolves the dispute.

Hold the note through an LLC

A limited liability company (LLC) is a business structure that features both a partnership or sole proprietorship and a corporation. The LLC itself is not taxed; its owners report business profits or losses on their personal income tax returns like partners in a partnership.

As with a corporation, though, all LLC owners are protected from personal liability for business debts and claims. This is why it is called "limited liability." If your business owes money or faces a lawsuit, only the company assets, not your personal assets, are at risk.

It is very easy to organize a LLC. In most states, you only need to file "articles of organization" with the appropriate state agency, normally a department of the office of the Secretary of State. Most states provide a fill-in-the-blank form that takes just a few minutes to prepare and submit online. A few states require you to publish your intention to form a LLC in a local newspaper before filing your articles of organization.

Although it is not a legal necessity, you should prepare an LLC operating agreement stating the rights and responsibilities of the LLC owners. You need to create a written operating agreement, or the laws of your state will govern your LLC.

The operating agreement should cover:

- How profits are to be divided.

- How major business decisions are made.

- Procedures for handling the departure and addition of members.

The main way a LLC differs from a partnership is LLC owners are not personally liable for the company's debts and liabilities. Creditors of the LLC usually cannot claim the owners' personal assets to pay off LLC debts. Partners in a partnership are not protected from liability unless they are designated as "limited" partners in their partnership agreement.

Though owners of limited liability companies must file formal articles of organization, pay a filing fee, and comply with certain other legal requirements, partners in a partnership do not need to file any formal paperwork or pay any special fees.

For both LLCs and partnerships, owners report business income or losses on their personal tax returns; the business itself is not taxed. Both types of businesses report income and losses on IRS Form 1065 and distribute copies to the business's owners.

Hold the note through a corporation

A corporation is very different from a partnership. It is a separate legal entity, distinct from its members. Two main types of corporations exist: the C Corporation and the S Corporation. Here is a look at both.

The C Corporation

Most standard businesses are C Corporations, which pay taxes at their own corporate income tax rates. C Corporations have the following characteristics:

- They file corporate taxes using IRS Form 1120.

- A board of directors elected by the shareholders controls the corporation.

- They conduct day-to-day activities through officers and employees. The directors delegate the authority to do so.

- Shareholders, who do not have authority over day-to-day operations, own the corporation. They do, however, have the power to appoint and remove directors.

- A board of directors, which is responsible for the long-term management and policy decisions of the corporation, guide them.

- Corporate officers elected by the board of directors run them, and they are responsible for conducting the day-to-day operational activities of the corporation.

- They often offer their employees unique fringe benefits, such as health insurance, retirement pensions, housing and relocation allowances, vacation time, stock ownership, and discounts on company goods or services.

- They must hold annual meetings. Corporate minutes of the meetings must be taken, officers must be appointed, and shares must be issued to shareholders.

- They are taxed on their own profits. Any profits paid out in the form of dividends are taxed again to the recipient as dividend income at the individual shareholder's tax rate.

The S Corporation

Owners who want the limited liability of a corporation and the "pass-through" tax treatment of a partnership will often make the S Corporation election. An S Corporation, also known as a "Subchapter S Corporation" for Subchapter S of Chapter 1 of the Internal Revenue Code, is a structure allowed by the IRS for corporations with less than 75 shareholders who are all U.S. citizens or resident aliens. In most cases, corporations that would benefit from S Corporation status are those that plan to distribute the majority of earnings to their shareholders in the year in which those earnings are realized.

An S Corporation begins its existence as a C Corporation. But, after the corporation has formed, it may elect S Corporation status by submitting IRS Form 2553 to the Internal Revenue Service. Once this filing is complete, the corporation is taxed in the same way as a partnership or sole proprietorship rather than as a separate entity.

To qualify for S Corporation status, the corporation must:

- Maintain only one class of stock.

- Maintain a maximum of 75 shareholders.

- Be comprised solely of shareholders who are individuals, estates, or certain qualified trusts and who consent in writing to the S Corporation election.

- Not have a shareholder who is a nonresident alien.

- Complete and file IRS Form 1120 to report its annual income to the IRS each year.

The difference between LLCs and S Corporations

An LLC, taxed in the same way as an S Corporation, has a number of advantages over the traditional straight S Corporation form of business organization. These additional benefits include the ability to have:

- More than 75 business owners.

- A nonresident alien as an owner.

- A corporation or a partnership as an owner.

- More than 80 percent ownership in a separate corporate entity.

- Disproportionate ownership — ownership percentages different from each respective owner's investment in the business.

- Flow-through business-loss deductions in excess of each respective owner's investment in the business.

- Owners and members active in the management of the business without losing their limited personal liability exposure.

Hold the note through a tenancy in common

Another way to hold a note is through a tenancy in common (TIC). A TIC is created when two or more people are legally granted interest in the same property. TIC is more flexible than joint tenancy, an arrangement in which two or more tenants hold equal shares in a property. If one of the joint tenants dies, his or her share of the property is equally divided among the surviving joint tenants. Under TIC, the shares held by the tenants do not all have to be equal or acquired at the same time. A tenant can sell his or her share without the mutual agreement of the others. If one tenant dies, the others do not automatically own the deceased's share. Instead it passes to his or her heirs.

The primary advantage of a TIC is it is easy to move investors in and out of the investment group while doing 1031 exchanges — and to preserve 1031 exchanges for those leaving the group. A 1031 exchange, named for Section 1031 of the Internal Revenue Code, is a real estate transaction in which capital gains tax is deferred because the investment property being sold is replaced with another investment property of a similar type. Capital gains tax on the profit from selling an investment property can range from 15 percent to 30 percent, which represents a substantial amount of money that the group could reinvest.

The disadvantage of a tenancy in common is each TIC is fully liable personally for all debts, lawsuits, and so forth, associated with the property because TICs are treated as general partnerships.

HOLDING NOTES IN A SELF-DIRECTED IRA

Individual Retirement Arrangements (IRAs) are tax-advantaged accounts that allow individuals to invest more money for retirement savings by deferring or waiving income tax on the earnings. A traditional IRA allows the investor to defer paying income tax on the contributions or earnings until the money is withdrawn. Contributions to a Roth IRA are made after income tax has been paid on them, but all earnings can be withdrawn tax free. The IRS regulates IRAs and imposes strict conditions, including annual limits on the amount you can contribute and additional tax penalties if you withdraw money before you reach the age of 59 ½. Banks, financial institutions, and stock brokerages administer IRAs. Most IRA plans offer a selection of traditional investment options, such as mutual funds, bonds, stocks and ETFs, but IRS guidelines allow almost any type of investment, including real estate. Self-directed IRAs let you choose and manage your own investments under the administration of a third-party trustee. A self-directed IRA can own and manage businesses and real estate, but all of its activities must benefit the IRA rather than the IRA's owner. You can withdraw your earnings without penalty after you reach retirement age. *The next chapter explains how to use your self-directed IRA to invest in real estate.*

Chapter 7: Getting the Most from Your IRA

As explained in the previous chapter, is a tax-advantaged investment account that allows individuals to save more for retirement by deferring or waiving income tax until money is withdrawn after the owner reaches the age of 59 ½. The IRAs administered by most banks and financial institutions offer a selection of mutual funds, stocks, and bonds, but you can hold a wide variety of investments in .

A self-directed IRA lets you manage your own investment account under the administration of a third-party trustee. A self-directed IRA can own almost any type of investment, including businesses and real estate, but all of its activities must benefit the IRA rather than the IRA's owner. For example, the IRA owner cannot use property owned by the IRA as a personal residence, and the IRA cannot buy property from members of his or her immediate family. All expenses associated with a property held by must be paid with money from the IRA. Money and assets in a self-directed IRA cannot be mixed with personal funds.

WHY USE IRA FUNDS FOR PRIVATE MORTGAGES?

When the stock market goes into decline, your rate of return on equity investments could be much lower than the average 7 percent, and you could even lose some of your capital. It takes months for the stock market to recover and years for you to recover from your losses. A two-year slump early in your working career could mean there will be substantially less in your IRA when you are ready to retire. Management fees for mutual funds and fees for stock transactions also eat into your returns. Funding private mortgages with a self-directed IRA offers an excellent way to grow your retirement account. For investors who have seen stock values sliding and retirement account balances crumbling, private mortgages with 10 to 16 percent returns look very attractive.

Conventional IRAs offer a menu of mutual funds representing various investment styles and market sectors, some of which might have been created specifically for those IRA plans. Once you have selected the mutual funds for your portfolio, you are at the mercy of the fund managers and have no further say in the investments they make. A self-directed IRA allows you to put your retirement funds into an investment you can see, select, control, and understand. You can apply your experience in business and the real estate market to increase your retirement savings.

Many companies now offer tax-deferred 401(k) plans that allow employees to make regular contributions out of their pay to retirement savings. When you leave an employer, you should roll over the funds from your 401(k) into a traditional or a Roth IRA administered by a bank or financial institution. IRAs give you more flexibility in planning for your heirs and in withdrawing your money when you need it. The company sets the rules governing 401(k)s, and they may be less liberal than IRS regulations. Some 401(k)s have high management fees and hidden costs that eat into your returns; when you open , you can select one that charges reasonable fees. Increased transparency will allow you to see your exact costs.

Income tax on your contributions to traditional IRAs is deferred until you withdraw those funds during retirement; you will be charged at your ordinary income tax rate on both the contributions and the earnings in your IRA. You pay income tax on contributions before they go into a Roth IRA, but you do not pay any taxes on the earnings. Only taxpayers in lower-income brackets can contribute to Roth IRAs. The income limit for 2010 was $177,000 for a married couple filing jointly, and $120,000 for an individual. But in 2010, the government allowed a one-time opportunity for all taxpayers, regardless of income, to convert traditional IRAs into Roth IRAs and pay the resulting income tax divided into two installments, one paid in 2011 and the other in 2012. If individuals with large balances in their traditional IRAs convert to a Roth IRA and use it to invest in private mortgages, all earnings will be tax free. A Simplified Employee Pension IRA (SEP-IRA) is designed for self-employed individuals and small companies. A SEP-IRA allows you to contribute up to 25 percent of your compensation, or $49,000, whichever amount is less. If you have employees, you must make contributions for them as well. A self-employed real estate practitioner who can make the maximum contributions can build up investment funds rapidly. Withdrawals from a SEP-IRA are treated in the same way as those of a traditional IRA for tax purposes.

Assets held in a retirement fund, including a self-directed IRA, are protected from creditors. The Employee Retirement Income Security Act of 1974 (ERISA) is a federal law that sets minimum standards for retirement and health benefit plans in private industry. ERISA protects assets held in qualified retirement plans from legal process, as long as the plan document has the proper "anti-alienation" clauses. Anti-alienation clauses do not allow ownership of assets to be transferred to a third-party, such as a creditor. Additionally, ERISA keeps these plans from being liquidated during a bankruptcy. The U.S. Supreme Court concluded in a recent case, Rousey v. Jacoway (April 2005), that IRAs were "exempt from the reach of their creditors." Bankruptcy laws have been amended to exempt all IRAs from collectors if the IRA holder goes bankrupt.

The idea that financing real estate inside is too complex to be viable is a myth. Using LLC to do real estate transactions is no more complex than using any other type of company structure. Your IRA can pool resources with other investors or form a partnership. Because of the tax-deferred status of , certain restrictions, discussed later in this chapter, exist.

THE MAJOR PLAYERS

In order to invest in real estate with , you must establish a self-directed traditional or Roth IRA. To prevent misuse of the tax benefits offered by and the manipulation of clients by financial institutions, the IRS has strict rules governing the way a self-directed IRA can be structured. For example, only a bank or an approved financial entity can hold the assets in your IRA, and it must submit annual reports to the IRS. This financial entity cannot interfere in investment decisions. You are not allowed to directly carry out transactions, such as buying and selling the assets in ; a professional intermediary must do this. While a custodian might manage invested in mutual funds, stocks, and bonds, a self-directed IRA typically requires the additional services of an administrator/trustee. The responsibilities of each are different.

Custodian

Your IRA custodian is the bank or financial institution that holds your IRA account. The custodian is responsible for keeping the accounts and reporting to you and to the IRA. According to IRS rules, custodian must remain neutral in regard to investment decisions, taking direction from the IRA owner and not attempting to influence or advise him or her. According to federal law, only a bank, savings and loan institution, credit union, or an institution or individual who has received approval from the IRS may act as an IRA custodian.

Trustee

A trustee represents a trust that holds assets on your behalf and has the authority to act on your behalf in certain matters. A trustee is obligated by law to act in your best interests.

Administrator

An IRA administrator handles the administrative details of an IRA account and acts as an interface between the IRA owner and the custodian or trustee. An administrator does not hold assets or have fiduciary authority over assets in the IRA. An administrator carries out the process of opening and closing account; receives contributions; executes rollovers, transfers, and distributions; and conveys the account holder's instructions regarding transactions.

Establishing a Self-Directed IRA

The "self-directed IRAs" many financial institutions advertise are simply IRAs that allow you to choose which stocks, bonds, and mutual funds to invest in. A completely self-directed Roth IRA offers the flexibility to invest in many types of assets, including real estate and business ownership. To distinguish themselves, some companies advertise a "truly self-directed IRA," meaning they are prepared to handle many types of investments and put you in charge of managing them. An IRA with "checkbook control" is an arrangement that lets you handle the financial transactions associated with your investment under the administration of a third-party trustee.

An IRA administrator is typically a company employing a staff of accountants, lawyers, and finance professionals. It might be a small company with a handful of employees or a large firm serving thousands of clients. You should choose an administrator equipped to handle transactions for the types of investments you plan to include in your self-directed IRA. You do not want to do the extra work of changing administrators later on when your investment plans have begun.

You can find potential administrators by typing "self-directed IRA" in an online search engine, inquiring at banks and brokerages, or asking professionals and friends for recommendations. Several questions can help you select the right administrator:

What kind of transactions can you handle?

Most administrators of self-directed IRAs can handle real estate transactions, but if you are interested in buying and selling mortgage notes, buying real estate options, or private lending, make sure the company is equipped to support you.

What is your typical turn-around time for funding a transaction?

Some investment opportunities, such as the purchase of property at foreclosure auctions, require immediate action. IRS rules prohibit temporary borrowing from personal funds to pay for an IRA investment so funds in the IRA must be easily available for such transactions. A company with a large number of clients might take days to respond to an order, resulting in the loss of investment opportunities.

What are the credentials of your staff?

An ideal administrator will have lawyers, accountants, and certified real estate professionals on staff. They should have experience as IRA advisers and receive ongoing training to keep abreast of the changes in IRS rules. The penalty for engaging in a prohibited transaction is severe; even if the transaction represents only a small portion of your IRA, the entire IRA will be deemed distributed and you will have to pay income tax and — if applicable — an early withdrawal penalty that tax year. Your administrator should be able to alert you to any possible contradictions of IRS rules.

How long have you been in business?

A company that has been in business for a long time will have an established reputation and a large, experienced staff. On the other hand, a smaller company might offer more personal attention and a faster response to your requests. You should know the background of a new business; its founders might have a wealth of experience or they could be newcomers to the field.

Is your company involved in any current, ongoing, or pending litigation?

A company being sued for mishandling someone else's investments is not a good choice for yours. Ask if the company is bonded for theft or fraud and insured for errors and omissions. Ask to see the company's annual financial statements, and look for footnotes referring to litigation or payments for legal fees or settlements.

Who do you consult when you need expert advice?

A good administrator will have access to experts outside the company who can give legal advice and answer questions in an unclear situation. Even a professional sometimes comes up with questions he or she cannot answer. For example, a complex tax issue. A competent professional knows when to seek additional counsel.

Do you provide education for investors?

Some administrators provide newsletters, information, and classes on their websites or the services of a financial adviser to help you get started.

Can you automatically transfer unused cash into a money-market account?

Some IRA administrators automatically place unused cash into a money-market account at the end of each day so it can earn interest until it is needed. This ensures the most efficient use of money that might not be needed immediately for business purposes.

What is your fee structure?

Administrative fees for a typical IRA are less than $100 per year, but fees for a self-directed IRA can range from several hundred to more than $1,000 a year for a $100,000 account, reflecting the additional services provided. A self-directed IRA incurs fees both from the IRA custodian and the administrator. Custodians normally charge a fee for each transaction and might also charge an annual fee. A fee-based administrator charges either a flat annual fee or a fee for each service or transaction, in addition to the custodian's fee. An asset-based administrator charges an annual fee based either on the value or the number and type of assets in the IRA. Some administrators charge a flat annual fee along with a fee for each transaction. There might also be a termination fee when you close your account or transfer to another IRA.

Paying fees with outside funds means more money stays in your IRA.

Many IRA owners pay IRA administrators' fees with outside funds in order to preserve as much cash as possible inside the IRA.

Can I access my account online?

Many IRA administrators offer the ability to make changes to an account and submit orders online. Viewing your account details easily whenever you need them can be helpful.

What kind of customer service do you offer?

If you want someone available to answer your questions, try calling the company customer service telephone number to see how responsive the staff is. Some administrators offer live chats online with customer service representatives. Not everyone needs to consult with his or her IRA administrator on a regular basis, but if you do, make sure you will be able to do so easily.

FUNDING A SELF-DIRECTED IRA

Annual IRA contribution limits restrict the amount available for investment in a self-directed IRA — $5,000 per year, $6,000 if you are older than 50, in 2010. You might have a substantial amount to invest if you are rolling over a 401(k) or other retirement plan, have inherited , or have already accumulated a substantial IRA balance. A self-employed individual establishing an SEP-IRA is allowed to contribute 25 percent of his or her wages — or up to 20 percent of income reported on IRS Schedule C (Form 1040): Profit or Loss from Business — up to a maximum of $49,000, in 2010. Before setting up a self-directed IRA, confirm that the amount in your account will suffice for the type of investment you are planning. If your account has a small balance, you could increase it by making some short-term investments with quick returns. You can leverage the money in your IRA by creating and investing in your own limited liability company, which then takes out a mortgage or a business loan to be paid back with rent or business income. Your IRA can also buy a partial interest, or partnership, in a company otherwise established with outside funds or in collaboration with a spouse or other family member. You will manage the company, but only the IRA's share of the profits can be deposited in the IRA account.

 All expenses must be paid from IRA funds.

IRS rules do not allow the use of personal funds to pay expenses associated with an investment your IRA owns. If you need cash to pay for maintenance, supplies, or service charges associated with real estate or a business owned by your IRA, you must ensure there is enough cash in your IRA account to cover these needs.

CHECKBOOK CONTROL

One of the limitations of a self-directed IRA is the owner must instruct the IRA custodian to carry out financial transactions on his or her behalf, resulting in delays, extra paperwork, and custodian transactional fees. To get around this difficulty, the owner of a self-directed IRA can set up a LLC that he or she manages and instruct the IRA custodian to invest in it. This is known as "checkbook control." The IRA owner has sole signing authority for the bank accounts of the LLC and can carry out financial transactions without the involvement of the IRA custodian. The profits of the LLC go directly to the IRA. This structure was officially sanctioned by a tax court case, Swanson v. Commissioner of Internal Revenue, 106 T.C. 76, in 1996. James Swanson, owner of Swanson's Tools, set up a company called Worldwide to export tools abroad. All shares of Worldwide were owned by an IRA set up by James Swanson, and the company received commissions for its export sales and paid dividends to the IRA. The IRS characterized this arrangement as "self-dealing" and declared them as "prohibited transactions." Swanson appealed and the court declared that the payment of dividends to the IRA, by a company wholly owned by the IRA, benefited the IRA and did not directly benefit James Swanson. This ruling set a precedent for self-directed IRAs to own a business managed by the IRA owner and receive income from that business without losing their tax-deferred status. The IRA owner finds a custodian that allows self-directed IRAs, sets up the LLC, and then directs the custodian to purchase membership interest in the LLC and transfer funds to the LLC bank account. The IRA owner writes a check from the LLC to purchase an investment that he or she then manages.

The IRA custodian is a nondiscretionary trustee, meaning it does not offer legal or tax advice or ensure that legal requirements are met. The IRA owner is responsible for making sure all codes, regulations, and legal requirements are complied with. It is essential for the owner of a self-directed IRA who sets up an LLC to seek out the independent advice of accountants, lawyers, and business advisers who are not affiliated with the IRA custodian and who understand the IRS rules concerning IRAs.

MAKING IRA INVESTMENTS THROUGH A LIMITED PARTNERSHIP

There are several reasons why a limited partnership is a good investment vehicle for a self-directed IRA:

1. Your IRA's funds will be in the partnership's name, making it easier to get cashier's checks for foreclosures or tax-lien auctions.

2. Real estate closings can be done more efficiently and require less explanation to the title company.

3. You will have better-protected assets.

Check with your CPA or tax adviser on the local, state, and federal tax implications of the entity you want your IRA to invest in. You will need a lawyer familiar with the prohibited transaction rules of Section 4975, as well as the plan assets regulations of ERISA.

BUYING FOREIGN PROPERTIES THROUGH YOUR IRA

Nothing in the IRS Code prohibits the purchase of property outside the United States. However, many IRA custodians will not allow foreign real estate investment purchases because the property is not easily inspected. If you have experience with foreign real estate and wish to invest in property in another country, find a custodian who:

• Allows you to write your own checks, reducing the transaction costs.

- Allows you to make your own investment decisions.

- Has a low, flat-rate custodial fee.

Additionally, you will want to have your IRA in the form of a limited partnership to protect you from any possible litigation.

CASE STUDY: PRIVATE LENDING OVERSEAS

Allan Bolton
GCA Private Capital Solutions
and Opportunities
Phone: 506-2251-2841
Toll-free: 1-877-605-8330
E-mail: info@gcacr.com
Website: www.gcacr.com

Seizing high quality opportunities with a strong focus on protecting your capital.

GCA member investors can participate in the following investing programs:

Private Lending:

Through the Private Lending Program, we assist individuals and companies with proven honesty and a history of successful operation that require debt financing to accomplish critical goals. At the same time, investors benefit by earning high yields on their investment, secured by prime assets worth considerably more than the amount committed by a private investor. In many instances, temporary cash flow problems, high financial leverage, past credit problems, unusual business situations, business size, restrained lending policies by financial institutions, and the need for a faster loan approval process make traditional funding sources unavailable or inappropriate.

For potential borrowers who own prime real estate assets in Costa Rica, we offer an alternative private funding solution. High-yield private loans are arranged between prospective borrowers and committed private investors.

We look for private lending opportunities with the following characteristics:

- The loan must be secured by prime real estate assets in Costa Rica. These assets must be highly desirable — having attributes that qualify as highly attractive for a specific target group — and relatively liquid.

- We only recommend investments for which you have a very strong equity cushion, and we insist on investing only when a considerable margin of safety exists. We recommend that our investors not lend more than 40 percent to 45 percent of the verifiable market value of the property offered as collateral. To determine market value for a potential investment, we engage experienced and conservative third-party appraisers who must justify their valuations with hard facts and not general opinions.

- The asset offered as collateral must have a high emotional value to its owners.

- A potential borrower must be competent, knowledgeable, and honest.

- The borrower must have a realistic exit strategy to pay back the loan offered.

- If recovered, the asset offered as collateral can be disposed quickly because of its prime characteristics for a well-identified target group.

We offer the following terms:

Loan Amounts: $100,000 USD to $10 million USD.

LTV: Maximum of 50 percent of verifiable market value of the offered collateral.

Term: three months to 24 months

Rate: 12 to 20 percent.

Closing points: five to seven.

Legal structure of the investment:

We prefer legal structures that allow a fast recovery of the asset with minimum cost to investors. As a result, we like to structure private loans under a Trust Agreement.

Protection of investors:

Our first commitment is to eliminate risk.

- We only recommend investments secured by prime real estate assets.

- We only recommend investments for which you have a very strong equity cushion. We are adamant about investing only when a considerable margin of safety exists.

- We only recommend investments in which the borrower is competent, knowledgeable, and honest.

- We only recommend investments for which a simple, realistic, and highly probable exit strategy exists.

- We never touch your money. All funds stay in your control until the mortgage paperwork is completed and escrow requires funding.

- You are never given a "hard sell" or pressured to put your money in an investment about which you do not feel confident and safe.

- You are never charged anything for the investment transaction or the management of your mortgage investment. Borrowers take care of all fees.

- We structure your investment in such way that in case of a borrower default, you can recover the asset in a fast, efficient, and cost-effective way.

- We recommend working only through third-party-managed escrow accounts.

What we do for investors

It is our goal to find the best loans for our investors. We pre-qualify the borrowers, do initial due diligence — to be partnered with your own, match the project to your profile, and send you an investment summary.

After thorough due diligence on a loan request and the borrower, we submit a summary of the loan and the borrower to you for your acceptance. If you find the loan opportunity practical and attractive, you will confirm your desire to fund the loan for the given term and at the interest rate in the summary.

Our team then sets up an escrow through a third-party firm, completes all legal paperwork, helps with the final signing, and then services the loan free of charge to our investors. Your funds will be written directly to the escrow company, and your name will appear on the deed of trust or private mortgage set up as a promissory note with the borrower's property as security and then recorded through the Public Registry of Costa Rica. Payments will then be made to you on a monthly basis through a collection account managed by an escrow account manager. The borrower pays all fees so the transaction does not cost you anything. The borrower also pays all servicing and management fees.

JV–Equity Real Estate Investment Opportunities

Our JV–Equity Real Estate Program assists real estate developers/operators of high integrity and a proven track record to secure the private capital required to build or acquire real estate intensive assets, businesses, or projects in Costa Rican market segments where very high returns are possible because of limited competition, very large demand of institutional quality, significant barriers to entry, low saturation, true product or service differentiation, and clear exit strategies. To minimize risk, we do not recommend investment in start-ups or in ventures where the critical permit processing stage has not been overcome — red tape risk is common in Costa Rica. This program offers loan amounts ranging from $100,000 USD to $20 million USD depending on business segment and investor type. Private investors have a preferred claim on profits. We look for opportunities with limited competition and a strong, growing demand for a highly differentiated real estate product. Currently, we are focusing on medical tourism real estate, select investments in the hospitality industry, and affordable housing for locals and low-income families. Our involvement in these projects extends to the investment execution stage through oversight management activities.

ENSURING THE TAX-DEFERRED STATUS OF THE ACCOUNT

The major benefit of investing with an IRA is that its tax-advantaged status allows you to increase your earnings. Because you are not paying income tax on the profits earned by your IRA investments, you have more money to reinvest. Income tax is paid on withdrawals from traditional IRAs when you take out the money during retirement and never on withdrawals from Roth IRAs. Always consult a CPA or attorney who knows retirement planning and tax law to ensure your IRA investments are structured in a way that do not violate IRA rules. One simple mistake might result in the sudden loss of your IRA's tax benefits. If you engage in a prohibited transaction in connection with your IRA, then the account stops being. The account is treated as though all the assets in it had been distributed to you at their fair market values on the first day of that year. You could find yourself owing taxes on large portions of what you thought was nontaxable income. Combined penalties and income taxes can range from 15 percent to more than 100 percent of the real estate's value. You could end up with a large taxable income for that year and find yourself in a higher tax bracket. If you are younger than 59½, you must also pay a 10 percent early withdrawal penalty.

Self-directed IRAs are in particular danger of violating IRS rules regarding prohibited transactions. The IRS stipulates that every transaction in a self-directed IRA must be for the primary benefit of the IRA. The purpose of this is to use tax privileges to generate retirement income for the owner, not to provide concessions or tax breaks to the IRA owner and his or her immediate family. Your IRA custodian, trustee, and administrator are also prohibited from using your IRA for their personal benefit.

You cannot pay yourself a salary from a company your IRA owns unless the company is structured so someone else decides your compensation. You are not allowed to commingle your personal funds with IRA funds or to loan money to your IRA. This means you cannot pay any expenses for property your IRA owns out of your personal bank account. A business your IRA owns cannot furnish free goods or services to you or your administrator. When you receive interest payments each month, the money must go straight to the IRA account. That interest can be reinvested in real estate or invested in other assets — as long as it stays within the IRA.

The penalty for a prohibited transaction is the immediate distribution of all assets in the IRA and the loss of its tax-free status.

Prohibited Transactions

Excerpt from Internal Revenue Service Publication 590, Traditional IRAs **.irs.gov/ publications/p590/ch01.html#en_US_publink10006397**

Generally, a prohibited transaction is any improper use of your traditional IRA account or annuity by you, your beneficiary, or any disqualified person.

Disqualified persons include your fiduciary and members of your family — spouse, ancestor, lineal descendant, and any spouse of a lineal descendant. The following are examples of prohibited transactions with a traditional IRA:

- *Borrowing money from it.*
- *Selling property to it.*
- *Receiving unreasonable compensation for managing it.*
- *Using it as security for a loan.*
- *Buying property for personal use (present or future) with IRA funds.*

FIDUCIARY

For these purposes, a fiduciary includes anyone who does any of the following:

- *Exercises any discretionary authority or discretionary control in managing your IRA or exercises any authority or control in managing or disposing of its assets.*
- *Provides investment advice to your IRA for a fee or has any authority or responsibility to do so.*
- *Has any discretionary authority or discretionary responsibility in administering your IRA.*
- *Has an effect on the account. If you or your beneficiary engages in a prohibited transaction in connection with your traditional IRA account at any time during the year, the account stops being as of the first day of that year.*
- *Has an effect on you or your beneficiary. If your account stops being because you or your beneficiary engaged in a prohibited transaction, the account is treated as distributing all its assets to you at their fair market values on the first day of the year. If the total of those values is more than your basis in the IRA, you will have a taxable gain that is includible in your income.*

- Borrows on an annuity contract. If you borrow money against your traditional IRA annuity contract, you must include in your gross income the fair market value of the annuity contract as of the first day of your tax year. You may have to pay the 10 percent additional tax on early distributions, discussed later.

- Pledges an account as security. If you use a part of your traditional IRA account as security for a loan, that part is treated as a distribution and is included in your gross income. You may have to pay the 10 percent additional tax on early distributions.

OWNING REAL ESTATE IN AN IRA

Any type of investment real estate can qualify for IRA investment, including apartment buildings, office buildings, and motels. If you purchase and hold real estate property with a self-directed IRA, there are additional rules you should be aware of:

- You may not personally own the property purchased by your plan. It has to be owned by your IRA.

- Properties included in IRAs cannot be the investor's personal residence or purchased from immediate family. This does not include your siblings, just your parents, children, and grandchildren.

- The IRS allows you to use the land or building but not while it is in your IRA. For instance, you could buy a retirement home, rent it to someone else, put the rental income in your IRA, and when you retire, take the house as a distribution. Then you could move in.

- You must use the property for investment purposes only.

- Your business may not lease, or be located in or on, any part of the property while it is held by your IRA.

- If the title is put in your name, you cannot "sell" it to your IRA.

Because it is a tax-advantaged account, you do not receive the usual tax deductions associated with owning and selling real estate. For instance, you cannot write off depreciation on your real estate investment. When you make a profit by selling a property in a traditional IRA, the earnings will be taxed at your personal income tax rate when you withdraw them from the account, rather than at the lower capital gains rate. On the other hand, you do not have to pay capital gains tax when you sell a property and buy another because the money remains in the IRA.

DISTRIBUTING YOUR PROPERTY

You can withdraw real estate from your IRA and use it as a residence or second home when you reach retirement age — age 59½ or older for a penalty-free withdrawal. At that time, you can elect either to have the IRA sell the property or take an in-kind distribution of the property.

In an in-kind distribution, your IRA custodian assigns the title to the property to you. You will then pay income tax on the current value of the property if it is held in a traditional IRA. If the property is held in a Roth IRA, you will not owe taxes at distribution. This makes a Roth IRA extremely attractive if you anticipate your real estate investments will appreciate over time.

CASE STUDY: USING AN IRA TO INVEST IN PRIVATE MORTGAGES

Jean
retired investor

Before I started investing in private mortgages, I had all my money in IRA funds. My bank talked me into switching to another mutual fund. When the stock market crashed so did my IRA. I lost half of my investment and to this day, I have never gotten it back. Luckily for me, my son had begun to invest in private mortgages, and he talked me into giving it a try, too. I did not understand it in the beginning, but I have a great broker and a great son. They explain everything to me. For me, it has been a great investment plan these last two years.

One thing that was a bit different about private mortgage investing was how I used my IRA money. There are not too many places that will be a trustee over an IRA that is going to be used for real estate investing. They simply do not believe in this kind of investing. However, my son recommended a great IRA trustee in California named Trust Administration Services. This meant I had to transfer my IRA money to the new trustee. For me, this was a bit complicated but only because of all the paperwork.

Remember, your IRA activity gets reported to the government so everything has to be done in a very proper order. Trust Administration Services answered all my questions and helped me get through the paperwork. Now that my money is there, it has been quite easy.

Except for my social security and my small pensions, I have all my money in private mortgage investing. I feel very safe. In fact, I even have the equity in my home working for me. My house is paid off, but I have taken an equity loan for about half of the value of my home and am using that money to earn money. The only drawback to using your home equity is you do have to pay your own bank for the equity loan even if your borrower is not paying you. For me, this is not an issue. I know that my incoming finances will cover me if the borrower does not pay. I also know the borrower will eventually pay, or I will foreclose. At that time, I get my money back. As I said, I feel very safe. Prior to investing in private mortgages, I was very concerned about getting long-term insurance. When you get older — elderly — you do think about being a burden on your kids. You wonder if you are going to lose all your money. Long-term insurance is very expensive. Nonetheless, I wanted to know that I could go into an assisted-living home or a nursing home if the need ever arose. My basic money is only $2,500 a month and almost half would be going to long-term insurance. With the money I am making now, I do not ever worry about it anymore. There is always money coming in. You can count on it month after month. You will not have to worry. The interest is substantial, reliable, and will more than pay for an assisted-living facility. Not only that, but my principal will not be touched. That means this money can go to my kids. The added bonus is that I am saving about $12,000 a year on insurance premiums. Now, instead of worrying about the future and spending money on insurance, I do wonderful things — like take trips.

If I had to give one tip to someone just starting out, it would be to find a good broker. I am very lucky. I have a good broker and a good son. A good broker is someone you have confidence in. A good broker is one who goes out of his or her way and visits the people borrowing the money. He or she knows the properties he or she brokers. He or she knows you and your level of comfort with different situations. When you have a good broker, you know that you can trust him or her.

I have an excellent broker. I had a mortgage on a million-dollar horse farm. The borrower had only needed $130,000 so this was a really good deal for me. However, the borrower had stopped paying. It looked like I might have had to foreclose. This was not too bad, since I knew that my loan-to-value ratio was excellent and that I was the primary investor, but no one likes the idea of foreclosure. This is where my broker came in. He talked with the guy, and we restructured the loan. I lent him a bit more money; however, we increased the interest, and he paid all of that interest for a year up front. I walked away with $52,000 in one day.

My broker understands real estate mortgages, and I know I can trust him. Even if we had to go to foreclosure, I know he has worked the mortgage in such a way that I will never lose my principal. He often works deals where I get points up front and points on the back end. That can be a few thousand dollars before I ever give them the mortgage. I am glad I am out of regular investing. I looked at the newspaper every day. I was a nervous wreck. With private mortgage investing, the risk is a lot less. In fact, there really is no risk as long as you keep your loan-to-value ratio at no more than 50 percent and check out property. Investing in this way allows me to live the lifestyle I want. I can spend on trips, or I can stay home. Whatever I choose. If I want to buy something extravagant, I can do it. I used to worry a lot. Being from the Depression era, I still do worry a bit but not like I used to.

Chapter 8: Selling Mortgages and Notes

Previous chapters explained how you can earn high rates of return by loaning money for short-term mortgages. You loan money to a borrower who cannot get a traditional bank loan, receive regular interest payments, and recover your capital at the end of the loan. This process is the most straightforward, but other ways to make money with private loans exist. Almost every mortgage can be sold to another lender, even if the payments are not being made on a timely basis. There are many situations in which a lender is willing to take cash payment of less than the face value of the mortgage and turn the mortgage and its interest payments over to you. This chapter explains how you can earn higher rates of return than the stock market by buying and selling mortgages.

BUYING A DISCOUNTED MORTGAGE

When a home is sold, you must record certain information at your county courthouse or the county clerk's office, including:

- Price.
- Taxes.
- Liens.
- Buyer's name.
- Seller's name.
- Amount of mortgage.
- Names of lenders.

All of this information becomes available to the public. Most counties now make this information available on their websites. Find where local real estate mortgages are recorded, and look for properties that have two mortgages — a primary and a secondary. The primary mortgage will typically be a financial institution, and the secondary is often an individual.

It is common for a seller to offer supplementary financing to a qualified buyer who does not have enough cash for the down payment required by the bank issuing the first mortgage. Suppose that Mrs. Jones is selling her house for $120,000. Mr. and Mrs. Smith want to buy the house. They both have stable jobs and good credit, and the bank has approved their mortgage, except for one thing: They are $5,000 short of the $18,000 down payment — 15 percent — required by the bank. The Smiths ask Mrs. Jones if she would loan them $5,000 at an interest rate of 10 percent with the entire loan to be paid back at the end of eight years. Mrs. Jones agrees because she wants to sell her house. The Smiths buy the house. They now have a primary mortgage with the bank and a secondary mortgage with Mrs. Jones, both on record at the county courthouse. The Smiths make an interest payment of $41.67 every month to Mrs. Jones. After four years, Mrs. Jones has received $2,000 in interest from the Smiths. By this time, she has become tired of keeping records, or perhaps she would like a lump sum of cash to use for her granddaughter's college tuition. This is where you step into the picture. While looking through courthouse records, you discover that the Smiths have a secondary mortgage with Mrs. Jones. You look up Mrs. Jones's phone number and call her. Here is what you will say:

You: "Hello, Ms. Jones, my name is _____. I am a real estate investor. I understand that you hold a mortgage for $5,000 on the property located at _____ St. here in (name of town). Is that correct?"

Ms. Jones: "Who are you anyway, and how do you know about any of that?"

You: "As I said, I am a real estate investor, and I saw your mortgage listed at the county courthouse. I wonder if you would like to sell that mortgage. You see, I pay cash for these kinds of mortgages. I would like to offer to buy that mortgage from you for cash. Are you interested?"

Ms. Jones: "That depends on what you are offering."

You: "Well, I could offer you $3,000." (Your offer should be between 60 and 75 percent of the loan in order to make a profit.) "How does that sound?"

Ms. Jones: "Why yes, I think I might be interested."

You: "Could I meet with you at your attorney's office to show you my proposal?" (Going to her own attorney will reassure Ms. Smith that this is a legitimate business deal.)

Because Mrs. Jones has already received $2,000 in interest payments from the Smiths, if she sells the mortgage to you for $3,000, she will have recovered her original $5,000. You will earn $2,000 in interest over the remainder of the mortgage's eight-year term and $5,000 when the mortgage matures — a total of $7,000 from your $3,000 investment. The following is an illustration demonstrating the potential return on this investment:

Face Value	$5,000
Purchase Price	$3,000
Term Balance	4 years
Original Interest Rate	10 percent
Monthly Interest Payment	$41.67
Annual Return from Interest	$500/$3,000 = 16.7 percent
Total Interest You Receive	$2,000
Discount on Face Value	$2,000
Total Profit	$4,000
Average Annual Return	($4,000/$3,000)/4 yrs = 19 percent

In this example, Mrs. Jones recovered the $5,000 she loaned the Smiths with the added benefit that she sold her house when she wanted to. Other individuals who hold secondary mortgages might accept a greater discount and sell to you at a loss if they need cash urgently, if their personal circumstances have made holding the mortgage inconvenient or if they have difficulty collecting monthly payments from the borrower.

SELLING MORTGAGES

You can also make a profit by buying a second mortgage at a discount from one person and selling it to another investor. Suppose Mr. Brown has retired and wants to sell his home, valued at $100,000, and buy a condominium in Florida for $50,000. Mr. Brown owns his home free and clear. You suggest he sell you his home in exchange for $50,000 cash to buy the condo and a $50,000 seasoned mortgage note paying 10 percent interest. This will give him monthly interest payments of $417 to supplement his social security. Interest income is not counted as earned income when calculating income limits for social security benefits so his benefits will not be affected. Mr. Brown agrees.

Now, find a mortgage with a face value of $50,000 or more, at 10 percent interest, with monthly payments of at least $417. Offer the mortgage holder $35,000 cash for this note to be paid at closing. If the mortgage holder agrees, the mortgage note should be placed in escrow along with a signed copy of the agreement — preferably notarized. At closing, your bank puts up the money for a first mortgage on Mr. Brown's home of 90 percent of the price, or $90,000. From this amount:

- You pay the mortgage note holder $35,000 for the note.

- You pay the seller of the property $50,000 cash and give him the $50,000 in mortgage notes.

- There is $5,000 left "on the table." This belongs to you, along with $10,000 in equity in the property you bought from Mr. Brown — the difference between the $90,000 mortgage and the $100,000 value.

If you found a new buyer for the home and bought and sold the property simultaneously at a double closing, you would walk away with $15,000 cash — in other words, the $5,000 left on the table and the $10,000 equity you sold to your buyer — his down payment.

Finding mortgage notes to buy and sell

You can find all of the information concerning privately held notes at the county courthouse. To make the time spent researching the courthouse records worthwhile, you will need to use an organized approach.

First, look at land records from the past two or three years online or at your county courthouse for properties with second mortgages, and collect the information you need, such as names and contact information and the amounts of the mortgages. Check records monthly to stay up to date and find the most recent notes. Find out how often your county courthouse updates its online databases. Find about 20 of these situations and make a list of them along with the name and contact information for the holders of the second mortgages.

If you do not want to do that kind of work yourself, you have two options when you search for second mortgages. You can get the information from a company that does all the research for you. Experience™ (**www.experian.com/ small-business/specialty-mailing-lists.jsp**) sells lists of leads generated from its database of more than 210 million people. For a monthly subscription fee, you can research mortgage information on HomeInfoMax (**www.homeinfomax. com**). NETRonline (**http://publicrecords.netronline.com/**) offers links to public records online and sells detailed information. You can also purchase single-day passes or subscriptions to research real estate records using KnowX® , a LexisNexis® company (**www.knowx.com/real/search.jsp?**).

Another effective way to find notes is through networking with social and business contacts. Nearly a third of all real estate transactions involve some kind of private financing. That means three out of every ten people you know with real estate hold a note or know someone who holds a note. Those who hold private notes often are not aware they can sell them, or if they are aware, they do not know who to sell to. Let everyone in your circle, including the local restaurant owner and the person behind the counter at your gas station, know that you buy and sell mortgages.

You can also find the information you need through real estate agents who have access to past transactions through the Multiple Listing System (MLS). If you do a search based on seller financing, you will get a list of potential notes.

Contacting the note holders

Once you have the information, begin contacting the note holders. It is very likely that a note holder will not accept your proposal the first time you present it, especially if it is a new note. Do not give up after a first refusal. Instead, keep organized records, and call him or her back at a later date. By then, the note holder might need cash or might have grown tired of "playing bank."

When you contact the note holder, give him or her a way to get in touch with you. One way to do this is through a follow-up letter. Suggest that this letter be put with the note so if circumstances change, the note holder will know who to contact.

Getting the agreement

If the note holder agrees to sell the note, you should quickly get the agreement in writing, sign it, and notarize it by all parties involved. The agreement should include a clause giving you the option to reject or accept the purchase. Once you have a written agreement, you can choose whether to go ahead with the purchase or abort it. Without the written agreement, however, that decision rests with the note holder.

After the agreement

Normally, the best way to make money is to go ahead and sell the note soon after you buy it before the circumstances of the loan change. As soon as you have the written agreement, begin to look for investors. Prospective investors will give you a proposal based on your verbal assessment of the note. However, before actual prices can be considered, documentation must be presented.

Documentation

Four different sets of documents are required to buy and sell notes:

- The original real estate transaction documents.
- Those created to evaluate the deal.
- Those created to close the deal.
- Post-closing documents.

Original documents

You need to see the original loan documents, including the deed of trust and the promissory note. It is especially important to examine the promissory note because that is what you actually purchase. The promissory note contains the following information:

- Loan amount.
- Payment amount.
- Interest rates.
- Financial terms.

Finally, you need to review the settlement statement, also known as the HUD-1. The HUD-1 contains:

- The sale price.
- The legal description.
- The amount of the down payment.

- The details of any other financing.

- If there is title insurance and from where.

- The hazard- nsurance carrier and amount.

- The real estate agencies involved in the original transaction and their commissions.

- The property taxes.

Looking at these three documents will help you determine if you really want to go through with buying the note. If any negative information comes to light and you choose to abort the transaction, contact the note holder in writing.

Documents used to evaluate the deal

Many of the documents used to evaluate the purchase of a note are similar to the documents used to determine if you are willing to provide a private mortgage. For instance, you need an appraisal of the property and, if it is a commercial property, you need to see the financial statements of the business.

You should also ask to see any "senior debt instruments." These are any mortgages, deeds, and similar liens that take priority over your note in case of foreclosure. Find out about the status of these debt instruments. For example, if you know the first mortgage is in default, you will probably be unwilling to buy the second mortgage note. This kind of information is available in public records.

Finally, you will need an estoppel affidavit. This is an affidavit sent to the note payer confirming the note terms, conditions, and the current status of the note. Be sure to send this with return receipt requested as proof that the affidavit was sent.

Closing documents

Closing documents depend upon what you plan to do with the note. If you are keeping the note, there will be one set of closing documents. If you plan to sell the note immediately, you will have what is known as a double closure, and you will need two of everything — one set of documents with you as the buyer of the note and another with you as the seller of the same note. You will also want to make sure your purchase assignment is recorded before your buyer's assignment is recorded so your purchase legally precedes your sale of the note.

Post-sale documents

If you are keeping the note, you will want to be immediately added to the insurance policy as a loss payee so if anything, such as a fire or flooding, happens to the property, you will receive your share of any compensation payments.

You must also send a letter informing the note payer you are the new note holder and instructing him or her about where to send the payments. You will also send the payer a letter from the former note holder that authorizes this transaction.

If you are a second note holder, you will also need to contact the senior note holders and let them know you are now a junior note holder. Ask them to inform you if a problem with the first note arises.

When you sell the note immediately, you will not need any post-sale documents, just cash the check.

You can buy and sell mortgage notes using the same organizational structures described earlier in this book, including partnerships, corporations, and IRAs. Although the process is different from directly investing in private mortgages, buying and selling mortgage notes is another way to create an investment vehicle based on real estate lending that provides you with high-interest yields. Successful buying and selling of notes requires a similar knowledge of real estate and familiarity with real estate contracts.

The following chapter returns to private mortgage lending and explains how to find and evaluate potential borrowers.

Chapter 9: Finding Potential Borrowers

You have money to invest — now you need to find borrowers. The first step is to identify the characteristics of the right borrower. You already know you are looking for borrowers with experience. Experienced borrowers are far more likely to succeed in carrying out the proposed business deal. They are not as likely to be caught off-guard if something does not go exactly as planned and will have various backup exit strategies.

Experience alone is not enough. Someone once said, "You can have 20 years of experience or the same experience 20 times." In other words, has your borrower merely been in the business a long time, or has he or she been continually learning and growing while in the business? You want a borrower who can demonstrate a good track record or compensate for his or her lack of experience with a lower LTV ratio, higher interest rate, or both.

One way to learn whether your real estate investors are experienced is to talk to others in your local investment community. Ask your investors for references, and then contact them. Check public records to see how many deals they have completed. Do a background check to see if they have any lawsuits against them.

Avoid doing business with anyone who:

- Will not give you any references.

- Does not want you to get an appraisal.

- Does not want you to see the property.

- Will not gather and present all the necessary paperwork.

If you have already started to work with a borrower who seems to be hiding something, it is not too late to back out. A legitimate borrower should have no difficulty providing you with a solid business plan and all the relevant documents. It is better to be safe than sorry; only agree to deals that adequately protect you and your money.

WHO ARE THE BEST BORROWERS?

Borrowers come in all shapes and sizes: first-time homebuyers, developers, speculators, and real estate investors. For the purpose of private mortgage investing, you will probably want to stick with real estate investors — experienced real estate investors. Real estate investors are looking for short-term loans because they either plan to quickly resell the property or to refinance with a loan on better terms. Landlords and homeowners are typically looking for 15- to 30-year loans, and you do not want to have your money tied up that long.

- Real estate investors are not "one-time shots." They tend to buy many pieces of property each year — often 30 or more. This means you only have to find a few good investors who will borrow from you repeatedly rather than a new borrower for each deal.

- Real estate investors are not looking for loans more than about 70 percent of the value of the property because they are buying it at reduced rates themselves. Homeowners, on the other hand, often need 80 percent or more. Developers need to borrow more than the current value of the property, since the land is vacant and they have yet to build on it. A loan with no more than a 70 percent LTV is a much safer investment than one with an 80 or 90 percent LTV.

- Real estate investors are willing to pay a higher interest rate to get the money they need when they need it. This translates into more profit for you.

While real estate investors should make up the bulk of your business, there might be occasions when you will loan to a landlord, a homeowner, or a developer. You will find you make more profit with less worry when you use mostly real estate investors.

Are There Enough Good Candidates for Private Mortgage Loans?

According to a report from the National Association of Realtors (NAR), of the almost 5 million homes sold in the U.S. in 2009, real estate investors bought 940,000, or almost 17 percent. About one in four real estate investors purchased more than one home in 2009. NAR also reported that its analysis of U.S. Census Bureau data shows there are 41.1 million investment homes in the U.S. and 75 million owner-occupied homes, meaning investors own 35 percent of all U.S. homes.

Increased restrictions on lending by banks and financial institutions during the Great Recession, which is the name of the recession that began in the United States beginning in December 2007, have created an increased demand for private mortgage loans. The potential national demand for private mortgages is in the hundreds of millions of dollars each year.

Network

Networking can and should play an important part in your search for real estate investors. Investors are spread out all over your community and the country; you cannot just walk to the "investor section" of town and pick someone out of the group.

To network effectively, you must build a database of acquaintances, as well as professionals, using personal contacts, investment professionals, industry and local organizations, libraries, media, and the Internet. You can meet business professionals by joining service clubs, such as the Rotary Club.

Friends and acquaintances

There is a strong possibility you already know potential real estate investors. They could be relatives or friends or perhaps people you know from church. You will never know who they are until you tell them what you do.

Local investment clubs

Go to a local real estate investing club. You can find a club near you by looking on REIClub.com™ (**www.reiclub.com/real-estate-clubs.php**) or on the National Real Estate Investors Association website (**www.nationalreia.com**), or by asking others in the real estate field. These clubs offer education and informative speakers.

Many of their members are active investors looking for loans.

A good club will have several hundred members and large attendance at its monthly meetings. Although you must pay a fee to join, real estate investors clubs provide many benefits, such as discounted subscriptions for computer research services and legal papers and special prices for remodeling materials, such as tile flooring.

Take your business cards along when you go to club meetings. This is a networking opportunity. Whenever you get the chance, let others in the group know you are a private lender. You could easily leave a meeting with four or five potential borrowers.

There is normally an information table where you can put your business cards or fliers advertising that you are looking for loan opportunities. Often, wholesalers put lists of properties there and will put you on their fax-out sheets for weekly updates.

Using the Internet

Look for real estate investors both locally and nationally on the Internet. If you type "real estate investors" in the Google™ search box, you will get more than 7 million results. Try keywords like "finding private lenders," and contact those sites as potential lenders.

Create your own website stating you are a private mortgage investor and asking real estate investors to contact you. Many domain name registries offer inexpensive website hosting and free do-it-yourself templates for basic websites. Include your website address on your letterhead, e-mail signature, and business cards. You can purchase a magnetic sign to stick on the back of your car advertising your business and URL.

Mortgage brokers, realtors, and appraisers

Even if there is no local real estate investment club, you can still get to know those involved in the real estate business in your area by calling on realtors and attending meetings of local business organizations, such as the Chamber of Commerce or the Better Business Bureau. Because you are not in direct competition with these business professionals, they may provide you with leads, and you can reciprocate by directing potential property buyers to them.

Hold a presentation

Another strategy is to gather a large group of potential investors and hold a presentation in a hotel conference room or restaurant. An event like this has several benefits:

- **Leveraging your time:** You save time by talking to more than one person at a time. You also save time by talking only to those who are pre-qualified. For instance, you can let them know from the outset that unless they have a specific amount to invest, the presentation is not for them. You can also mail invitations to lists of real estate investors, such as membership lists of real estate investor clubs.

- **Meeting in an attractive location:** Holding a presentation or luncheon allows you to meet your clients in a "nicer" venue than your office and helps gain their confidence and respect.

- **Having a controlled atmosphere:** The meeting location provides a place where you are in control of the situation and will not be interrupted by distractions, such as ringing telephones.

- **Answering everyone's questions at once:** People often ask questions you have not thought to answer. Not only that, some people do not want to show what they do not know by asking a question. If one person asks a question, they all learn from the answer. Everyone in the group gets educated at once.

- **Clients feel no pressure:** Even when you are very careful, a one-on-one meeting can come across as a high-pressure sales pitch to a client. In a relaxed presentation, people can listen without the feeling they are being put on the spot.

- **Your presentation will be more professional:** Because you will be presenting to a large group, you are more likely to make effort to refine your presentation. The experience will build your confidence and professionalism.

- **People will socialize afterward:** Because it is not a high-pressure event, people will linger afterward, ask more questions, and develop personal relationships with you. Those who linger may turn into your next investors.

Use "bird dogs"

"Bird dogs" are people who search out bargains for real estate investors. Some private mortgage investors hire "bird dogs" to hunt up leads in return for a referral fee if the deal goes through. The referral fee is worth it because time is money, and having someone else looking for leads will save you time. A "bird dog" might be a novice trying to break into the mortgage investing business and needs experience or someone already involved with real estate investors.

Look for ads and fliers

You see the ads of private real estate investors all the time in the local paper, in online classifieds, and on roadside signs. They usually say something like, "Got houses? Must sell? Fast cash." Call the number on the ad, and let them know you are a private mortgage investor. They may need your help on a deal, or they may know of a real estate investor looking for a good private loan.

Do not be shy; ask anyone and everyone if they know any area real estate investors, and before long, you will be connected with successful investors.

Finding suitable borrowers will become easier as you become involved in private mortgage lending. Real estate investors will spread the word, and you may develop a working relationship with one or two investors who come back to you for loans repeatedly. If you work with a broker, the broker will come to know your investment style and recommend appropriate opportunities.

This chapter has discussed how to identify and evaluate potential borrowers. *The next chapter is about evaluating the real estate property that will be used as collateral for your investment.*

CASE STUDY: INTERVIEW WITH REAL ESTATE INVESTORS CLUB

REIClub.com
www.reiclub.com

REIClub.com (**www.reiclub.com**) has been the pioneer in creative real estate investing education for more than 10 years. We are a premiere website learning portal for real estate investors.

By providing free training, business tools, how-to articles, and an active discussion forum, we essentially become the link for many to learn new and creative ways to achieve real estate wealth.

We strongly believe you do well by learning from others and with others, so much so, we offer a national listing of REIAs and Cash Flow Clubs to encourage people to network locally with other investors. Other great investor resources we take pride in providing are access to hard money, transactional funding, and private money lenders, as well as up-to-date real estate training seminars.

Private mortgage loans are typically short-term, from a few months to three years. Real estate investors are good candidates for these loans because they resell their properties or find more long-term financing quickly and because they understand the real estate market. How has the economic slowdown affected the strategies of real estate investors?

With the implosion of the banking and securities industry, the days of easy credit, instant equity, and everyone's 401(k) ballooning, investors have been forced to self-correct. Investors have resorted to becoming more creative in their deal structuring and more savvy in their acquisition techniques, and they are forming more partnerships and turning to cash, private lending, and notes to financially support their deals. Cash is king now.

They are constantly seeking out individuals who can fund short-term transactions for a day to 36 months. This is a unique time in history, with record devaluations, foreclosures, short sales, and the impending commercial meltdown rearing its ugly head so deals abound. Real estate investors are more open now than ever before to paying a premium for access to cash and credit and creating private notes.

Investors are uniquely positioned to help homeowners, landlords, other investors, and people with private money all make good in this situation. What we have now are well-trained, in-it-to-win-it, specialized investors who know what they are doing. That is the only way they are surviving. They are retraining themselves and their staff on new laws, investing techniques, forming strategic alliances with title companies and loss-mitigation firms, and constantly positioning themselves to gain access to and work with private money.

How has the banks' tightening of restrictions on credit affected real estate investors? Has it increased the demand for private loans?

Yes, absolutely. The tightening of the credit belt has caused an unequivocal rise of the need and use of private loans. This is a great thing for those who have cash, self-directed IRAs, and money they would otherwise invest in the stock market available at their disposable to lend. What is so great about private lending is you can set your own rules for use, define your terms, and set your repayment schedule.

Private loans in some societies have been the backbone for business ventures and real estate investments for centuries.

The demand for private loans has never been higher in the past three decades in our opinion. We hear the cry for them and the use of them in our forums, training seminars, and in the increasing listing of the number of private moneylenders on our "Hard Money Resources Page."

The "credit crunch," as the media has dubbed it, has shaken out many of the unskilled and "lucky" investors getting rich just because. As a private money mortgage investor or lender, you work with the higher caliber investor who is professional, who does it full-time, and who is trained to navigate the tumultuous water we now tread. They will seek our private money with new fervor.

How can private mortgage lenders locate real estate investors who might be potential borrowers?

You can always advertise on **www.reiclub.com**. We have a "Hard & Private Money Resources" page that continually ranks in the top five of the search engines for private money resources where investors look. It is the third most visited page on our site.

Second, connect with your local real estate brokers and real estate investment clubs. They offer great sources for information on who are great, ethical, and savvy investors active in today's market.

Last, start networking with title companies. They play a vital role in recording the necessary documents to properly document your financial instruments. Do not underestimate the power of the title company. They know who are doing deals and, for a small fee, can provide you with data on investors and other private moneylenders.

How are real estate investors responding to the large number of foreclosure sales and short sales?

Some are sitting on the sidelines. The overwhelming response has consisted of three actions that almost guarantee success in today's market: education, marketing, and funding.

1. **Education** — Most people are re-educating themselves in the perpetually changing rules that govern short sales and foreclosures. They have also formed alliances, working closely with lawyers who can advise and assist with the loss-mitigation process and interpret banking regulations. Others seek out mentors, attend training seminars, and invest in training their staff.

2. **Marketing** — All successful investors realize the need to reach potential buyers, sellers, and private moneylenders on a regular basis to maintain their network. Transactions are taking longer to complete because larger parties and more paperwork are involved in most short sale and foreclosure deals. You need to secure multiple buyers if one walks because the deal is taking too long to close.

3. **Funding** — Transaction funding is on the rise. It is very common for real estate investors to only need money for one to 45 days. Savvy investors help homeowners in short sales and foreclosure situations by procuring end buyers. Currently laws state the investor must take clear and legal possession of the title. That means they have to close on the buy transaction, wait for a day to 45 days to close the transaction, ideally private money or what has come to be known as transactional funding.

They do so by obtaining short term financing, ideally private money, or what has come to be known as transactional funding. They do not mind paying points, percentage of the amount borrowed, and other miscellaneous fees. In the end, everyone wins. The private money lender gets his or her principal plus interest back relatively quickly to start another loan, the investor makes money on the spread, the old home owner is saved, and the new home owner is happy because he or she got a great deal.

What advice would you give to private mortgage lenders?

Think now, and think win-win. Real estate investors need you. You need real estate investors. Other than a bank CD that usually locks you down for a six-month minimum, where else could you invest your principal and get a guaranteed return of full principal plus interest?

With the use of transactional funding, you can avail yourself to real estate investors, especially those specializing in short sales and foreclosures. You will have many opportunities where you can earn great returns relatively quickly and usually have your entire principal back in less than 60 days. You can essentially lend the same money over and over again.

Your money. Your rules. Your success. All you have to do is write the check.

Chapter 10: Verifying Property Information

When you decide to become a private mortgage lender, you take the responsibility of due diligence: assessing an investment and verifying it meets your criteria and is accurate. A mortgage originator is the person or company that helps the borrower complete the mortgage transaction. You may act as the mortgage originator, or you may work with a broker who represents you. If you have decided to work alone, you must gather all of the relevant information. If you work with a mortgage broker, a good portion of the due diligence will be the broker's responsibility. But, at least initially, you will want to verify some of the paperwork yourself. As you develop a relationship of trust with the broker, you will have to do less due diligence yourself but never give it up completely. You should always have first-hand information concerning your investments and know exactly how you intend to make money from them.

THE APPRAISAL

The first step when carrying out due diligence is an appraisal of the property and the subsequent report. This needs to be a complete report, using the three methods:

- Market approach.
- Cost approach.
- Income approach.

The market approach is the most significant, but getting all three will help confirm the report's accuracy. If either the cost or income approach is lower than the market approach, use the lowest appraised value to determine the maximum LTV ratio. By using the lowest appraisal to calculate your LTV, you will avoid loaning more than you can recover in case of default.

You can hire an appraiser, or you can learn to do the appraisals yourself. Either way, you should understand the different appraisal approaches and what they tell you, as well as the different ways to get "comps" — prices at which comparable properties have recently sold.

The market approach

With the market approach, the value of the property is determined by recent sales of comparable properties in that market. For the best results, you will want to get at least four comps to determine the market appraisal portion of the report.

There are three different methods of getting comps: doing your own research, using service companies, and accessing the MLS. You can do your own research by examining public records at the courthouse or online; checking newspaper listings — not all localities list sales information; looking at appraisals on tax records — often undervalued and useless for your purpose; using Internet searches — often outdated; or, by far the best way, knowing the neighborhood.

The longer you are in the investment business, the more you will know about the property values of particular neighborhoods. You can also learn about specific neighborhoods and communities by talking with realtors, attending open houses, viewing floor plans, and looking at online listings and virtual tours. Once you have done this often enough in a particular area, you can get a feel for the value of the house just by driving by.

Service companies sell data about home sales in different areas online. Do not simply accept online companies' comps as accurate; check the figures by doing your own research. Once you have established that a service company's appraisal figures are accurate, you will only have to spot check properties occasionally. Remember that not all online databases are updated regularly so look for a site that updates regularly.

Having access to the Multiple Listing Service (MLS) used by realtors is invaluable. If you do not have direct access to the MLS, you can often find someone in the real estate business who does and who will do searches for you for a fee. Instead of asking for a comp, ask them to print out the data sheets for you and determine your own comp values.

You can gain access to the MLS yourself by becoming a realtor or obtaining an associate membership. In some areas, you are allowed to access the MLS without a real estate license. If you do not have a license and cannot get an associate membership, you can develop a good working relationship with someone who does. A realtor who specializes in commercial properties is a good contact because he or she does not need to use the MLS daily like a residential realtor, and that will give you easier access to it.

Once you have at least four comps, you can determine the market value of your investment property by looking at the price for which each property sold. Compare its location to the location of your property. Be alert for any circumstances that might have affected the price, such as a pre-foreclosure sale, damage to the property, or details of construction, such as the type of roof or flooring or the presence of a pool or a screened porch.

The income approach

The income approach also requires four comps — rental comps — to determine the value of the property. The income approach evaluates the amount of income your investment property will return if rented out. This is important because your borrower will make payments out of this income if the property is rented out and because you might end up renting it out yourself if the borrower defaults.

In order for your appraisal to be valid, you must find similar properties in the neighborhood for rent, know the operating expenses associated with those rents, and have vacancy and collection loss data. You can get rental comps by contacting landlords directly or by using a service such as Rentometer™ (**www.rentometer. com/pages/rental_comps**) or RentJungle™ (**www.rentjungle.com**). Once you have identified comparable properties, you can look at public records to get their sale prices. You will probably not get all the information for each comp property, but you will need sufficient information to determine the "typical" numbers for your property.

You can use the form below to evaluate rental income and operating expenses for a rental property.

Annual Property Operating Data

Property Address:_____

Date: _____

Prepared by:_____

INCOME	$	%	Comments
Gross Scheduled Rent Income			
Other Income			
TOTAL GROSS INCOME			
VACANCY & CREDIT ALLOWANCE			
GROSS OPERATING INCOME			
EXPENSES			
Accounting			
Advertising			
Inslurance (fire nad liability)			
Janitorial Service			
Lawn/Snow			
Legal			
Licenses			
Miscellaneous			
Property Management			
Repairs and Maintenance			
Resident Superintendant			
Suppulies			
Taxes			
Real Estate			
Personal Property			
Payroll			
Other			
Trash Removal			
Utilities			
Electricity			
Fuel Oil			
Gas			
Sewer and Water			
Telephone			
Other			
TOTAL EXPENSES			
NET OPERATING INCOME			

The cost approach

The cost approach involves estimating the replacement value of a property as separate components — land and improvements. Here is how it works:

1. Estimate the value of the land as if it were a vacant property.

2. Estimate the replacement cost of the building.

3. Estimate the building's loss in value from depreciation.

4. Subtract the building's depreciation from the estimated replacement cost.

5. Calculate the value of the property by adding the estimated land value to the depreciated value of the building.

By compiling and reviewing information from all three approaches, you can get a fairly accurate estimate of the property's value, as well as its business potential. It is also important to evaluate the growth potential of the area by looking at county and city planning and development projections and by reading news articles on local business conditions. If the property will be rented out, determine the strength of rental demand in that area. You can do this by visiting local rental agencies and by observing rental listings online and in the media. Aggressive advertising campaigns and listings that remain unchanged for weeks indicate that demand is slow and landlords are actively searching for tenants. Little or no advertising and rental listings that disappear from week to week mean that rental property in that area is being snapped up. A drive through the neighborhood is very revealing: Look for vacant properties and "for lease" signs that indicate a surplus of rentals in the area.

After you have completed this research, if you still believe the investment is solid, you should conduct a physical inspection of the property.

PHYSICAL INSPECTION

An appraisal will not tell you everything about a property, nor should you place your trust in a piece of paper. Before committing yourself to a loan, conduct a physical inspection of the property and of the area in general. If you are inexperienced, hire a building inspector to accompany you. Here are a few of the things you should look for and consider:

- **Structural inspection:** If the property appears to need repairs, consult a building inspector or contractor for estimates. Note any major repairs that were not part of the appraisal so you can adjust the appraisal value accordingly.

- **Handicap accessibility:** If the property you are buying is a commercial property, you will want to verify that it complies with the handicap accessibility requirements under the Americans with Disabilities Act (ADA).

- **Drainage and retaining walls:** Check both the condition and the design of drainage and retaining walls, and look for any potential problems, such as signs of flooding, erosion, or leakage.

- **Roads:** Check to see if the property has adequate access from the public street. Projected road improvements could significantly change the desirability of the property. Road construction may present obstacles to customers wishing to enter the property.

- **Public transit:** Access to public transportation can increase the value of the property.

- **Wells:** If an on-site well provides water to the property, quality/potability and quantity — measured in gallons per hour — need to be determined. In some cases, the output of the well may limit the development of the property.

EXAMINE FINANCIAL DOCUMENTATION

If the property you are considering is either commercial or a multi-family rental property, you definitely want to see the financial documentation for that property because loan payments will come out of the property's business income. Keep in mind you do not care about the financial situation of the borrower — just the financial situation of the property. A property not bringing in enough income to cover insurance, maintenance, and loan payments is a poor investment risk. Knowing the financial status of the business helps you determine whether to loan the money.

What kind of financial documentation do you want to see?

- Rent rolls.

- Leases.

- Current and past financial statements.

- Expense projections.

- Licenses.

- Contracts that affect the property.

- Estoppel certificates — no defaults, no prepaid rent, status of security deposits, and so on — from each of the tenants prior to closing.

APPRAISALS ARE SUBJECTIVE

Appraisals are subjective. It is unlikely that two appraisers will give you the same figures for the same reasons. Factors that affect the appraiser's valuation, beyond the actual home and its appearance, include:

- Local taxes.

- Plat survey: size of lot, topography and landscape, easements.

- Deed: Is the title clear? Are there any deed covenants that would limit use or resale opportunities?

- List of improvements, especially to kitchen and bathrooms. Do you have permits, if required, for the alterations?

- Homeowner warranties.

- Value and condition of neighborhood houses.

- Zoning of, and plans for, any nearby vacant land.

- Age of neighborhood.

- Ease of access to work, schools, shopping, and recreation.

- Adequacy and cost of utilities.

- Adverse influences, such as proximity to highways, high-tension wires, and commercial areas.

- Present and proposed assessments.

Additionally, the appraiser will consider the following:

- Local supply and demand: How many homes are for sale in the immediate neighborhood? How quickly are they being sold? What are the current market trends? What is the reason for the sale of this particular piece of property?

- Economic conditions: What is the economy like in the region? Are there currently strikes or factory closings? Have there been any recent rezonings, or are there any scheduled? Are any factories leaving the area? Are any factories coming into the area?

- Politics: What state and local government actions are affecting property values? Have any school bonds been passed or been recently proposed? Have there been any property reassessments? Are taxes on the rise?

For each investment opportunity, you must go through the due diligence process. It might seem time consuming and require considerable effort, but this work is the foundation for your success as an investor. Once you have signed the loan contract, your money is committed. Overlooking a detail, such as a zoning permit or the closure of a local factory whose employees were a major source of business in the area, could result in failure. Even after you determine that a business proposition is sound, it is important to protect your investment from unexpected pitfalls with insurance. *The next chapter discusses the types of insurance you should include in a private loan contract.*

CASE STUDY: APPRAISALS ARE UNRELIABLE

Bud
Private mortgage investor of 25 years.

I got started in private mortgage investing in 1982. I was in apartment buildings, and I sold out and met a mortgage broker. In all my 25 years, I have only lost on one building, and that was due to fraud. It taught me a valuable lesson — inspect everything.

I think private mortgage investing is great. Why? Because you are in control. With stocks and bonds, you never really know what you have. You rely totally on someone else's opinion, but that is not the case with real estate. Real estate is tangible. I can go out and see it for myself. It is stable. Every now and then, I do the more traditional real estate deals, but only if a good deal comes up. Private mortgage investing, however, is much better. You just cannot pass it up.

Some people only like certain kinds of deals. For instance, some people only want commercial property, while others only want single-family dwellings. I am willing to look at just about anything — from mobile homes to construction loans. I see every loan as an individual deal. As long as there is equity in the property, it has the potential for a good, solid investment.

This is where the appraisals come in. Appraisals are supposed to let you know how much equity is actually in the property. In general, however, I do not like most appraisals. Appraisers are doing a job, typically for the person wanting the loan. They will ask the borrower what they want to borrow and what the loan-to-value ratio needs to be, and somehow, they get a figure that is almost on the dot of what the borrower needs it to be. For instance, an appraiser, with the help of comps, can come up with a price of $50/foot for a 30-year-old mobile home. Some are pretty sneaky that way.

This is why I always check out the property myself. I even check out the non-local ones. After you are in business a while, you can almost look at a building and know what it is going to be. In addition to the property itself, it is all about location.

Let me share with you one deal that sounded good on paper but just was not good at all. There was an out-of-town piece of property with a $250,000 home on it. It was a new home, and the appraisal was very good. By the photos, I would have said it was a really good deal. But, I drove the 60 miles to see the property. Everything within a mile and a half of this new house was junk. There were trailers in horrible condition and run-down, unkempt homes. It was terrible. The house itself was great, but the location was awful. Who would you be able to sell this house to if you had to foreclose? No one.

The appraiser had used comps from three miles out. It is true that homes three miles out would make this home appraise at a higher value. In this case, three miles was just too far. My advice: Go and see the neighborhood.

That does not mean I will not do deals that are not local. I will do it if I know the area. However, if things out of town go bad, it does make foreclosure more difficult. When you first getting started, I would suggest staying local.

Let us talk for a minute about taxes and insurance. Some people like to have it escrowed. I guess I can understand that, but I just do not like the hassle and the cost. Once you do escrowed money, you need a special account. I prefer to handle it on my own. In fact, I like to do most of my private mortgage investing "solo," with the exception of finding a good broker. I do not like investing in loans with others because of the hassle. I also do not feel the need for loan-servicing companies. I like private mortgage investing because of the ease and the control. Once I start partnering with others, my control gets lost.

This is even true for direct-deposited payments. I want to see the check come in. Then, I use a simple ledger sheet to record the payment, the interest, and the date. This way, I know what has been done and if someone is late. I do not have to mess with anyone else.

That said, I do use mortgage brokers. I look for someone who gets his or her paperwork together. Once I have established a working relationship, I usually stay with that person because they know me and my needs. That person knows which properties to run by me. And, I trust that person to find me good deals.

HERE ARE A FEW MORE TIPS:

1. If you have to live or eat from the money you invest, then you should not invest. Investment money has to be extra.

2. If you have equity in your home, use it. You can currently get a home equity loan for 3 percent and invest that money out for no less than 12 percent. You might as well have your equity making money.

3. High-cost mortgages can get risky because of legal issues. Be sure to have a good lawyer to keep you out of trouble.

Chapter 11: Insuring Your Investment

Private mortgage lending uses real estate property as collateral to ensure you recover your capital, even if your borrower defaults on the loan. Many investment opportunities involve lending to a real estate investor who plans to make money from the property to pay back your loan. What happens if the real estate property backing your loan is damaged or destroyed? What if it turns out the seller of that property had forged the title deed, and it legally belongs to someone else? Your borrower will no longer have assets to pay back the loan, and you will no longer have a property to sell to get your money back.

Your mortgage loan contract should contain clauses requiring the borrower to purchase, at his or her expense, title insurance and property insurance with you as the beneficiary. Insurance protects your investment. If, after your borrower has purchased a property with money from your loan, a third party comes along and proves he or she is the legal owner of the property, both you and your borrower could lose your entire investment. You would certainly face a protracted legal battle. What will happen if the property is burned to the ground because of a lightning strike, or the ground floor is covered by water during a flood? Without insurance, you could become the owner of a charred ruin on a vacant lot instead of a desirable rental property. This chapter explains what you need to know about title insurance and property insurance.

TITLE INSURANCE

A title is a legal document establishing ownership of land and real estate property. A title free of any liens — claims — or legal questions is a requirement for the sale of real estate. Such a title is called a "perfect title," "clear title," "good title," or "just title." Title companies are businesses that research legal records to ensure a title is clear and provide title insurance. If at some time in the future, the title is found to be illegal or "imperfect" — for example, if someone proves a signature was forged and the land really belongs to someone else — title insurance will pay for legal costs and settlement of the claim. If the owner must relinquish the property because of a bad title, depending on the type of insurance, insurance will compensate the lender for the unpaid portion of a mortgage and might also reimburse the money the buyer has invested in the property.

Title insurance is necessary of both the lender and the borrower. You will want to get a lender's title insurance policy. These are also known as loan policies, and they cover the amount loaned by the lender. The amount of the policy decreases as the loaned amount is paid off. In the case of private mortgage interest-only loans, the amount of the policy will remain the same throughout the life of the loan because the principal is not due to be paid off until the end of the loan. The coverage continues in effect for as long as you have an interest in the covered property, and the cost varies depending upon the value of the property. You do not need to worry about the cost because the borrower pays for this insurance.

Suppose a property is worth $100,000, and you loaned $65,000 to the borrower. Your lender's title insurance will only cover the $65,000 and not the full value of the property.

If even the slightest possibility of a claim against your title arises, contact your title insurer or the agent who issued your policy. Title insurance covers the costs of investigation, litigation, and settlement of an adverse claim. Legal fees often cost more than the settlement itself so title insurance is an important protection for your investment.

Not all states require or even authorize title insurance. Check with a local real estate broker or real estate attorney to determine the laws and availability of title insurance in your area.

Common title problems

A title company checks out the title thoroughly before issuing title insurance, often going as far back as 50 years. In about 25 percent of the cases, problems are found and fixed on the title before the insurance is issued. Even when a comprehensive title search has been performed, problems can still occur with the title after closing. Such problems include:

- Mistakes in the public record.

- Undisclosed heirs claiming to own the property.

- Forged deeds.

- A party to the contract was not competent or did not have the authority to enter into a contract.

- A deed was executed under expired or false power of attorney.

- Deed not joined in by a necessary party: co-owner, heir, spouse, corporate officer, or business partner.

- Undisclosed but recorded prior mortgage or lien.

- Undisclosed but recorded easement or use restriction.

- Erroneous or inadequate legal descriptions.

- There is no right of access to the property.

- Fraud in connection with the execution of documents.

- Undue influence on a grantor or executor.

- False impersonation by those purporting to be owners of the property.

- Problems with wills concerning the seller's ownership of the property: a will not properly probated; mistaken interpretation of wills and trusts; birth of heirs after the date of a will.

- Conveyance by a minor.

- Confusion because of similar or identical names.

- Dower or courtesy rights of ex-spouse or former owners.

- Delivery of deeds after the death of a grantor.

- Off-record legal matters, such as claims for adverse possession or prescriptive easement.

- Deed to land with buildings encroaching on land of another.

- Incorrect survey.

- Silent — off-record — liens, such as mechanic's or estate tax liens.

- Pre-existing violations of subdivision laws, zoning ordinances, or CC&Rs (Covenants, Conditions and Restrictions) — the documents setting forth the rules for a homeowners association.

- Forced removal of improvements because of a lack of building permit.

- Post-policy construction of improvements by a neighbor on insured land.

Title insurance offers you financial protection against all of these possible events. The title company will negotiate any settlements and pay the claims and legal fees.

The borrower can also purchase a title insurance policy, known as the "owner's policy," covering the full value of the property. Borrower title insurance pays for any legal fees and settlements associated with claims against the title and reimburses the borrower if he or she has to relinquish ownership of the property. In many states, borrowers are not required to purchase title insurance, but private mortgage lenders always require a borrower to have title insurance. If the borrower loses ownership of the property, he or she will also lose the income generated by the property used to pay back the loan. In case of default, you cannot foreclose on the property, or you cannot sell it because the title is tied up in a legal battle. The borrower pays for owner's title insurance.

 Private mortgage lenders often require 125 percent title insurance.

For added security, lenders like Doug Brown, a private mortgage investor for five years, and Matt Tabacchi require 125 percent title insurance. This means the borrower must have title insurance worth 125 percent of the current value of the property. When asked why, Doug stated:

It is a protection against inflation and rising real estate prices. Imagine for a moment you have loaned money on a $100,000 piece of property. In the ensuing years, the property becomes worth $125,000. Now, assume you have to foreclose on the property and in the process, a title defect is found. You will only get the amount of money the title insurance stated — not the true value of the property. Requiring that the borrower get 125 percent title insurance costs you nothing and can protect you against rising costs.

PROPERTY INSURANCE

Property insurance provides financial protection against the loss of, or damage to, real and personal property caused by the perils covered in the policy. Fire and hazard insurance protect against the most common causes of real property destruction. In the case of catastrophes, such as fire, explosion, theft, or vandalism, property insurance helps cover your costs, whether for repairs to damaged property or to replace what you have lost.

Events that cause damage are known as "perils" or "causes of loss" and include weather-related events, such as lightning strikes or hail, and human causes, such as robbery or vehicular accidents. Two types of policies are available: a named-perils policy, which covers losses resulting from only those perils named in the policy, and an all-risk policy, also known as special form coverage, which offers coverage for all perils except those specifically excluded.

As a private mortgage lender, you would be better off with all-risk policies, which typically have higher premiums. The problem is that this type of insurance is extraordinarily expensive, and some properties will not meet the insurance company's requirements for it even if the borrower can afford to pay. Therefore, you will probably have to accept a named-perils policy that covers the main causes of damage, such as fire and windstorm.

Do not forget flood insurance.

If the property is in a floodplain, you should demand the borrower also get federal flood insurance.

Insurance policies can pay out in one of two ways: replacement cost or actual cash value (ACV). If you are covered for the actual cost of replacing your property, this is known as a replacement cost basis. The alternative, actual cash value reimbursement, is based on the replacement cost minus physical depreciation of the property before it was lost or damaged.

The premiums for ACV policies tend to be lower because they pay out less, but the reimbursement could be inadequate if you actually need to replace items. Therefore, it is better to get replacement cost insurance.

Title insurance protects you from loss if there are legal challenges to ownership of the property, and property insurance protects you from financial loss if the property is burned, flooded, or damaged in any way. Insurance is not the only protection you need for your investment, however. *The following chapters discuss other steps you should take to ensure your investment brings in the expected returns.*

Protect Yourself From Mortgage Fraud

People like con man Matthew Bevan Cox are the reason why you should always carefully check out every aspect of a mortgage deal.

Sentenced in November 2007 to serve 26 years in federal prison and pay $12 million in restitution to his victims, he was indicted on 42 counts of mortgage fraud and may have signed for as many as 100 fraudulent mortgages. Using aliases and stolen identities, he would rent or agree to purchase properties, then fraudulently erase prior mortgage liens and assume the identities of the owners to apply for new mortgage loans. He sometimes used stolen identities or paid straw borrowers to obtain multiple mortgage loans on the same property. He would then abscond with the loan money, laundering it through a complex system of cashier's checks and bank accounts, and leave the true property owners holding the bag. Charming and self-effacing, he knew how to dress and act in a way that won the complete confidence of his victims. He often recruited petite blond female accomplices to pose as his real estate agent or girlfriend and add to his appearance of innocence. He found his victims by searching real estate listings and county court documents for situations he could turn to his advantage.

Mortgage fraud is on the rise: The incidence of mortgage fraud has increased dramatically since 2007. Mortgage fraud includes submitting falsified documentation to misrepresent a borrower's financial status, the overvaluing of a property to obtain a loan for more than the property is worth, and the theft of money through mortgage loans.

You can protect yourself by verifying that all loan documents are legitimate originals and that all names, addresses, and property descriptions are accurate. Know your borrowers — do background checks and credit checks, ask for references, and verify their income statements. Insist that the borrower purchase title insurance, and examine county records to see if there are any liens on the property.

Chapter 12: More Safety Measures for the Private Lender

Physical damage to the property used as collateral for a loan is not the only hazard in private mortgage investing. Your success depends on the successful fulfillment of the terms of the loan contract signed by you and your borrower. Loan contracts are full of legal clauses covering every possible eventuality, including the death of your borrower and the appropriation of the property by the county for a road development project. The clauses of a loan contract can be worded to your advantage, or they can favor your borrower. Documents that support a loan contract, such as title deeds, appraisals, inventories, and surveys, may contain errors that make the contract invalid. Successful private mortgage lenders know how to protect their investments by safeguarding contracts and legal documents and ensuring their accuracy. This chapter discusses several legal and practical measures you can take to protect your investment.

REAL ESTATE ATTORNEYS ARE WORTH THE PRICE

Unless you have a great deal of legal experience or you are working with a trusted broker, you need the services of an experienced real estate attorney. A real estate attorney can help you assess an investment opportunity, avoid pitfalls, and draw up a loan contract that will cover all eventualities and make sure you accomplish your investment objectives. The attorney's fees are well worth the security of having legal protection if something goes wrong.

Mortgage note and deed of trust

Mortgage notes and deeds of trust with which a loan is secured are the tools of the trade for a private mortgage investor. The language in a mortgage note or deed of trust determines how and when the loan will be paid off and exactly what will happen if the borrower defaults or if something happens to the property. A faulty note — one in which important details have been left out or misstated — can have disastrous consequences. This is why it is absolutely necessary to have a real estate attorney — one who represents you — draw up these forms. Because most private notes are individually tailored to a particular situation, there is no such thing as a "standard form" that you can use.

A mortgage note should clearly state the following information:

- Names of both the borrower and the lender, spelled correctly.

- Correct address of the property.

- The loan amount.

- Interest rate.

- Any interest rate adjustment criteria.

- Payment schedule.

- Minimum payment due on each payment date.

- Date when final payments are due.

- Any penalty for late payments.

- Whether there is a penalty for early payoff.

- Any other conditions imposed by the lender.

The note must be signed and dated by the borrower.

Every state has different legal requirements so the wording will be different in each state. A competent real estate attorney will know these differences and will produce a document that works best for you.

You should consider investing only in states that are "lender friendly." A lender-friendly state should:

- Allow non-judicial foreclosures.

- Not have laws that unfairly penalize lenders for minor errors or omissions, such as failing to follow an exact procedure to notify a borrower of a late payment.

- Not have laws that make lending money for a mortgage burdensome by insisting on too many disclosures or qualifications.

You will find a list of states with non-judicial foreclosure in Chapter 2.

MORTGAGE RENEWALS

When you loan out money, you loan it for a specific time. Most private mortgage loans are 360/120 loans if they are principal and interest, meaning the loan is amortized over 360 months, 30 years, and it balloons at 120 months, or ten years. To balloon means the entire principal that is owed at ten years is due on that balloon date. If mortgage loans are interest-only loans, the typical loan is for five years with the principal due at the end of the five-year period.

If you had a 360/180, you would know the loan is amortized over 30 years and balloons at 15 years.

Suppose you do a $100,000 loan at 360/60. That means that in five years, the borrower either has to pay you off or refinance. Now, if the borrower paid perfectly — did not miss a payment and always paid on time — for five years, you have the opportunity to give him or her a mortgage renewal. Instead of making the borrower pay off the loan ("calling the balloon due"), you can let the borrower continue making monthly payments and keep the loan for an additional time. Whether you offer a mortgage renewal to the borrower is completely up to you. There is no right or wrong answer. If you do not want your capital for another purpose and feel content with the monthly interest payment you are receiving, you can renew the mortgage and avoid the work of looking for a new investment.

MORTGAGE COMMITMENT LETTER

A mortgage commitment letter is simply an approval from the investor. Suppose a broker sends Jack a loan package for a borrower who needs $100,000. If Jack agrees he wants to make this loan, he will give the broker a mortgage commitment letter. The letter does not require Jack to follow through: He can put provisions in the mortgage commitment that he is agreeing based on the results of the appraisal, the title search, and the inspection. The broker who receives this letter can then commit to the borrower. These letters are important to real estate investors because their deals often hinge on coming up with money for a purchase in a very short time. Many foreclosure auctions require full payment within a few days.

See Appendix A for a sample mortgage commitment letter.

DISCLOSURE FORMS

Disclosure forms are exchanged between the broker and the borrower and contain any information that might affect the loan. As an investor, you will receive a copy of all these signed disclosure forms. If a problem ever arises with the borrower, you have proof of what the borrower knew and what he or she signed.

For instance, one form shows that the borrower knows how much must be paid monthly, to whom, and where. This form also states that late charges, returned check fees, and the insurance and taxes are the responsibility of the borrower.

Disclosures also show the borrower the interest rate to be paid and the number of payments to be made. The borrower will signify whether he or she is going to occupy the property, confirm he or she has not been coerced into taking insurance from a specific company, and verify he or she received a copy of the Consumer Handbook on Adjustable-Rate Mortgages. These are just a few of the various disclosures signed by the borrower.

Appendix A contains some of the standard disclosure forms.

USURY LAWS

States have usury laws that affect mortgages. Each state has different standards for the type and the maximum amount of interest that can be charged, based on the particular kind and size of the loan. State usury laws change regularly.

For instance:

In Illinois, the state's high court overturned a 2004 Illinois Appellate Court decision that the Illinois Interest Act applies to virtually all mortgages made in the state. The 1974 law bars lenders that charge interest greater than 8 percent from charging additional fees exceeding 3 percent of the principal.

Disagreeing with the Appellate Court, the Illinois Supreme Court ruled that federal law pre-empts the Illinois Interest Act. In effect, the state's usury law now no longer applies to any home loans.

In Florida, usury laws only affect property that is "homesteaded" — property that is the primary residence of the borrower. Even when the property is a primary residence, you can charge high interest rates as long as you stay within the limits and have the right legal forms signed.

It is very important that your real estate lawyer know the usury laws of the state in which you invest.

FORECLOSURE

As with usury laws and the wording on notes and deeds, foreclosures differ from state to state. A good attorney will know the laws of the states in which you will lend.

Here are your three main concerns when involved in a foreclosure:

- Judicial versus non-judicial foreclosure.
- Time allowed before an auction can be held.
- Existence of redemption rights.

If you have loaned money in a judicial foreclosure state, you will have to go through a court hearing in order to auction the property. A non-judicial state allows you to notify the borrower, wait the specified time, and then auction the property. This is a much cheaper and easier way to foreclose.

States also differ on the time that must be allowed to elapse before an auction can be held. For private mortgage investors, the shorter the time, the better. The sooner you can recover your capital and reinvest it, the better.

The right to redemption allows the borrower who was foreclosed upon to reclaim the property if he or she can get the payments up to date and pay off any penalties, interest, and legal fees within a specified time. Long redemption periods are friendlier to borrowers than to lenders because if the borrower fails to come up with the payments, the lender will not earn interest during that time. It is best to lend money in states with short or nonexistent rights to redemption.

FINDING A GOOD ATTORNEY

When looking for an attorney, ask for referrals from friends, business acquaintances, and other real estate investors. After you select two or three real estate attorneys, you can look up their qualifications on Martindale.com® (**www.martindale.com**) or Law.com (**www.law.com**). You can also go to the clerk of the courthouse in your area and ask to review cases in which those attorneys have been involved. Note how many of those cases they won or lost.

Questions to ask a prospective attorney

The important thing when choosing a real estate attorney is that you are comfortable with him or her and believe the attorney can see things from your point of view. You must be confident that he or she will advise you correctly.

The following questions will help you determine whether a particular attorney is a good "fit" for you:

1. **What experience do you have in creative real estate investing, such as private mortgage lending?** The attorney should understand and be open to creative real estate investing.

2. **How much of your practice is in real estate?** Depending on your market size, it should be at least 30 to 50 percent. In smaller communities, there would be less need for an attorney to devote all of his or her practice to real estate.

3. **Do you have other real estate investors as clients?** If so, ask if you can contact them for references.

4. **What are your fees?** The size of the law firm is not an important factor, but larger firms usually charge more because of their overhead, and they are not as available to you as a smaller firm. Be careful of low quotes promising everything for an improbably low price. While some real estate attorneys are extremely competitive in price, you get what you pay for. You might need an attorney who can take the time to go over documents with you and educate you. The low-cost/high-volume attorneys are best for buyers and sellers who already have a thorough understanding of real estate transactions.

5. **Do you work with other real estate professionals?** The attorney

should be able to recommend and refer you to other professionals, such as CPAs, mortgage brokers (for refinances), and so forth.

6. **Are you familiar with closing practices in the geographic area involved?** Because each state, and sometimes localities within a state, has different real estate laws, this is a very important question.

USE A FIREPROOF SAFE

It is important to keep your original note in a safe place, such as a safe-deposit box or a fireproof safe in your home. Make a photocopy to keep with your trust deed and other escrow papers.

There are two reasons for this precaution. First, the note is not recorded in the county recorder's office. The deed of trust is. If you lose your deed of trust, you can simply get another copy at the recorder's office. If the original note is lost, you cannot sell the note, and the borrower could bring a legal defense against you in a foreclosure case.

Second, your note is a negotiable instrument that can be endorsed on the back like a check. Do not leave it lying around where it might fall into the wrong hands.

DIRECT DEPOSIT/AUTOMATIC ELECTRONIC PAYMENTS

Some investors feel more comfortable knowing the payments are set up to automatically draft out of the borrower's account. This does not guarantee the investor will be paid, but since it is an automatic draft, the borrower is likely to ensure there is enough money in the account to avoid an overdraft.

Additionally, having an automatic payment set up is good for the borrower. Many people do not seem to recognize that paying bills late can damage their credit rating, according to a national poll by the Direct Deposit and Direct Payment Coalition. The survey found that 35 percent had been late with major credit card payments, 19 percent had been late on car-loan payments, and 17 percent were late with payments to gas station or department store accounts. Only about half of those polled, though, identified a negative impact on their credit rating when asked to name "any possible consequences of paying bills late."

About 35 percent of the FICO credit score is based on payment history, which includes details of both timely and late or missed payments. Lenders often rely on the FICO score when deciding whether to approve a loan or other form of credit. If the borrower has a less-than-stellar credit rating, paying the investor on time for 12 months will give him or her a good track record. One way to be sure the payments are on time is to set up an automatic draft.

ADDITIONAL COLLATERAL

Although not a common practice in private mortgage investing, it is possible to ask for additional collateral besides the property when loaning out money. Perhaps the borrower needs money that amounts to a 75 percent LTV ratio but also owns another piece of property free and clear. You can lower your LTV by writing a loan agreement that adds that second piece of property as collateral. Going above a 65 percent LTV can be unwise in certain cases so unless you are experienced or have a trustworthy broker, it is best to stay away from these kinds of deals.

REQUIRE A SURVEY

It is important to distinguish between a survey and an appraisal, both of which are charged to the borrower. An appraisal assists the investor in assessing the value of the property to determine whether a mortgage should be made and in what amount. The appraisal will analyze the condition of the house, its location, structural soundness, and comparable sales in the area.

A survey confirms the marketability of the house. The surveyor determines whether the house is within the property borders, whether there are any encroachments on the property by neighbors, and the extent to which any easements on the property may affect legal title.

The typical survey obtained by most purchasers when they go to closing is called a "house location" survey. Title insurance excludes coverage encroachments, overlaps, boundary line disputes, and any other matters that would be disclosed by an accurate survey and inspection of the premises. The title insurance industry takes the position that a house location survey is not an accurate survey and thus will reject many claims regarding boundary disputes. So, to make your title insurance as good as possible, it is best to require a survey.

The process of private mortgage lending is relatively simple: You are giving short-term loans to a few individual lenders, each with a unique business proposition, and collecting interest. As you have seen in past chapters, however, you must do a certain amount of work to safeguard your investment capital. You can succeed in private mortgage lending if you select your borrower carefully, properly appraise and inspect the property, prepare your legal documents with care, and make certain the buyer purchases title insurance and property insurance. As in any business venture, you must also keep accurate financial records so you always know how your investment is doing. *The next chapter discusses technical aspects of mortgage investing, such as bookkeeping and taxes.*

CASE STUDY: TIPS FOR SUCCESSFUL PRIVATE MORTGAGE INVESTING

Doug Brown
Private mortgage investor

I learned about private mortgage investing from my father-in-law. I tried to do a bit of research, but there was not much out there. And what was there was very simplistic. So, I had to rely on people I knew and basic concepts. Therefore, I started slowly with one mortgage and then moved my IRA funds into it and then finally the equity from my home. If you have a vast amount of money, you can use private mortgage investing as your sole income. For most people, it is not feasible to come up with enough accumulated savings or equity. This does not mean, however, that they cannot be involved. Anyone with at least $10,000 can get started. The more the better, but if you have $10,000 sitting around without any immediate need, you can put it to work for 12 percent or more.

I firmly believe in using the equity in your home. Oh, I have heard people say they are "earning" money, since their home is increasing in value. But, in reality, how are you going to actually get at that equity without selling your home? The problem with selling is you will need to live somewhere else, and you have to pay the escalated price to live somewhere else. By pulling out the equity, all the stuff you never see and that does very little for you can be put to work making money. At the time of publication, in early 2011, you can borrow at 6 to 7 percent, thus making about 7 to 9 percent interest. Not only that, but your home is still increasing in value.

The risk, should the mortgage default to you, is that you have to continue making your payments on your equity loan or mortgage. You have to have enough financial resources to pay for up to six months if the loan defaults. If you cannot, then stay away. As far as the kind of land to invest in, it simply does not matter to me. I personally try to stay away from mobile homes because they are mobile. In other words, my investment could simply move away. However, mobile homes are registered, just like a car, so this is not too much of a concern. The critical thing is loan-to-value ratio and to be sure the property is valued correctly.

I do not find most appraisals accurate because it depends so much on who does the appraisal. If the appraisal is bank order, it leans to the bank. A homeowner's appraisal will lean toward the homeowner. Let me give you an example. I bought a commercial building about a year ago, and the appraisal was rushed through. The appraiser never went into the house. The appraisal was the exact amount of the sales contract. He just copied it. It was worth nearly $100,000 more. Appraisals are simply very subjective. And the hotter the real estate market, the more subjective the appraisals.

That is why I inspect most of my properties. I used to inspect all of them, but now I only inspect about 90 percent because I trust my broker and know the area. He is a great broker because he goes a step further. He does not disappear once a deal has been brokered. If things go awry, he helps straighten them back out.

I do not worry much about the safety of my private mortgage investments. It is the safest investment vehicle I have ever encountered as long as you follow the parameters. Of course, I am someone that puts everything on the line every day. If you are a bit more concerned about safety, you can always escrow insurance and taxes and have your payments direct-deposited to your bank. Everyone has different comfort levels. If you want to know your money is under your pillow, then you have to do what you feel comfortable with.

Here are a few other tips I would like to share so you can become a successful private mortgage investor:

- It is important to work with a broker. Dealing directly with clients would be difficult. Since the borrower pays the broker's fees anyway, you simply cannot lose.

- Do not do anything you are not comfortable with.

- See each property personally.

- Keep your LTV less than 70 percent. This makes everything secure, even in a foreclosure.

- Start small, and see how it goes.

Chapter 13:
Bookkeeping and Taxes

Keeping a detailed, well-organized, and legible payment record showing the date each payment was received and a breakdown of the principal, interest, and late charge for each amount received is important to maintaining the value of your note.

If you ever decide to sell your note, you must show the payment history to a prospective note buyer so the note buyer can verify the payment patterns of the note payer.

The amount of risk is a key factor in determining the selling price of a note. If the payments on a "seasoned" note, which is a note with a payment history over an extended period, have been made consistently on time, the value of the note will be greater than if the payments have been late or delinquent because the perceived risk of the note is lower. A buyer who needs a steady income may not want to purchase a note if the payments have been erratic.

Other benefits of keeping detailed records include:

- Ease of calculating taxes at the end of the year.
- Records to prove delinquency in case of foreclosure.
- Ability to calculate payoffs.

For each payment you should record:

- Amount of interest.
- Amount toward principal.
- Late fees.

- Other fees.

- Date of payment.

SOFTWARE TO USE

Mortgage broker software automates the work of organizing borrower information, managing and recording payments, calculating fees, generating letters and documents, scheduling daily tasks, and tracking remortgage opportunities. Some software facilitates the sending of e-mails and automated communications to clients.

A number of mortgage software programs are available with a wide range of features and prices. Try a free trial of one of the fast and simple programs first and upgrade as you need to.

NoteSmith® loan-servicing software is a product of Princeton Investments, Inc. According to the NoteSmith website (**www.notesmith.com**), the software is designed for individual note investors and tracks notes, discounted notes, leases, rent, and other cash flows. NoteSmith is designed for Windows® 95, 98, Me, NT, 2000, XP, Vista, and 7.

NoteSmith Pro® has additional features for small loan companies, landlords, and investors with sophisticated needs. NoteSmith Net® is designed for multiple, simultaneous users on a local area network.

Some other good mortgage software providers are:

- **Credex Systems (www.credexsystems.com):** A complete loan-origination and loan-servicing system that can be used in a single location or multiple locations.

- **ISGN LSAMS™ (www.dynatek.com/Products/LSAMS.htm):** A highly flexible loan-servicing application that services both mortgage and consumer loans.

- **Loan Administrator Pro (www.laproiq.com/):** LA Pro easily integrates with existing general ledger systems and facilitates core processing, loan origination, and documentation. Versions are available on most popular databases, including MS Access and MS SQL Server.

- **Pipeline Solutions (www.pipesoft.com):** Complete loan-processing software application with free demo download.

- **Twenty-First Century (www.21stcenturycompany.com):** A complete loan-servicing application that includes investor tracking with distribution payments and 1099 tax forms. It has interfaces for loan origination, general ledger system, Excel spreadsheets, report writers, and custom programs.

CALCULATING PAYOFFS

A payoff is the payment in full of the outstanding balance of a mortgage. Mortgage payments are paid in arrears — in other words, each payment is for the previous month. Take a sample mortgage with an original balance of $100,000 at 10 percent interest for 180 months. The monthly payments are $1,074.61. The interest accrues from the payment date until the next payment date.

So, to determine a payoff, you have to know the daily rate. A daily rate is figured by:

Original principal X (the interest rate divided by 365)

In this case, $100,000 X 10%/365 = $27.40 per day.

Once you know the daily rate, you can calculate the payoff using this formula:

Principal balance + (days past payment X daily rate)

Assume the 60th payment was made, and the principal balance is $81,316.29. If the mortgage were paid off 10 days after the last payment due date, then the payoff would be:

$81,316.29 + (10 X $27.40) = $81,590.29

Tax Deductions

In addition to high rates of return, private mortgage investing presents some opportunities to claim certain income tax deductions that will save you money and increase your wealth. For example, by organizing your investment activities as a home business, you can take deductions for office equipment and for the use of your home. You possibly can also claim deductions associated with the type of loans in which you are investing. IRS regulations are strict and detailed, but if you meet the qualifications, you might be able to deduct thousands of dollars from your taxable income. A tax adviser or a good tax preparation software program can help you identify potential deductions.

Home-based business

You can deduct the expenses of your private mortgage investing activities from your taxable income by starting a home-based business. If you have a full-time job in addition to a home-based business, your deductions may exceed your home-based business income by thousands of dollars. That means that your home business would report a net loss for the year. A home-based business allows you to claim tax deductions for expenses, such as computer equipment, books, and office supplies, as long as they are used primarily for your business. You can even deduct the cost of travel and business lunches associated with your investment activities. If you are in the 28 percent tax bracket, this amounts to a 28 percent discount on the cost of anything that qualifies as a business expense. An item that seemed too expensive at $100 becomes a bargain at $72 ($100 minus the $28 you will save by deducting the $100 from your taxable income).

The IRS often targets home-based businesses for audits so you must keep receipts, contracts, income statements, expense reports, and any other documents that support your claims for legitimate business expenses. Consult your accountant for help in identifying and documenting your home-based business expenses.

1. The standard charge for the first phone line in your house cannot be deducted as a business expense. If you use your home phone for business, you can deduct only the extra business costs — for example, long-distance calls and call waiting. You will also have to document your business use. Better idea: Get a separate business phone.

2. Document the business use of your personal car by keeping track of business miles driven and the purpose of each trip. Trips are deductible at the rate of 50 cents a mile (in 2010), plus parking and tolls, according to IRS rates. You can also deduct a portion of your car-loan interest.

    Instead of taking a mileage rate deduction, you can take a deduction for the actual expenses of using your car. These include depreciation, lease payments, registration fees, gas, insurance, repairs, oil, garage rent, licenses, tires, tolls, and parking fees.

    If you purchase a vehicle for business use, you can take a Section 179 deduction in the year you buy the car and put it into service. You must use the car more than 50 percent for business purposes, and subtract the personal use from the price of the car. You can also claim special depreciation allowance and a depreciation deduction for a car you use for business. The total amount of Section 179 deduction, special depreciation allowance, and depreciation deduction that could be claimed for 2009 was $10,960. This limit was reduced if the business use of the car was less than 100 percent. Your car can be a valuable source of tax savings. If your car is used 75 percent of the time for business, 75 percent of the expenses related to that car would be deductible. For more information, see the IRS publication *Topic 510 - Business Use of Car* (**www.irs.gov/taxtopics/tc510.html**).

3. You can deduct the expense of attending business conventions but only for yourself. You cannot deduct your spouse's expenses unless he or she is employed by the business and has a legitimate reason for being there.

4. The travel cost of a business trip combined with a vacation cannot be written off unless the trip's primary purpose is business. If you do some business during a trip, however, you can deduct a pro rata portion of your hotel bill and meals and direct expenses of doing business, such as photocopying or taxi fares.

   Suppose you took a trip from New York to Los Angeles primarily for business purposes. You were away from home from Feb. 12 through Feb. 22. Three of those days were spent vacationing and seven days conducting business — including two travel days. Suppose your airfare was $650 and your meals and lodging cost $75 per day. You could deduct 70 percent of your transportation expenses — seven out of ten days — and $75 per day for the seven business days because you were away from home for more than seven days, and more than 25 percent — three out of ten days — of your time was devoted to business. Only 50 percent of your meals would be deductible.

   For more information, see IRS *Publication 463 (2009), Travel, Entertainment, Gift, and Car Expenses* (**www.irs.gov/publications/p463/index.html**).

5. Your home office can be a room or a portion of a room, but that area must be used exclusively and regularly as your primary place of

business. If you use your dining room table as an office, do not expect a write off.

The amount of the deduction depends on the percentage of floor space used. If your office takes up, say, 20 percent of your house, you can write off 20 percent of everything involved — mortgage interest; rent; real estate taxes; homeowner's insurance; home maintenance, such as house painting and the bills for heat, water, electricity, trash removal, and a home security system. You also can depreciate your office space.

Unused deductions can be carried forward to future years.

For more information, see the IRS publication *Topic 509 - Business Use of Home* (**www.irs.gov/taxtopics/tc509.html**).

6. You can deduct medical and dental expenses by hiring your spouse, then setting up a medical reimbursement plan for your employees and their families. You cannot cover yourself directly, but you can be covered as a member of your spouse's family. The reimbursement plan does not require you to buy insurance. Instead, you reimburse your employees' out-of-pocket medical and dental bills and deduct these amounts from your taxable income. This works for most small businesses but not for S Corporations.

7. Each employee can put as much as $5,000 of earned income a year into a tax-deferred individual retirement account (IRA). By paying your spouse $5,000, you can jointly put $10,000 away. If you and your spouse are older than 50, you can contribute an additional $1,000.

8. You can take advantage of higher limits on tax-deductible contributions to Simplified Employee Pension IRAs (SEP-IRAs) retirement plans available to self-employed people — up to $49,000 in 2010.

9. Convert your business to an S Corporation to reduce self-employment taxes. As business income rises, consider converting to a C Corporation to take advantage of additional fringe benefits.

Depreciation

Commercial and investment real estate properties are allowed an annual tax deduction to account for decrease in the value of the property because of deterioration, aging, and the wear-and-tear of daily use. This loss in value is called depreciation. Depreciation is regarded as the cost of replacing the deteriorating property and is recorded as a business expense each year on your tax return. Only the value of the building and improvements on the property can be depreciated because land does not decrease in value over time. The appraised market value of the buildings and improvements is divided by a specific number of years to determine the amount you can deduct each year. This method of calculating depreciation is known as the "straight-line method." Residential income property must be depreciated over a 27.5-year period, and commercial income property must be depreciated over 39 years.

Because depreciation is recorded as a business expense, no cash is actually spent. It reduces your taxable income while your real income remains the same. The tax deduction for depreciation is available to those who invest in income-producing property, which means your borrower will be the one taking these deductions. But, as a private mortgage lender, you might become eligible for this deduction if you take possession of a property or actively participate as the investor's business partner.

Other real estate deductions

Other tax deductions available to real estate investors include:

- Real estate taxes and mortgage interest on an investment property are fully tax deductible.

- Operating expenses, such as utilities, insurance, repairs, and condominium common charges are deductible.

- Rental fees paid to brokers are deductible, although they must be spread out over the life of the loan.

TAX CONSIDERATIONS

Managing your taxes is integral to successful real estate investing. Know the tax regulations and how you can manipulate your own situation to your advantage. A professional tax adviser can help you set up your business to make the most of potential tax deductions. Tax laws are constantly changing; your accountant should be well versed in the constantly evolving tax code.

Rental property

The IRS treatment of income and losses from rental property is complex. If you qualify as a real estate professional or are directly involved in managing the rental, losses from the rental are regarded as "active" and can be written off in the year they occur. If you own all or part of a rental property but are not actively managing it, your involvement is considered "passive," and you cannot deduct your losses until you sell the property or you bring in enough income to offset the losses. If you are simply loaning money to a real estate investor, you might not be able to write off any losses. But, if you become involved in the management of the rental property, your circumstances might change, making you eligible for certain tax deductions.

1. If you spend a majority of your time in the rental property business, meeting the half personal services and 750-hour tests on rental real estate losses, you qualify as a "real estate professional," and you can write off your rental losses in the year they are incurred. If a taxpayer who owns a rental property materially participates in each rental real estate activity, losses are deductible only up to $25,000 — if your Modified Adjusted Gross Income (MAGI) is less than $100,000. The deduction is phased out for MAGI between $100,000 and $150,000.

2. You must include in your gross income all amounts you receive as rent. Rental income is any payment you receive for the use or occupation of property. You can deduct expenses of renting property from your gross rental income. You normally deduct your rental expenses in the year you pay them.

3. Report rental income on your return for the year you actually receive it. Include advance rent in your rental income in the year you receive it, regardless of the period covered or the method of accounting you use.

4. If your tenant pays any of your expenses, the payments are rental income, and you must include them in your income. You can deduct the expenses if they are deductible rental expenses as defined by the IRS tax rules.

5. If you receive property or services instead of money as rent, include the fair market value of the property or services in your rental income. If the services are provided at an agreed-upon or specified price, that price is the fair market value unless evidence to the contrary exists.

6. If you have any personal use of a vacation home or other dwelling unit you rent out, you must divide your expenses between rental use and personal use according to the amount of time you use the property for each purpose.

S Corporation

In general, an S Corporation does not pay a tax on its income. Instead, its income and expenses are passed through to the shareholders, who then report these items on their own income tax returns.

If you are an S Corporation shareholder, your share of the corporation's current-year income or loss and other tax items is taxed to you whether or not you receive any amount. The S Corporation should send you a copy of a Schedule K-1 (Form 1120S) showing your share of the S Corporation's income, credits, and deductions for the tax year. You must report your distributive share of the S Corporation's income, gain, loss, deductions, or credits on the appropriate lines and schedules of your Form 1040.

Investment clubs

A real estate investment club is a group of people who pool their money to invest in real estate. It is normally organized as a partnership and is treated as a partnership for federal tax purposes. In some cases, the club chooses another form of organizational structure and is taxed as a corporation or a trust.

Tax reporting for note holders

The amount of interest received each year by the seller or note holder must be reported to the IRS on Schedule B of Form 1040 (**www.irs.gov/pub/irs-pdf/ f1040sb.pdf**). This is a very simple process if the note holder has an amortization schedule for the loan, which summarizes the interest portion of each payment received.

A portion of the principal received each year must also be reported to the IRS on Schedule D of Form 1040 (and supporting Form 6251 for Installment Sales) (**www.irs.gov/pub/irs-pdf/f1040sd.pdf**). This is not as simple as the tax reporting for interest.

The total amount of the gain on the sale of a note is called the "realized gain." Realized gain is the net sales price minus the cost. The amount of the realized gain reported each year on the note holder's tax return is called "recognized gain."

The amortization schedule for your note shows the amount of interest and principal reduction for each payment and the yearly totals.

Tax reporting for partial sales and split-funded sales is somewhat more complicated than for a full sale. You should consult your tax adviser for the tax reporting method for these types of sales.

1031 tax-deferred exchange

A 1031 tax-deferred exchange allows you to roll over all of the proceeds received from the sale of an investment property into the purchase of one or more other like-kind investment properties. At closing, proceeds from a sale are transferred to a third party — called a facilitator or qualified intermediary — who holds them until they are used to acquire the new property. A 1031 exchange is often referred to as a Starker Exchange.

In a 1031 tax-deferred exchange, capital gains taxes are deferred if all of the exchange funds are used to purchase like-kind investment property. This deferment is like getting an interest-free loan for the amount you would have paid in income tax for the profit from a cash sale. Instead, you are able to reinvest this money in a new property. This helps you move into properties of higher value because the amount of your capital increases each time you perform a 1031 exchange. You do not pay income tax until the final sale when you cash out of your investment.

A 1031 exchange is possible only when you sell real estate held for investment purposes. You cannot use it for the sale of your personal residence. In a like-kind exchange, both the property you give up and the property you receive must be held by you for investment or for productive use in your trade or business.

Exchanged properties must be like-kind. For a real estate exchange, this means real property for real property but not necessarily land for land or a rental house for another rental house.

Look at the IRS rules for specific information about what types of properties qualify as like-kind (**www.irs.gov/businesses/small/industries/article/0,,id=98491,00.html**).

Proceeds from a property sale not used to purchase new investment property are taxed as a cash sale.

Selling too many properties too quickly

One problem with selling too many properties too quickly is the IRS could say that your real estate business is your trade, subject to ordinary income and self-employment taxes.

Self-employment tax, a social security and Medicare tax primarily for individuals who work for themselves, is similar to the social security and Medicare taxes withheld from the paychecks of most employees. The self-employment tax rate costs you 15.3 percent of your profits. If you work for an employer, the employer pays 7.65 percent of your salary, and you pay the other 7.65 percent from your wages. When you are self-employed, you must pay the entire amount yourself. Your future social security and Medicare benefits will be based on these contributions so the tax is not a loss, but it is money that will no longer be available to you for investment.

To take advantage of the low 15 percent long-term capital gains tax rate (LTCG), you must keep the investment property for at least a year before selling. If you sell before a year passes, your profit will be taxed as short-term capital gains (STCG) at your ordinary income tax rate of up to 35 percent. This could eat up a significant amount of your profits.

End-of-year list

If you or your company, corporation, partnership, or trust is in a trade or business and you receive mortgage interest incident to your trade or business and you receive interest payments from individuals and these individuals paid you more than $600 in interest in a calendar year, you must:

1. Provide an IRS Form 1098 by Jan. 31 of each year to each individual who paid you at least $600 of mortgage interest in the last year.

2. Send a copy of the Form 1098 to the IRS along with the Summary Form 1096 by Feb. 28.

Just as each private mortgage lending opportunity is unique, the nature of your involvement with your borrower and with your business partners might change from time to time. It is important to be aware of the tax ramifications of real estate investment and to know when you might become eligible for tax deductions. A tax adviser can help you make the most of your investments. You should also understand your obligations to report to the IRS when you receive interest payments from your borrowers and when you buy or sell a note. As you gain experience, you will develop a natural awareness of the business and tax consequences of your investment activities.

CASE STUDY: PRIVATE MORTGAGE INVESTING BEATS THE STOCK MARKET

Chuck
Private mortgage investor

I love private mortgage investing as opposed to other traditional investment vehicles. The stock market is up and down and must be checked daily. Not only that, it costs to trade. Tax liens require as much or more research than the stock market. Neither is terribly safe. The benefits of investing in private mortgages are they are a very low-risk investment, and the return on investment is much greater than normal. Private mortgages are great. They produce a great return on investment with George Washington doing all the work.

My son entered the mortgage business ten years ago. We discussed private investing, and I started out with a small mortgage loan. I became addicted to the point of becoming a mortgage broker. I talked to my CPA, and not only did he agree it was worth pursuing, but he also became a private investor.

Interest rates run between 12 and 15 percent, depending on the type of property and the credit rating of the borrower. Terms vary between interest only, which is my preference, to 30-year amortization schedules. A 5- or 10-year balloon is normally included.

There are fees involved in private mortgage investing. The good part is the borrower pays them. Fees include origination fees, inspection fees, lawyer fees, appraisals, and the like.

My favorite borrowers are realtor/builders. They spend their own personal dollars on building the house, and I lend them money to finish it. These loans last nine to 15 months, and they are interest only. The investment stays intact, and the interest is great. In a word, they are easy — easy to service.

I have a borrower who I have lent money to for five years. A couple of times, the money never left the title company, meaning I have my money working for me every day. I take the payoff and have it back out there making interest immediately. I highly recommend construction loans. However, I do not just do construction loans. Any and all real property is a candidate, but the type of property determines the interest rate and terms offered to the borrower.

For the average person in, or trying to get in, the mortgage business, it is well worth the effort to find a brokerage firm you trust and are confident in. When a mortgage is paid off, I want those funds reinvested as soon as possible. This is where a good brokerage firm is a must. I have had funds change borrowers the same day, and I have not seen or touched the money. The bottom line is I did not lose a day of interest. Even so, I always, always, always personally look at the properties. I take pictures and research the area for my own personal investments. This is my policy, and I think it would be a good policy for anyone investing in private mortgages to adopt.

There are many different things that can kill a loan, from lack of pride of ownership to finding out the borrower lied on the application. This is where a good brokerage firm shines. The process starts when a client looking to borrow money approaches the broker. The broker takes a loan application, and, from that point on, they start doing research. A good broker will do research until the day of closing. They will want to be sure they give true information to their investor. A good broker leans toward investor satisfaction because the investors are there for the long term, and the borrowers are here for right now.

Besides having a good mortgage broker, title insurance is a must. No investment should be made without proper title work and documentation. Would you really lend money to your brother-in-law's brother with just a handshake and expect to get paid back? If you would, I have a bridge for sale at a fantastic price. One of the basic requirements is the investor is the first mortgagee with clear and free title. The title company guarantees this with the title insurance. There is no reason to neglect this insurance, since it is at the borrower's expense. It is mandatory in some states but not in all. So, if you live in a state where this is not mandatory, be sure to get it anyway.

As for what money to invest, I think using both IRA money and home equity can be great ideas. If the IRA produces less than 12 percent, it makes sense to get that money into private mortgage investing because the return is greater with the same or less risk. The paperwork is a bit more complicated, but a good broker or attorney can get the job done.

You can also use money from your home equity. This is an individual decision and is determined by your level of investing knowledge and understanding of the risks involved. When you choose to use your home equity, even if the borrower does not make his or her payment on time, you must still make your payment. Since it is a bit more risky, it is not something I would recommend just starting out. You do not want to go so far out on a limb that if someone stubs a toe, you are in trouble.

How much should you start with? I started with a $10,000 loan that lasted six months. With the origination fee and interest, I received $700 profit. The original investment never left the title company. My broker reinvested this money at a higher interest rate. I was hooked. Crawl before you walk, before you run is a good adage for beginners and is what I recommend.

The only other thing I would recommend is excellent bookkeeping. I use a software program called NoteSmith and keep handwritten ledger sheets on each account just in case my computer fails.

You simply cannot go wrong with property — they do not make any more dirt. Even if you do not get into it at the right price today, down the road, it is going to get to the right price. Private mortgage investing is truly the way to watch your investments consistently increase.

Conclusion

Are you ready to add private mortgage investing to your own portfolio? You are probably anxious to start bringing in double-digit earnings in the safe, secure realm of private mortgages. Private mortgages are a reliable and a profitable investment opportunity as long as you take the time to learn about the real estate business and to research potential investments. This book is an introduction to the important aspects of private mortgage lending. It is up to you to investigate the possibilities that exist in your local community or through brokerages and investment clubs. You can succeed if you follow the precautions described in this book and move with care to protect your capital.

CASE STUDY: PRIVATE MORTGAGE INVESTING DURING THE CURRENT FORECLOSURE CRISIS

Doug Brown
Private mortgage investor

I think you have to be a lot more careful with private mortgage investing these days. Attitudes are changing. Two decades ago, people felt a moral obligation to repay debts; they would move heaven and earth to pay off what they owed. Today, there is a lot of talk about "walking away" — a person who does not want to make payments anymore just mails you the keys and says, "Here, you can have the house."

This is especially true for people who bought overpriced houses during the housing bubble from 2004 through 2006. Now, some of those homes are only worth half what the buyers paid for them. You have to check out prospective borrowers very carefully — do they really know what they are doing? Is the property really worth as much as they say it is? Does the borrower have a sound plan for paying off the loan when it is due?

Another problem is the appraisers. They received a lot of the blame for the foreclosure crisis. Instead of looking at the real value of the house, they would just ask you, "How much is it in the contract?" Then, they would want to appraise it at that amount. They might say a house was worth $250,000 when it was really worth $200,000. If you make a loan based on that appraisal, your loan-to-value is going to be too high. If you have to foreclose on a house now with so many properties on the market, it might take you a long time to sell it and get your money back, even if you are offering a bargain price. Plus, you have all the headaches of maintaining the property and trying to find renters until the house sells.

There are a lot of opportunities for real estate investors in the current housing market, and they are having trouble borrowing from the banks. If you find an experienced real estate investor who has a good business plan, that might be the best kind of borrower. An individual who cannot get a mortgage because he or she is self-employed and does not have a steady income or some other collateral could also be a good investment. Just do a thorough background check, inspect the property yourself, and make sure the appraisal is correct — do not rely too much on other people's judgments. After all, it is your money.

As you enter the private mortgage market, seek out the guidance of seasoned private mortgage investors and reap the benefits of their years of experience. After you have made several loans, you will become familiar with real estate property in the area where you invest, and you will be able to accurately assess potential borrowers. Do not hesitate to use the services of professionals, such as mortgage brokers, real estate attorneys, appraisers, and realtors — the fees they charge is money well spent to guarantee the success of your investment.

Private mortgage investment is not passive investing; you will make short-term loans for periods of several months to a few years, and each time a loan is paid off, you will have to locate a new borrower so you can reinvest. If you are not prepared to do this yourself, work with a mortgage broker or partner with another private mortgage investor. Here are some tips for working with a mortgage broker:

- **Know your mortgage broker.** The selection of your mortgage broker is probably the single most important decision you can make — especially at the outset of your private mortgage investing endeavors. Your broker is also in a position to refer you to a good accountant, appraiser, and real estate attorney.

- **Start small.** Increase your capital outlay as you gain confidence and practical experience.

- **Diversify.** Unless you have a large amount of money to invest, you probably cannot live on your private mortgage interest. Think of private mortgage interest as supplemental income that fits neatly between your stock dividends and bond interest.

- **You do not have to go at it alone.** If you are more comfortable investing with a group, you can partner up with other like-minded investors in a number of partnership and corporate configurations.

- **Keep your finger in the pie.** Be as "hands on" as you can. Drive by the property. Get to know the neighborhood. Learn to do your own appraisals. Become an expert at due diligence.

- **Keep your eyes on the prize.** Concentrate on the property appraisal, rather than the borrower's credit score, and never forget the five all-important investment parameters.

- **Read and reread this book.** Soon you will know the most important precepts by heart, and your confidence will rise, along with your income.

Hundreds of worthy borrowers out there need your services. There are many situations in which a little help from you, a private mortgage lender, can make a big difference in someone's life. So, feel good about what you are doing, and enjoy the ride!

Appendix A: Sample Real Estate Forms

SAMPLE MORTGAGE

The following sample mortgage document is the Fannie Mae/Freddie Mac and Freddie Mac Single-Family Uniform Instrument Form 3001 for Alabama. It is one of the standardized forms (Uniform Instruments) used for all Fannie Mae/Freddie Mac mortgages. All of the Fannie Mae/Freddie Mac mortgage forms can be found at **www.freddiemac.com/uniform/unifsecurity.html#highlights**. This is only intended to be an example of the language and content of a typical mortgage form. You should use a form customized for the laws of the state in which you are lending money. Consult a real estate lawyer or an experienced private mortgage broker when drawing up your own mortgage contracts.

Date: _____

Mortgagor: _____

Address: _____

City: _____ State: _____ ZIP: _____

Mortgagee: _____

Address: _____

City: _____ State: _____ ZIP: _____

1. Amount of Lien: "Note".

Mortgagor is indebted to Mortgagee for the amount of $_____ (U.S. Dollars) and has agreed to pay this amount, plus interest, according to the terms of a certain note (the "Note") given by Mortgagor to Mortgagee, dated _____ _____ (Date).

2. Description of Property Subject To Lien: "Premises".

To secure the payment of the Secured Indebtedness defined in this mortgage agreement, Mortgagor grants, sells, and conveys to the Mortgagee the property located in _____ County, in the State of _____, described in detail in Exhibit "A" attached to and made a part of this document, together with all buildings, structures, and other improvements now located, or to be located in the future, on, above, or below the surface of that property, or on any part and parcel of that property; and, together with all and any of the tenements, easements, riparian, and littoral rights, and appurtenances belonging to or associated in any way with that property, whether owned currently or acquired by Mortgagor in the future, and including all rights of ingress and egress to and from adjoining property (currently existing or arising in the future) together with the reversion or reversions, remainder and remainders, rents, issues, and profits from them; and all the estate, right, title, interest, claim, and demand of any kind of Mortgagor in respect to the property and every part and parcel thereof; and, together with all machinery, apparatus, equipment, fittings, fixtures, whether actually or constructively attached to the property specified in this mortgage agreement, and including all trade, domestic, and ornamental fixtures, and articles of personal property of every kind and nature ("Equipment"), now owned or acquired in the future by Mortgagor and located now or in the future in, upon or under that property or any part of that property, and used or usable in connection with any present or future operation of the property; and, together with all the common elements shared with any parcel, unit or lot which is all or part of the property.

ALL the foregoing is covered by this Mortgage and will be collectively referred to as the "Premises" for the purpose of this agreement.

The Premises are hereby granted to the Mortgagee to have and to hold, for the use and benefit of the Mortgagee, forever.

3. Uniform Commercial Code Security Agreement.

It is agreed that if the nature of any of the property mortgaged in this agreement is such that a security interest in it can be realized under the Uniform Commercial Code, this instrument shall constitute a Security Agreement, and Mortgagor agrees to join with the Mortgagee in the execution of any financing statements and to execute any and all other documents that may be required for the completion or renewal of such security interest under the Uniform Commercial Code.

4. Redemption.

If Mortgagor promptly pays or causes to be paid to Mortgagee, at its address listed in the Note, or at any other place designated by Mortgagee, Mortgagee's successors or assigns, with interest, the principal sum of

_____DOLLARS ($_____) when the note reaches maturity, as stated in said Note, or sooner, unless maturity date is amended or extended according to the terms of the Note executed by Mortgagor and payable to the order of Mortgagee, then the lien on the property shall cease and be void. Otherwise, the lien shall remain in full force and effect.

5. Agreements of Mortgagor.

a) Secured Indebtedness.

This Mortgage is given as security for the Note and also as security for any and all other sums, debts, obligations, and liabilities arising under the Note or this Mortgage, or under any amendments, modifications, or supplements to the Note or Mortgage, and for any renewals, modifications, or extensions of any or all of the foregoing obligations and liabilities (all of which are collectively referred to as the "Secured Indebtedness"). The entire Secured Indebtedness is equally secured with and has the same priority as any other amounts owed by Mortgagor at the date of this agreement.

b) Performance of Note, Mortgage.

Mortgagor shall observe and comply with all provisions of this agreement and of the Note, and shall promptly pay to Mortgagee, in U.S. dollars, the Secured Indebtedness with interest as set forth in the Note. This Mortgage and all other documents constitute the Secured Indebtedness.

c) Payments Other Than Principal and Interest.

Mortgagor is responsible to pay, when due and payable, (1) all taxes, assessments, and other charges levied on, or assessed against the Premises, this instrument or the Secured Indebtedness or any interest of the Mortgagee in the Premises or associated obligations; (2) premiums on insurance policies covering the Premises against loss from fire and other hazards, as required by this agreement; (3) ground rents or other lease rentals; and (4) any other sums related to the Premises or the indebtedness secured hereby, for which Mortgagor is responsible.

d) Insurance.

Mortgagor shall keep the Premises insured at its sole cost and expense against all hazards as is customary and reasonable for properties of a similar type and nature located in _____ County, _____.

e) Maintenance.

Mortgagor shall maintain the Premises in good condition and repair and shall not commit or allow any damage to be done to the Premises.

f) Prior Mortgage.

With regard to the Prior Mortgage, Mortgagor hereby agrees to:

(i) Pay promptly, when due, all installments of principal and interest and all other sums and charges payable under the Prior Mortgage;

(ii) Promptly perform and observe all of the terms, covenants, and conditions required by Mortgagor under the Prior Mortgage, within the period provided in the Prior Mortgage;

(iii) Promptly notify Mortgagee of any default or any notice claiming any event of default by Mortgagor in the performance or observance of any term, covenant, or condition required by such a Prior Mortgage.

(iv) Mortgagor will not request or accept any voluntary future advances under the Prior Mortgage without Mortgagee's prior written consent, which shall not be unreasonably withheld by Mortgagee.

6. Defaults.

a) Event of Default.

Any one of the following events, if it is not resolved within_____ days after written notice of the event for a monetary default, or _____days after written notice from Mortgagee for non-monetary defaults, shall constitute an "Event of Default":

(i) Mortgagor does not pay the Secured Indebtedness, or any part of the Secured Indebtedness, or the taxes, insurance, and other charges, as set forth in this agreement, when these become due and payable;

(ii) Any statement of Mortgagor contained in this agreement, or contained in the Note, is found to be untrue or misleading in any material respect;

(iii) Mortgagor materially fails to observe and carry out the covenants, agreements, obligations, and conditions set out in this Mortgage or in the Note;

(iv) Foreclosure proceedings (whether judicial or otherwise) that affect the priority of this Mortgage are instituted on any mortgage or any lien of any kind secured by any portion of the Premises.

b) Options of Mortgagee Upon Default.

Upon the occurrence of any Event of Default, the Mortgagee may immediately do any one or more of the following:

(i) Declare the total Secured Indebtedness, including without limitation all payments for taxes, assessments, insurance premiums, liens, costs, expenses, and attorney's fees as set forth in this agreement, to be due and collectible at once, by foreclosure or otherwise, without notice to Mortgagor. Mortgagor expressly waives the right to receive such notice.

(ii) Pursue any and all remedies available under the Uniform Commercial Code. It is agreed that ten (10) days' notice of the time, date, and place of any proposed sale shall be reasonable.

(iii) If Mortgagee elects declare the Secured Indebtedness to be due and payable in full at once as provided for in Paragraph 2.02(a) above, or as may be provided for in the Note, or any other provision of this Mortgage, the Mortgagee may pursue all rights and remedies for the collection of such Secured Indebtedness granted by this Mortgage or by any other agreement, law, equity, or otherwise, to include, without limitation, the institution of foreclosure proceedings against the Premises under the terms of this Mortgage and any applicable state or federal law.

7. Prior Liens.

Mortgagor shall keep the Premises free from all prior liens (except for those consented to by Mortgagee in writing).

8. Notice, Demand, and Request.

A written notice, demand, or request, delivered according to the provisions of the Note relating to that notice, shall constitute fulfillment of those provisions.

9. Meaning of Words.

The words "Mortgagor" and "Mortgagee," whenever used in this agreement, include all individuals, corporations (and if a corporation, its officers, employees, or agents), trusts, and any and all other persons or entities, and the respective heirs, executors, administrators, legal representatives, successors, and assigns of the parties hereto, and all those holding under either of them.

The pronouns used in this notice refer to either gender and both singular and plural, where appropriate. The word "Note" may also refer to one or more notes.

10. Severability.

If any provision of this Mortgage or any other Loan Document is found to be invalid or unenforceable under the law, the remaining provisions of the document in which that provision is contained shall continue to be valid and subject to enforcement in the courts without exception.

11. Governing Law.

The terms and provisions of this Mortgage are governed by the laws of the State of _____. Interest, or payment in the nature of interest for any debt secured in part by this Mortgage, shall not exceed the maximum amount permitted by law. Any payment in excess of the maximum amount shall be applied to the Secured Indebtedness or disbursed to Mortgagor as set forth in the Note.

12. Paragraph Headings.

The captions and paragraph headings in this document are used only for convenience and for reference and shall have no effect upon the construction or interpretation of any provision in this contract or on determining the rights or obligations of the Mortgagor or Mortgagee.

13. Attorney's Fees.

For purposes of this Mortgage, attorneys' fees include, but are not limited to, fees incurred in all matters of collection and enforcement, construction and interpretation, before, during, and after suit, trial, proceedings, and appeals. Attorneys' fees may also include hourly charges for paralegals, law clerks, and other staff members operating under the supervision of an attorney.

IN WITNESS WHEREOF, the Mortgagor has caused this instrument to be duly executed as of the day and year first above written.

Signature of Mortgagor: _____

Date: _____

Signature of Mortgagee: _____

Date: _____

STATE OF _____, COUNTY OF _____

The foregoing instrument was acknowledged before me, this

_____ day of _____, 20 _____.

_____ Notary Public

(SEAL) State of _____

My Commission Expires: _____

SAMPLE PROMISSORY NOTE

$ _____

DATE: _____

This note is given a "Good Faith Deposit" as outlined in the attached Contract to Purchase Real Estate between

_____

and _____

dated _____ relating to the property listed as _____
_____.

When requested the undersigned, hereinafter called the Payer, promises to pay the amount of $_____ without interest, to _____ or his assigns, hereinafter call the Payee.

This note is to be payable immediately once the Payee and Payer agree to the conditions, contingencies and inspections outlined in the said contract are met.

In the event that this note goes unpaid for any length of time and collection action is taken, the undersigning Payer agrees to pay the Payee of this note all legal fees associated with the collections efforts. These fees included but are not limited to, cost of suit, including attorney's fees.

_____
Witness

_____
Buyer

_____
Witness

_____
Seller

Name of Mortgage Holder: _____

Address of Mortgage Holder: _____

_____

SAMPLE COMMITMENT LETTER

Dear _____,

Below are the details of the mortgage that _____ (mortgage company) is arranging for you for the address listed above. Please review these details carefully and contact us with any discrepancies.

Amount of Mortgage	$ _____.____
Interest Rate	_____% per year, to be compounded on monthly basis
Principal Payment	$ _____.____ per month
Interest Payment	$ _____.____ per month
Total Monthly Payment	$ _____.____ per month
Date Payments Begin	_ _/_ _/_ _ _ _
Terms	_____ year(s)
Options for Prepayment	€No prepayment penalty. Can be paid off at any time with a penalty of _____. €Other _____.
Fee for Placement	$ _____.____ due to _____ from any proceeds.
Fee for Processing	$ _____.____ due upon signing.
Mortgage Subject To:	1. Approval of all documents by attorney. 2. Adequate insurance coverage; Lender name on Windstorm, Hazard, and Flood. 3. Survey. 4. Credit Report. 5. Financial statement and current #1040. 6. Current inspection of interior and exterior. 7. Lender approval of draw schedule for any remodeling. 8. Recorded parking easement.

This commitment expires 10 days from date of issue.

Sincerely,

_____

Name of Mortgage Company

_____

Role in Company

_____

Date Signed

AGREEMENT FOR PURCHASE & SALE OF REAL ESTATE

Date: _____

Seller: _____

Address: _____

City: _____ State: _____ ZIP: _____

Buyer: _____

Address: _____

City: _____ State: _____ ZIP: _____

This Agreement is hereby made as of this date by and between the abovementioned Seller and Buyer.

1. Property.

Both parties listed above hereby agree that the Seller will sell, and the Buyer will buy the following property which is located in _____
County and _____ State. The address is known by the following address: _____
_____
_____.

This sale will also include the following personal property, fixtures, and appliances:

_____
_____
_____
_____
_____

The following items are excluded and unless listed below, all other items will be included whether or not they are affixed to the property or structures.

_____
_____
_____

_____

_____

The Seller specifically warrants that the property, improvements, building or structures, the appliances, roof, plumbing, heating, and/or ventilation systems are in good and working order. This clause shall survive closing of title.

2. Purchase Price.

Total purchase price to be paid by the Buyer will be $_____ and will be payable as follows:

A non-refundable earnest money deposit of $_____

Balance due at closing $_____

Owner financing from the Seller $_____

New loan $_____

Subject to existing loans $_____

The sale price is subject to an appraisal to be completed by Buyer and/or an agent of Buyer's choice.

3. Deposit.

The Buyer's deposit will be held in escrow by the agent of the Buyer's choice. If default of this Agreement shall occur, Seller will retain the deposit as his/her compensation without any further contact between the parties.

4. New Loan.

This Agreement is conditional upon the Buyer's ability to obtain a new loan in the amount due to the Seller at time of closing, a total amount of $_____. Buyer must provide to the Seller written proof of a loan commitment on or before the following date: _____ (month) _____ (day), _____ (year).

5. Seller Financing.

Buyer shall execute a promissory note in the amount of $_____. In the event of default, a recourse shall be against the property, and there shall be no personal resource against the Borrower. As a security for presentation of the promissory note, the Buyer shall provide the Seller with a mortgage, deed of trust, or other routine security agreement which shall be secondary to a new first mortgage not to exceed $_____.

6. The Closing.

The Closing will be held on or about _____ (month) _____ (day), _____ (year), at the time and place designated by the Buyer. Buyer will also choose the escrow, title, and/or closing agent. The Seller hereby agrees to convey the title by a general warranty deed.

7. Possession.

The Seller will surrender the possession of the property in clean condition and free of all personal effects and debris on or before _____ (month) _____ (day), _____ (year). In the event that the possession is not delivered at closing, the Buyer has all rights to withhold proceeds from the sale in the amount of $_____ as security. The Seller will be responsible for damages in the amount of $_____ per day for each day that the property is occupied beyond the date listed above. This clause shall survive the closing of the title.

8. Execution in Counterparts.

This Agreement may be executed in counterparts and by faxed signatures. This Agreement will be effective as of the date of the last signature.

9. Inspection of the Property.

This Agreement is subject to a final inspection and approval of the property by the Buyer in writing on or before _____ (month) _____ (day), _____ (year).

10. Access to the Property.

The Buyer will be entitled to the property's key and have access to show partners, lenders, inspectors, and/or contractors prior to closing. The Buyer may also place appropriate signage on the property prior to closing for prospective tenants and/or assigns.

Date of Signing By All Parties: _____

_____   _____
Seller   Buyer

_____   _____
Seller   Buyer

BUYER'S PURCHASE CONTRACT

Date: _____

Seller: _____

Social Security Number: ____-____-____

Address: _____

City: _____ State: _____ ZIP: _____

Buyer:_____
Social Security Number: ____-____-____

Address: _____

City: _____ State: _____ ZIP: _____

Purchaser: _____

The Seller agrees to sell and the Purchaser agrees to buy the real estate property listed below including all improvements and personal property as stipulated below:

Street Address_____,

_____ (City), _____

(County),_____

(State), _____ (ZIP)._____

Legal description of Property: _____

_____.

The following personal property is included:

_____   _____

_____   _____

_____   _____

The purchase price will be paid as follows:

    Deposit: $_____

    Cash to Seller at Closing: $_____

Existing Loans and Liens: $_____

New Loan to Seller at Closing: $_____

Purchase Price: $_____

1. Deposit.

A deposit must be made to either a licensed Title Company or attorney within 48 hours of the Seller's acceptance.

2. Loans.

The Purchaser will take title subject to the following loans on terms agreeable to the Purchaser:

a. Loan to _____

Balance $_____

Interest rate: _____ %, Monthly Payment $_____

Loan Number _____

Date of last payment: _____

Loan current through _____

b. Loan to _____

Balance $_____

Interest rate: _____ %, Monthly Payment $_____

Loan Number _____

Date of last payment _____

Loan current through _____

Other liens: _____

Any overstatement of the above amounts of loans and liens will be added to note to Seller. Any understatement will be deducted from the balance due to the Seller at Closing.

3. Payment of Balance.

Balance due to the Seller in the amount of $ _____ shall be paid as follows: _____

_____ with an interest rate of _____%.

4. Date of Closing and Title Transfer.

The closing of this sale will occur at _____ (location) on or before _____ (date).

5. Title.

Seller(s) agrees to transfer the title free and clear of all encumbrances except those listed in this Agreement. Seller will pay any state taxes or stamps required to record deed and mortgage. Seller is responsible to furnish title insurance in the amount of the purchase price, verifying that no encumbrances or exceptions exist except for those already noted in this Agreement.

6. Prorations.

Purchaser's and Seller's portions of loan interest, property taxes, insurance, and rents will be prorated based on the Closing Date.

7. Security Deposits.

Seller will give any security deposits made by existing tenants to Purchaser at closing.

8. Impound Accounts.

All impound accounts for taxes and insurance are included in the purchase price and shall be transferred to Purchaser at closing. Seller will be charged for any deficiency in these accounts on the date of closing.

9. Inspection.

Purchaser will have complete access to inspect the Property and submit a written list of necessary repairs to the Seller. Seller will pay costs of performing these repairs.

10. Insurance.

Seller must insure Property and maintain it in its current condition until Closing. If damage occurs to the Property before closing, the Purchaser may opt to close and collect the insurance proceeds from the Seller.

11. Appliances.

Seller agrees that the house and all the mechanical systems of the Property are in good working order at closing. Ownership of appliances and other personal property will be transferred to Buyer at Closing by presentation of a Bill of Sale free of encumbrances.

12. Defaults.

In the event that Purchaser defaults on this contract in any way, Seller shall retain deposit. In the event the Seller defaults on this contract, the Purchaser may pursue all remedies allowed under law and Seller agrees to be responsible for all costs incurred by Purchaser in pursuing these remedies.

13. Assignees and Successors

The terms and conditions of this contract shall bind all successors, heirs, administrators, trustees, executors, and assignees of the Seller and Purchaser.

14. Other Terms and Conditions:_____

_____

_____

_____

_____

_____

_____

_____

The Seller and Purchaser both have read and agreed to the aforementioned terms and conditions of this agreement.

_____   _____
Seller   Seller

_____   _____
Purchaser   Purchaser

UNIFORM RESIDENTIAL LOAN APPLICATION

Reprinted with permission from Freddie Mac (**www.freddiemac.com/uniform/unifurla.html**).

Form RD 410-4
(Rev. 10-06)

Position 3

Form Approved
OMB No. 0575-0172

APPLICATION FOR RURAL ASSISTANCE (NONFARM TRACT)

Uniform Residential Loan Application

This application is designed to be completed by the applicant with the lender's assistance. Applicants should complete this form as "Applicant #1" or "Applicant #2", as applicable. All Applicants must provide information (and the appropriate box checked) when ☐ the income or assets of a person other than the "Applicant" (including the Applicant's spouse) will be used as a basis for loan qualification or ☐ the income or assets of the Applicant's spouse will not be used as a basis for loan qualification, but his or her liabilities must be considered because the Applicant resides in a community property state, the security property is located in a community property state, or the Applicant is relying on other property located in a community property state as a basis for repayment of the loan.

I. TYPE OF MORTGAGE AND TERMS OF LOAN

Mortgage Applied for:	☐ V.A. ☐ FHA	☐ Conventional ☐ USDA/Rural Housing Service	☐ Other:	Agency Case Number	Lender Account Number
Amount $	Interest Rate %	No. of Months	Amortization Type: ☐ Fixed Rate ☐ GPM	☐ Other (Explain): ☐ ARM (Type):	

II. PROPERTY INFORMATION AND PURPOSE OF LOAN

Subject Property Address (Street, City, State, ZIP)			No. of Units
Legal Description of Subject Property (Attach description if necessary)			Year Built

Purpose of Loan	☐ Purchase ☐ Refinance	☐ Construction ☐ Construction-Permanent	☐ Other (Explain):	Property will be: ☐ Primary Residence ☐ Secondary Residence ☐ Investment

Complete this line if construction or construction-permanent loan.

Year Lot Acquired	Original Cost $	Amount Existing Liens $	(a) Present Value of Lot $	(b) Cost of Improvements $	Total (a + b) $ 0.00

Complete this line if this is a refinance loan.

Year Acquired	Original Cost $	Amount Existing Liens $	Purpose of Refinance	Describe Improvements ☐ Made ☐ To be made	
				Cost: $	

Title will be held in what Name(s)	Manner in which Title will be held	Estate will be held in: ☐ Fee Simple ☐ Leasehold (Show expiration date)

Source of Down Payment, Settlement Charges and/or Subordinate Financing (Explain)

III. APPLICANT INFORMATION

Applicant #1	Applicant #2
Name (include Jr. or Sr. if applicable)	Name (include Jr. or Sr. if applicable)
Social Security Number / Home Phone (Incl. Area Code) / DOB mm/dd/yy / Yrs. School	Social Security Number / Home Phone (Incl. Area Code) / DOB mm/dd/yy / Yrs. School
☐ Married ☐ Separated ☐ Unmarried (Include single divorced, widowed) / Dependents (Not listed by Applicant #2) No. Ages	☐ Married ☐ Separated ☐ Unmarried (Include single divorced, widowed) / Dependents (Not listed by Applicant #1) No. Ages
Present Address (Street, City State, ZIP) ☐ Own ☐ Rent No. Yrs.	Present Address (Street, City, State, ZIP) ☐ Own ☐ Rent No. Yrs.
Mailing Address if different from Present Address	Mailing Address if different from Present Address

If residing at present address for less than two years, complete the following:

Former Address (Street, City State, ZIP) ☐ Own ☐ Rent No. Yrs.	Former Address (Street, City, State, ZIP) ☐ Own ☐ Rent No. Yrs.

Freddie Mac Form 65	Page 1 of 10	Fannie Mae Form 1003

According to the Paperwork Reduction Act 1995, an agency may not conduct or sponsor, and a person is not are required to respond to a collection of information unless it displays a valid OMB control number. The valid OMB control number for this information collection is 0575-0172. The time required to complete this information collection is estimated to average 1-1/2 hours per response, including the time for reviewing instructions, searching existing data sources, gathering and maintaining the data needed, and completing and reviewing the collection of information.

IV. EMPLOYMENT INFORMATION

Applicant #1			Applicant #2		
Name & Address of Employer	☐ Self-Employed	Yrs./Mos. on the job	Name & Address of Employer	☐ Self-Employed	Yrs./Mos. on the job
		Yrs./Mos. employed in this line of work/profession			Yrs./Mos. employed in this line of work/profession
Position/Title/Type of Business		Business Phone (Incl. Area Code)	Position/Title/Type of Business		Business Phone (Incl. Area Code)

If employed in current position for less than two years or if currently employed in more than one position, complete the following:

Name & Address of Employer	☐ Self-Employed	Dates (From - To)	Name & Address of Employer	☐ Self-Employed	Dates (From - To)
		Monthly Income $			Monthly Income $
Position/Title/Type of Business		Business Phone (Incl. Area Code)	Position/Title/Type of Business		Business Phone (Incl. Area Code)
Name & Address of Employer	☐ Self-Employed	Dates (From - To)	Name & Address of Employer	☐ Self-Employed	Dates (From - To)
		Monthly Income $			Monthly Income $
Position/Title/Type of Business		Business Phone (Incl. Area Code)	Position/Title/Type of Business		Business Phone (Incl. Area Code)

V. MONTHLY INCOME AND COMBINED HOUSING EXPENSE INFORMATION

Gross Monthly Income	Applicant #1	Applicant #2	Total	Combined Monthly Housing Expense	Present	Proposed
Base Empl. Income*	$	$	$ 0.00	Rent	$	
Overtime			0.00	First Mortgage (P&I)		$
Bonuses			0.00	Other Financing (P&I)		
Commissions			0.00	Hazard Insurance		
Dividends/Interest			0.00	Real Estate Taxes		
Net Rental Income			0.00	Mortgage Insurance		
Other (Before completing see the notice in "describe other income," below			0.00	Homeowner Assn. Dues		
			0.00	Other		
Total	$ 0.00	$ 0.00	$ 0.00	Total	$ 0.00	$ 0.00

***Self Employed Applicant may be required to provide additional documentation such as tax returns and financial statements.**

Describe Other Income **Notice:** *Alimony, child Support, or separate maintenance income need not be revealed if the Applicant #1, (A 1) or Applicant #2 (A2) does not choose to have it considered for repaying this loan.*

A1/A2		Monthly Amount

VI. ASSETS AND LIABILITIES

This Statement and any applicable supporting schedules may be completed jointly by both married and unmarried Applicants if their assets and liabilities are sufficiently joined so that the Statement can be meaningfully and fairly presented on a combined basis; otherwise separate Statements and Schedules are required. If the Applicant #2 section was completed about a spouse, this Statement and supporting schedules must be completed about that spouse also.

Completed ☐ Jointly ☐ Not Jointly

ASSETS Description	Cash or Market Value	Liabilities and Pledged Assets. List the creditor's name, address and account number for all outstanding debts, including automobile loans, revolving charge accounts, real estate loans, alimony, child support, stock pledges, etc. Use continuation sheet, if necessary. Indicate by (*) those liabilities which will be satisfied upon sale of real estate owned or upon refinancing of the subject property.		
		LIABILITIES	Monthly Payment & Months Left to Pay	Unpaid Balance
Cash deposit toward purchase held by.	$	Name and Address of Company	$ Payment/Months	$
List checking and saving accounts below				
Name and Address of Bank, S&L, or Credit Union				
		Acct. No.		
		Name and Address of Company	$ Payment/Months	$
Acct. No.	$			
Name and Address of Bank, S&L, or Credit Union				
		Acct. No.		
		Name and Address of Company	$ Payment/Months	$
Acct. No.	$			
Name and Address of Bank, S&L, or Credit Union				
		Acct. No.		
		Name and Address of Company	$ Payment/Months	$
Acct. No.	$			
Name and Address of Bank, S&L, or Credit Union				
		Acct. No.		
		Name and Address of Company	$ Payment/Months	$
Acct. No.	$			
Stocks & Bonds (Company name/number & description)	$			
	$			
	$	Acct. No.		
	$	Name and Address of Company	$ Payment/Months	$
Life insurance net cash value Face amount: $	$			
Subtotal Liquid Assets	$			
Real estate owned (Enter market value from schedule of real estate owned)	$	Acct. No.		
Vested interest in retirement fund	$	Name and Address of Company	$ Payment/Months	$
Net worth of business(es) owned (Attach financial statement)	$			
Automobiles owned (Make and year)	$			
	$			
	$	Acct. No.		
	$	Alimony/Child Support/Separate Maintenance Payments Owed to:	$	
Other Assets (Itemize)	$	Job Related Expense (Child care, union dues, etc.)	$	
	$			
	$			
	$	**Total Monthly Payments**	$	
Total Assets a.	$	Net Worth (a minus b) $	Total Liabilities b.	$

VI. ASSETS AND LIABILITIES (cont.)

Schedule of Real Estate Owned *(If additional properties are owned, use continuation sheet.)*

Property Address *(Enter S if sold, PS if pending sale or R if rental being held for income)* ⇓	Type of Property	Present Market Value	Amount of Mortgage & Liens	Gross Rental Income	Mortgage Payments	Insurance Maintenance Taxes & Misc.	Net Rental Income
		$	$	$	$	$	$
Totals		$ 0	$ 0	$ 0	$ 0	$ 0	$ 0

List any additional names under which credit has previously been received and indicate appropriate creditor name(s) and account number(s):

Alternative Name	Creditor Name	Account Number

VII. DETAILS OF TRANSACTION		VIII. DECLARATIONS				
a. Purchase price	$	If you answer "Yes" to any questions a through i, please use continuation sheet for explanation.	**Applicant #1**		**Applicant #2**	
b. Alterations, improvements, repairs			**Yes** **No**		**Yes** **No**	
c. Land *(if acquired separately)*		a. Are there any outstanding judgments against you?	☐ ☐		☐ ☐	
d. Refinance *(incl. debts to be paid off)*		b. Have you been declared bankrupt within the past 7 years?	☐ ☐		☐ ☐	
e. Estimated prepaid items		c. Have you had property foreclosed upon or given title or deed in				
f. Estimated closing costs		lieu thereof in the last 7 years?	☐ ☐		☐ ☐	
g. PMI, MIP, Funding Fee		d. Are you a party to a lawsuit?	☐ ☐		☐ ☐	
h. Discount *(if Borrower will pay)*		e. Have you directly or indirectly been obligated on any loan which resulted in foreclosure,				
i. Total Costs *(Add items a through h)*	$0.00	transfer of title in lieu of foreclosure, or judgment? (This *would* include such loans as home mortgage loans				
j. Subordinate financing		SBA loans, home improvement loans, educational loans, *manufactured (mobile)* home loans, any mortgage,				
k. Borrower's closing costs paid by Seller		financial obligation, *bond, or loan guarantee.* If "Yes." provide details, including date, name, and address of				
l. Other Credits *(Explain)*		Lender, FHA or V.A. case number, *if any, and* reasons for the action.)	☐ ☐		☐ ☐	
		f. Are you presently delinquent or in default on any Federal debt or any other loan				
		mortgage, financial obligation, bond, or loan guarantee? If "Yes," give details as				
		described in question e. above.	☐ ☐		☐ ☐	
		g. Are you obligated to pay alimony, child support, or separate maintenance?	☐ ☐		☐ ☐	
		h. Is any part of the down payment borrowed?	☐ ☐		☐ ☐	
		i. Are you a co-maker or endorser on a note?	☐ ☐		☐ ☐	
m. Loan amount *(Exclude PMI, MIP Funding Fee financed)*		j. Are you a U.S. citizen?	☐ ☐		☐ ☐	
		k. Are you a permanent resident alien?	☐ ☐		☐ ☐	
n. PMI, MIP, Funding Fee financed		l. Do you intend to occupy the property as your primary residence?	☐ ☐		☐ ☐	
o. Loan amount *(Add m & n)*	$0.00	If "Yes," complete question m. below.				
		m. Have you had ownership interest in a property in the last 3 years?	☐ ☐		☐ ☐	
		(1) What type of property did you own-principal residence (PR), second home				
		(SH), or investment property (IP)?				
p. Cash from/to Borrower *(Subtract j, k, l, & o from i)*		(2) How did you hold title to the home-solely by yourself (S), jointly with your				
		spouse (SP), or jointly with another person (O)?				

Freddie Mac Form 65	**Page 4 of 10**	Fannie Mae Form 1003

IX. ACKNOWLEDGMENT AND AGREEMENT

Each of the undersigned specifically represents to Lender and to Lender's actual or potential agents, brokers, processors, attorneys, insurers, services, successors and assigns and agrees and acknowledges that: (1) the information provided in this application is true and correct as of the date set forth opposite my signature and that any intentional or negligent misrepresentation of this information contained in this application may result in civil liability, including monetary damages, to any person who may suffer any loss due to reliance upon any misrepresentation that I have made on this application, and/or in criminal penalties including, but not limited to, fine or imprisonment or both under the provisions of Title 18, United States Code, Sec. 1001, et seq.; (2) the loan requested pursuant to this application (the "loan") will be secured by a mortgage or deed of trust on the property described herein, (3) the property will not be used for any illegal or prohibited purpose or use; (4) all statements made in this application are made for the purpose of obtaining a residential mortgage loan; (5) the property will be occupied as indicated herein; (6) any owner or servicer of the Loan may verify or reverify any information contained in the application from any source named in this application, and Lender, its successors or assigns may retain the original and/or an electronic record of this application, even if the Loan is not approved; (7) the Lender and its agents, brokers, insurers, servicers, successors and assigns may continuously rely on the information contained in the application, and I am obligated to amend and/or supplement the information provided in this application if any of the material facts that I have represented herein should change prior to closing of the Loan; (8) in the event that my payments on the Loan become delinquent, the owner or servicer of the Loan may, in addition to any other rights and remedies that it may have relating to such delinquency, report my name and account information to one or more consumer credit reporting agencies; (9) ownership of the Loan and/or administration of the Loan account may be transferred with such notice as may be required by law; (10) neither Lender nor its agents, brokers, insurers, servicers, successors or assigns has made any representation or warranty, express or implied, to me regarding the property or the condition or value of the property; and (11) my transmission of this application as an "electronic record" containing my "electronic signature," as those terms are defined in applicable federal and/or state laws (excluding audio and video recordings), or my facsimile transmission of this application containing a facsimile of my signature, shall be as effective, enforceable and valid as if a paper version of this application were delivered containing my original written signature.

Applicant's Signature	Date	Applicant's Signature	Date
X		X	

X. INFORMATION FOR GOVERNMENT MONITORING PURPOSES

The following information is requested by the Federal Government for certain types of loans related to a dwelling in order to monitor the lender's compliance with equal credit opportunity, fair housing and home mortgage disclosure laws. You are not required to furnish this information, but are encouraged to do so. The law provides that a lender may discriminate neither on the basis of this information, or on whether you choose to furnish it. If you furnish the information, please provide both ethnicity and race. For race, you may check more than one designation. If you do not furnish ethnicity, race, or sex, under Federal regulations, this lender is required to note the information on the basis of visual observation or surname. If you do not wish to furnish the information, please check the box below. (Lender must review the above material to assure that the disclosures satisfy all requirements to which the lender is subject under applicable state law for the particular type of loan applied for.)

BORROWER ☐ I do not wish to furnish this information	CO-BORROWER ☐ I do not wish to furnish this information
Ethnicity: ☐ Hispanic or Latino ☐ Not Hispanic or Latino	Ethnicity: ☐ Hispanic or Latino ☐ Not Hispanic or Latino
Race ☐ American Indian or Alaska Native ☐ Asian ☐ Black or African American	Race ☐ American Indian or Alaska Native ☐ Asian ☐ Black or African American
☐ Native Hawaiian or Other Pacific Islander ☐ White	☐ Native Hawaiian or Other Pacific Islander ☐ White
Sex: ☐ Female ☐ Male	Sex: ☐ Female ☐ Male

To be Completed by Interviewer	Interviewer's Name (Print or type)	Name and Address of Interviewer's Employer
This application was taken by: ☐ face-to-face interview ☐ by mail ☐ by telephone ☐ Internet	Interviewer's Signature	Date	
	Interviewer's Phone Number (Incl. Area Code)	

Continuation For/Residential Loan Application

Use if you need more space to complete the Residential Loan Application Mark A1 for Applicant #1 or A2 for Applicant #2	Applicant #1 (A1)	Agency Account Number:
	Applicant #2 (A2)	Lender Account Number:

FEDERAL TRUTH IN LENDING
DISCLOSURE STATEMENT

Creditor:	Borrower(s):	Account Number:
_____	_____	_____
_____	_____	_____

Annual Percentage Rate: The cost of your credit as a yearly rate.	Finance Charge: The dollar amount the credit will cost you.	Amount Financed: The amount of credit provided to you or on your behalf.	Total of Payments: The amount you will have paid after you have made all payments as scheduled.
_____%	$_____	$_____	$_____

Your payment schedule will be:

Number of Payments	Amount of Payments	When Payments are Due
	$	

- Variable rate: If checked, your load contains a variable rate feature. Disclosures about the variable rate feature have been provided to you earlier.

- Demand Feature: If checked, this obligation has a demand feature.

- Insurance: You may obtain property insurance from anyone you want that is acceptable to the creditor. If checked, you can get insurance through _____. You will pay $ _____ for 12 months hazard insurance coverage. You will pay $ _____ for 12 months flood insurance coverage.

Security: You are giving a security interest in _____ property located at_____.

Assignment of brokerage account and pledge of securities

Personal property: stocks and lease

Assignment of life insurance policy

Other: _____

Late Charges: If a payment is late, you will be charged _____% of the payment.

Prepayment: If you pay off early, you may/will not have to pay a penalty. You may/will not be entitled to a refund of part of the finance charge.

Assumption: Someone buying your house may, subject to conditions, be allowed to/cannot assume the remainder of the mortgage on the original terms.

See your contract documents for any additional information about nonpayment, default, and required repayment in full before the scheduled date, prepayment refunds and penalties, and assumption policy.

ACKNOWLEDGMENT.

By signing below you are acknowledging that you have received a completed copy of this Federal Truth in Lending Statement prior to the execution of any closing documents.

Borrower	Date
Borrower	Date

Definition of Truth in Lending Terms.

Annual Percentage Rate

This is not the Note rate for which the borrower applied. The Annual Percentage Rate (APR) is the cost of the loan in percentage terms taking into account various loan charges of which interest is only one such charge. Other charges which are used in calculation of the Annual Percentage Rate are Private Mortgage Insurance (PMI) or FHA Mortgage Insurance Premium (when applicable) and Prepaid Finance Charges (loan discount, origination fees, prepaid interest, and other credit costs). The APR is calculated by spreading these charges over the life of the loan, which results in a rate higher than the interest rate shown on your Mortgage/Deed of Trust Note. If interest were the only Finance Charge, then the interest rate and the Annual Percentage Rate would be the same.

Prepaid Finance Charges.

Prepaid Finance Charges are certain charges made in connection with the loan and which must be paid upon the close of the loan. These charges are defined by the Federal Reserve Board in Regulation Z, and the charges must be paid by the borrower. Non-inclusive examples of such charges are: Loan origination fee,

"Points" or Discount, Private Mortgage Insurance or FHA Mortgage Insurance, Tax Service Fee. Some loan charges are specifically excluded from the Prepaid Finance Charge, such as appraisal fees and credit report fees. Prepaid Finance Charges are totaled and then subtracted from the Loan Amount (the face amount of the Deed of Trust/Mortgage Note). The net figure is the Amount Financed as explained below.

Finance Charge.

The amount of interest, prepaid finance charge, and certain insurance premiums (if any) which the borrower will be expected to pay over the life of the loan.

Amount Financed.

The Amount Financed is the loan amount applied for less the prepaid finance charges. Prepaid finance charges can be found on the Good Faith Estimate. For example, if the borrower's note is for $100,000 and the Prepaid Finance Charges total $5,000, the Amount Financed would be $95,000. The Amount Financed is the figure on which the Annual Percentage Rate is based.

Total of Payments.

This figure represents the total of all payments made toward principal, interest, and mortgage insurance (if applicable).

Payment Schedule.

The dollar figures in the Payment Schedule represent principal, interest, plus Private Mortgage Insurance (if applicable). These figures will not reflect taxes and insurance escrows or any temporary buydown payments contributed by the seller.

Disclosure Notices.

Borrower(s): _____

Property Address: _____

( ) Occupancy Statement.

This is to certify that I/we do not intend to occupy the subject property as my/our primary residence.

I/We hereby certify under penalty of U.S. Criminal Code Section 1010 Title 18 U.S.C., that the above statement submitted for the purpose of obtaining mortgage insurance under the National Housing Act is true and correct.

(   ) **Fair Credit Reporting Act.**

An investigation will be made as to the credit standing of all individuals seeking credit in this application. The nature and scope of any investigation will be furnished to you upon written request made within a reasonable period of time. In the event of denied credit due to an unfavorable consumer report, you will be advised of the identity of the Consumer Reporting Agency making such report and of right to request within 60 days the reason for the adverse action, pursuant to provisions of section 615(b) of the Fair Credit Reporting Act.

(   ) **Equal Credit Opportunity Act.**

The Equal Credit Opportunity Act prohibits creditors from discriminating against credit applicants on the basis of race, color, religion, national origin, sex, marital status, age (provided the applicant has the capacity to enter into a binding contract); because all or part of the applicant's income derives from any public assistance program; or because the applicant has in good faith exercised any right under the Consumer Credit Protection Act. Income which you receive as alimony, child support, or separate maintenance need not be disclosed to this creditor unless you choose to rely on such sources to qualify for the loan. Income from these and other sources, including part-time or temporary employment, will not be discounted by this lender because of your sex or marital status. However, we will consider very carefully the stability and probable continuity of any income you disclose to us. The Federal Agency that administers compliance with this law concerning this creditor is: _____

_____.

(   ) **Right to Financial Privacy Act.**

I/We acknowledge that this is notice to me/us as required by the Right to Financial Privacy Act of 1978 that the Veterans Administration (in the case of a VA Loan) or Department of Housing and Urban Development in the case of an FHA Loan has a right of access to financial records held by financial institutions in connection with the consideration or administration of assistance to me/us. Financial records involving my/our transactions will be available to the VA (in the case of a VA Ioan) or in HUD (in the case of an FHA loan) without further notice or authorization but will not be disclosed or released to another government agency or department without my/our consent, except as required or permitted by law.

(　) Information Disclosure Authorization.

I/We hereby authorize you to release to _____
___ for verification purposes, information concerning:

(　) Employment History, dates, title(s), income, hours worked, etc.

(　) Banking (checking & savings) account of record.

(　) Mortgage loan rating, (opening date, high credit, payment amount, loan balance, and payment).

(　) Any information deemed necessary in connection with consumer credit report for real estate transaction.

This information is for the confidential use of this lender in compiling a mortgage loan credit report. A copy of this authorization may be deemed to be the equivalent of the original and may be used as a duplicate original.

(　) Anti-Coercion Statement.

The insurance laws of _____ (state) provide that the lender may not require the applicant to take insurance through any particular insurance agent or company to protect the mortgaged property.

The applicant, subject to the rules adopted by the Insurance Commissioner, has the right to have the insurance placed with an insurance agent or company of his choice, provided the company meets the requirements of the lender. The lender has the right to designate reasonable financial requirements as to the company and the adequacy of the coverage.

I have read the foregoing statement, or the rules of the Insurance Commissioner relative thereto, and understand my rights and privileges and those of the lender relative to the placing of such insurance. I have selected the following agencies to write the insurance covering the property described above: _____
_____.

(　) Flood insurance Notification.

Federal regulations require us to inform you that the property used as security for this loan is located in an area identified by the U.S. Secretary of Housing & Urban Development as having special flood hazards and that in the event of damage to the property caused by flooding in a federally-declared disaster, federal disaster relief assistance, if authorized, will be available for the property.

At the closing you will be asked to acknowledge your receipt of this information. If you have any questions concerning this notice, please contact your loan officer.

Important: Please notify your insurance agent that the "loss payee" clause for the mortgagee on both the hazard and flood insurance must read as follows, unless otherwise advised: _____

_____

_____.

( ) Consumer Handbook on Adjustable Rate Mortgages.

I/We hereby acknowledge receipt from _____of a copy of the book titled *Consumer Handbook on Adjustable Rate Mortgages* published by the Federal Reserve Board and the Federal Home Loan Bank Board, which is provided in addition to other required adjustable rate mortgage disclosures.

I/We hereby certify that I/we have read the Notices set forth above and fully understand all of the above.

Borrower Signed   Date

Borrower Printed   Date

Borrower Signed   Date

Borrower Printed   Date

Acknowledgement of Notice to Borrower.

Pursuant to the Florida Fair Lending Act

If you obtain this high-cost home loan, the lender will have a mortgage on your home. You could lose your home and any money you have put into it if you do not meet your obligations under the loan.

Mortgage loan rates and closing costs and fees vary based on many factors, including your particular credit and financial circumstances, your employment history, the loan-to value requested, and the type of property that will secure your loan. The loan rate and fees could also vary based upon which lender or broker you select. As a borrower, you should shop around and compare loan rates and fees.

You should also consider consulting a qualified independent credit counselor or other experienced financial adviser regarding the rates, fees, and provisions of this mortgage loan before you proceed. You should contact the United States Department of Housing and Urban Development for a list of credit counselors available in your area.

You are not required to complete this agreement merely because you have received these disclosures or have signed a loan application.

Borrowing for the purpose of debt consolidation can be an appropriate financial management tool. However, if you continue to incur significant new credit card charges or other debts after this high-cost home loan is closed and then experience financial difficulties, you could lose your home and any equity you have in it if you do not meet your mortgage loan obligations.

Remember that property taxes and homeowners' insurance are your responsibility. Not all lenders provide escrow services for these payments. You should ask your lender about these services.

Also, your payments on existing debts contribute to your credit rating. You should not accept any advice to ignore your regular payments to your existing creditors.

Borrower	Date
Borrower	Date

Borrower's Certification & Authorization.

Certification.

I/We the undersigned hereby certify the following:

1. I/We have applied for a mortgage loan from _____. In applying for the loan, I/We completed a loan application containing various information on the purpose of the loan, the amount and source of the down payment, employment and Income information, and assets and liabilities. I/We

certify that all of the information is true and complete. I/We made no misrepresentations in the loan application or other documents, nor did I/We omit any pertinent information.

2. I/We understand and agree that _____ _____ reserves the right to change the mortgage loan review process to a full documentation program. This may include verifying the information provided on the application with the employer and/or the financial institution.

3. I/We fully understand that it is a Federal crime punishable by fine or imprisonment, or both, to knowingly make any false statements when applying for this mortgage, as applicable under the provisions of Title 18, United States Code, Section 1014.

Authorization to Release Information.

To Whom It May Concern:

1. I/We have applied for a mortgage loan from _____ _____. As part of the application process, _____ _____ may verify information contained in my/ our loan application and in other documents required in connection with the loan, either before the loan is closed or as part of its quality control program.

2. I/We authorize you to provide to _____ _____ ____and to any investor to whom _____ _____ may sell my mortgage, any and all information and documentation that they request. Such information includes, but is not limited to, employment history and income; bank, money market, and similar account balances; credit history; and copies of income tax returns.

3. _____ or any investor that purchases the mortgage may address this authorization to any party named in the loan application.

4. A copy of this authorization may be accepted as an original.

5. Your prompt reply to _____ or the Investor that purchased the mortgage is appreciated.

Borrower's Signature X_____ Social Security #_____

Printed Full-Name_____ Date ___/___/___

                  First   Middle   Last

Current Home Address_____

                      Number   Street   City   State   ZIP Code

Notice to Applicant of Right to Receive Copy of Appraisal Report.

Date	Loan Number	Property Address

You have the right to receive a copy of the appraisal report to be obtained in connection with the loan for which you have applied, provided that you have paid for the appraisal. We must receive your written request no later than 60 days after we notify you about the action taken on your application or you withdraw your application. If you would like a copy of the appraisal report, please contact our office at:

Company Name
Address
City, ST ZIP

Borrower		Date	
Borrower		Date	
Borrower		Date	
Borrower		Date	

Equal Credit Opportunity Act Notice.

Property Address:	Loan Number:

The federal Equal Credit Opportunity Act prohibits creditors from discriminating against credit applicants on the basis of race, color, religion, national origin, sex, marital status, age (provided the applicant has the capacity to enter into a binding contract); because all or part of the applicant's income derives from any public assistance program; or because the applicant has in good faith exercised any right under the Consumer Credit Protection Act. The federal agency that administers

compliance with this law concerning this creditor is: _____
_____ (name and address of appropriate agency).
Alimony, child support, or separate maintenance income need not be revealed if
you do not wish to have it considered as a basis for reporting.

Borrower	Date
Co-Borrower	Date

The Housing Financial Discrimination Act of 1977 Fair Lending Notice.

Property Address:	Lender:
Property Address:	Date:

It is illegal to discriminate in the provision of or in the availability of financial
assistance because of the consideration of:

1. Trends, characteristics, or conditions in the neighborhood or
    geographic area surrounding a housing accommodation, unless the
    financial institution can demonstrate in the particular case that such
    consideration is required to avoid an unsafe and unsound business
    practice; or

2. Race, color, religion, sex, marital status, domestic partnership, national
    origin, or ancestry.

It is illegal to consider the racial, ethnic, religious, or national origin composition
of a neighborhood or geographic area surrounding a housing accommodation or
whether or not such composition is undergoing change, or is expected to undergo
change, in appraising a housing accommodation or in determining whether or
not, or under what terms and conditions, to provide financial assistance.

These provisions govern financial assistance for the purpose of the purchase, construction, rehabilitation or refinancing of one- to four-unit family residences occupied by the owner and for the purpose of the home improvement of any one- to four-unit family residence.

If you have any questions about your rights, or if you wish to file a complaint, contact the management of this financial institution or the Department of Real Estate at one of the following locations:

ACKNOWLEDGEMENT OF RECEIPT.

I/We received a copy of this notice.

Borrower	Date
Co-Borrower	Date

Credit Authorization.

To all consumer-reporting agencies and to all creditors and depositories of the undersigned:

1. Please be advised that the undersigned, and each of them, has made application to: _____ (Company Name) requesting an extension of credit to the undersigned. Therefore, the undersigned, and each of them, hereby authorizes you to provide credit report and/or a disclosure to Lender or any agent or balance. The undersigned also authorizes you to disclose your deposit or credit experiences with the undersigned to Lender or to third parties.

2. In addition, the undersigned, and each of them, hereby authorizes Lender to disclose to any third party, or any agent or employee thereof, information regarding the deposit or credit experience with any of the undersigned.

3. A photographic or carbon copy of this authorization bearing a photographic or carbon copy of the signature(s) of the undersigned may be deemed to be equivalent to the original hereof and may be used as a duplicate original.

Borrower's Signature X_____ Social Security #_____

Printed Full-Name_____ Date ___/___/___
              First   Middle   Last

Co-Borrower's Signature X_____ Social Security #_____

Printed Full-Name_____ Date ___/___/___
              First   Middle   Last

Notice to the Home Loan Applicant Credit Score Information Disclosure.

Borrower(s) Name and Address:	Lender Name and Address:

In connection with your application for a home loan, the lender must disclose to you the score that a consumer-reporting agency distributed to users and the lender used in connection with your home loan, and the key factors affecting your credit scores.

The credit score is a computer-generated summary calculated at the time of the request and based on information that a consumer reporting agency or lender has on file. The scores are based on data about your credit history and payment patterns. Credit scores are important because they are used to assist the lender in determining whether you will obtain a loan. They may also be used to determine what interest rate you may be offered on the mortgage. Credit scores can change over time, depending on your conduct, how your credit history and payment patterns change, and how credit-scoring technologies change.

Because the score is based on information in your credit history, it is very important that you review the credit-related information that is being furnished to make sure it is accurate. Credit records may vary from one company to another.

If you have questions about your credit score or the credit information that is furnished to you, contact the consumer reporting agency at the address and telephone number provided with this notice, or contact the lender, if the lender developed or generated the credit score. The consumer-reporting agency plays no part in the decision to take any action on the loan application and is unable to provide you with specific reasons for the decision on a loan application. If you have questions concerning the terms of the loan, contact the lender.

One or more of the following credit bureaus provided a credit score that was used in connection with your home loan application.

Credit Bureau #1: _____

| Phone: _____
Fax: _____
Model Used: _____
Range of Possible Scores:
____to____ | **Borrower**

Name:_____
Score:_____Date:_____
Key Factors: _____ | **Co-Borrower**

Name:_____
Score:_____Date:_____
Key Factors: _____ |

Credit Bureau #2: _____

| Phone: _____

Fax: _____

Model Used: _____

Range of Possible Scores:
____to____ | **Borrower**

Name:_____

Score:_____Date:_____

Key Factors: _____ | **Co-Borrower**

Name:_____

Score:_____Date:_____

Key Factors: _____ |

Credit Bureau #3: _____

| Phone: _____

Fax: _____

Model Used: _____

Range of Possible Scores:
____to____ | **Borrower**

Name:_____

Score:_____Date:_____

Key Factors: _____ | **Co-Borrower**

Name:_____

Score:_____Date:_____

Key Factors: _____ |

I/We have received a copy of this Credit Score Information Disclosure

Borrower   Date   Co-Borrower   Date

Experian	Trans Union	Equifax Credit Information Services
PO Box 2002	PO Box 1000	PO Box 740241
Allen, TX 75013	Chester, PA 19022	Atlanta, GA 30374
1-888-397-3742	1-800-888-4213	1-800-685-1111

SERVICING DISCLOSURE

(Source: www.fdic.gov/regulations/laws/rules/6500-2525.html)

Name of Lender:	Date:

NOTICE TO FIRST LIEN MORTGAGE LOAN APPLICANTS: THE RIGHT TO COLLECT YOUR MORTGAGE LOAN PAYMENTS MAY BE TRANSFERRED. FEDERAL LAW GIVES YOU CERTAIN RELATED RIGHTS. IF YOUR LOAN IS MADE, SAVE THIS STATEMENT WITH YOUR LOAN DOCUMENTS. SIGN THE ACKNOWLEDGMENT AT THE END OF THIS STATEMENT ONLY IF YOU UNDERSTAND ITS CONTENTS.

Because you are applying for a mortgage loan covered by the Real Estate Settlement Procedures Act (RESPA) (12 U.S.C. § 2601 et seq.) you have certain rights under that Federal law.

This statement tells you about those rights. It also tells you what the chances are that the servicing for this loan may be transferred to a different loan servicer. "Servicing" refers to collecting your principal, interest, and escrow account payments, if any. If your loan servicer changes, there are certain procedures that must be followed. This statement generally explains those procedures.

Transfer practices and requirements

If the servicing of your loan is assigned, sold, or transferred to a new servicer, you must be given written notice of that transfer. The present loan servicer must send you notice in writing of the assignment, sale or transfer of the servicing not less than 15 days before the effective date of the transfer. The new loan servicer must also send you notice within 15 days after the effective date of the transfer. The present servicer and the new servicer may combine this information in one notice, so long as the notice is sent to you 15 days before the effective date of transfer. The 15-day period is not applicable if a notice of prospective transfer is provided to you at settlement. The law allows a delay in the time (not more than {{6-30-05 p.7048}} 30 days after a transfer) for servicers to notify you, upon the occurrence of certain business emergencies.

Notices must contain certain information. They must contain the effective date of the transfer of the servicing of your loan to the new servicer, and the name, address, and toll-free or collect call telephone number of the new servicer, and toll-free or collect call telephone numbers of a person or department for both your present servicer and your new servicer to answer your questions. During the 60-day period following the effective date of the transfer of the loan servicing, a loan payment received by your old servicer before its due date may not be treated by the new loan servicer as late, and a late fee may not be imposed on you.

Complaint Resolution

Section 6 of RESPA (12 U.S.C. § 2605) gives you certain consumer rights, *whether or not your loan servicing is transferred.* If you send a "qualified written request" to your servicer, your servicer must provide you with a written acknowledgment within 20 Business Days of receipt of your request. A "qualified written request" is a written correspondence, other than notice on a payment coupon or other payment medium supplied by the servicer, which includes your name and account number, and the information regarding your request. Not later than 60 Business Days after receiving your request, your servicer must make any appropriate corrections to your account, or must provide you with a written clarification regarding any dispute. During this 60-Business Day period, your servicer may not provide information to a consumer reporting agency concerning any overdue payment related to such period or qualified written request.

A Business Day is any day in which the offices of the business entity are open to the public for carrying on substantially all of its business functions.

Damages and Costs

Section 6 of RESPA also provides for damages and costs for individuals or classes of individuals in circumstances where servicers are shown to have violated the requirements of that Section.

Servicing Transfer Estimates

1. The following is the best estimate of what will happen to the servicing of your mortgage loan:

A. We may assign, sell, or transfer the servicing of your loan while the loan is outstanding. [We are able to service your loan[.][,] and we [will][will not] [have not decided whether to] service your loan.].
[or]

B. We do not service mortgage loans[.][,] and we have not serviced mortgage loans in the past three years.] We presently intend to assign, sell or transfer the servicing of your mortgage loan. You will be informed about your servicer.

INSTRUCTIONS TO PREPARER: The model format may be annotated with further information that clarifies or enhances the model language. The following model language may be used where appropriate:

> We assign, sell, or transfer the servicing of some of our loans while the loan is outstanding depending on the type of loan and other factors. For the program you have applied for, we expect to [sell all of the mortgage servicing] [retain all of the mortgage servicing] [assign, sell or transfer _____% of the mortgage servicing].

> {{6-30-05 p.7049}}

2. For all the first lien mortgage loans that we make in the 12 month period after your mortgage loan is funded, we estimate that the percentage of such loans for which we will transfer servicing is between: _____ [0 to 25%] or [NONE] _____ 26 to 50% _____ 51 to 75% _____ [76 to 100%] or [ALL] [This estimate [does] [does not] include assignments, sales or transfers to affiliates or subsidiaries.] This is only our best estimate and it is not binding. Business conditions or other circumstances may affect our future transferring decisions.

3. [3(A). We have previously assigned, sold, or transferred the servicing of first lien mortgage loans.]

[or]

3. [3(B). This is our record of transferring the servicing of the first lien mortgage loans we have made in the past:

Year	Percentage of Loans Transferred (Rounded to nearest quartile--0%, 25%, 50%, 75% or 100%).
20__	_____%
20__	_____%
20__	_____%

[This information [does] [does not] include assignments, sales, or transfers to affiliates or subsidiaries.]]

_____   _____
[Signature Not Mandatory]   Date

[INSTRUCTIONS TO PREPARER: Select either Item 3(A) or Item 3(B), except if you chose the provision in 1(B) stating: "We do not service mortgage loans, and we have not serviced mortgage loans in the past three years," all of Item 3 should be omitted.

> The information in Item 3(B) is for the previous three calendar years. The information does not have to include the previous calendar year if the statement is prepared before March 31 of the next calendar year. If the percentage of servicing transferred is less than 12.5%, the word "nominal" or the actual percentage amount of servicing transfers may be used. If no servicing was transferred, "none" may be placed on the percentage line; if all servicing was transferred, "all" may be placed on the percentage line.]
> {{6-30-05 p.7050}}

ACKNOWLEDGMENT OF MORTGAGE LOAN APPLICANT

I/we have read this disclosure form, and understand its contents, as evidenced by my/our signature(s) below. I/we understand that this acknowledgment is a required part of the mortgage loan application.

_____   _____
APPLICANT'S SIGNATURE   Date

_____   _____
CO-APPLICANT'S SIGNATURE   Date

Sample Amortization Schedule

This amortization schedule was created using the following terms:

Credit rating: Good
Loan amount: $150,000
Interest rate: 5.5%

Loan term: 30 years

Year	Interest	Principal	Balance
2010	$4,796.58	$1,165.21	$148,834.79
2011	$8,133.84	$2,086.36	$146,748.43

2012	$8,016.15	$2,204.05	$144,544.38
2013	$7,891.83	$2,328.37	$142,216.01
2014	$7,760.49	$2,459.71	$139,756.30
2015	$7,621.74	$2,598.46	$137,157.84
2016	$7,475.17	$2,745.03	$134,412.80
2017	$7,320.33	$2,899.87	$131,512.93
2018	$7,156.75	$3,063.45	$128,449.48
2019	$6,983.95	$3,236.25	$125,213.22
2020	$6,801.40	$3,418.80	$121,794.42
2021	$6,608.55	$3,611.65	$118,182.77
2022	$6,404.83	$3,815.38	$114,367.40
2023	$6,189.61	$4,030.59	$110,336.80
2024	$5,962.25	$4,257.95	$106,078.85
2025	$5,722.07	$4,498.13	$101,580.72
2026	$5,468.34	$4,751.86	$96,828.86
2027	$5,200.30	$5,019.90	$91,808.95
2028	$4,917.14	$5,303.07	$86,505.89
2029	$4,618.00	$5,602.20	$80,903.68
2030	$4,301.99	$5,918.21	$74,985.48
2031	$3,968.16	$6,252.04	$68,733.43
2032	$3,615.49	$6,604.71	$62,128.72
2033	$3,242.94	$6,977.26	$55,151.46
2034	$2,849.36	$7,370.84	$47,780.62
2035	$2,433.59	$7,786.61	$39,994.01
2036	$1,994.37	$8,225.84	$31,768.18
2037	$1,530.36	$8,689.84	$23,078.34
2038	$1,040.19	$9,180.01	$13,898.32
2039	$522.36	$9,697.84	$4,200.48
2040	$57.93	$4,200.48	$0.00

SAMPLE APPRAISAL

APPRAISAL OF REAL PROPERTY

LOCATED AT:
4822 Mindora Drive
Lot 108, Tract 13028, Book 393, Page 7-11, APN:7527-006-035
Torrance, CA 90505

FOR:
Professional Enterprises
1234 Any Street, Any City, CA 98765

AS OF:
10/06/2004

BY:
Daniel M Christian

DESKTOP RESTRICTED USE APPRAISAL REPORT

File No. Sample-Restricted
Loan No.

FOR INTERNAL RISK ANALYSIS
VALUE ESTIMATED FROM PUBLIC RECORD DATA ONLY, NO PROPERTY INSPECTION PERFORMED UNLESS OTHERWISE STATED.

Intended Purpose: ☐ Portfolio Evaluation: ☐ QC/Audit: ☒ Junior Lien: ☐ REO/Foreclosure: ☐ Other: _____
Data Source(s) Used: ☐ Lender ☒ Tax Record ☒ Appraiser Files ☒ MLS ☐ Other: _____
Interest: Fee Simple

CLIENT AND PROPERTY IDENTIFICATION

Client/Lender: Professional Enterprises   Address: 1234 Any Street, Any City, CA 98765
Borrower/Applicant: Smith   Client contact: John Joseph
Property Address: 4822 Mindora Drive   City: Torrance   State: CA   ZIP: 90505
Census Tract: 6512.01   APN: 7527-006-035   County: Los Angeles
Property Type: ☒ Tract SFR ☐ Custom ☐ Condominium ☐ Townhouse ☐ Multifamily ☐ Other:

MARKET AREA AND COMPARABLES

Market Value Trend:
☐ Increasing ☒ Stable
☐ Declining

Typical Market Price Range: $ 550,000 to $ 1,250,000
Typical Market Property Age: 1 yrs. to 75 yrs.

FEATURE	SUBJECT			COMPARABLE #1			COMPARABLE #2			COMPARABLE #3		
Address	4822 Mindora Drive Torrance, CA 90505			22723 Linda Drive Torrance, CA			21602 Evalyn Avenue Torrance, CA			21824 Barbara Street Torrance, CA		
Proximity to Subject				0.30 miles			0.60 miles			0.63 miles		
Sale Price	$			$ 652,000			$ 679,000			$ 670,000		
Price/Gross Living Area				613.00			578.00			570.00		
Date of Sale	N/A			07/01/2004			09/22/20043			06/30/2004		
Location	Average			Average			Average			Average		
Site/View	8,999/None			5,100/None			5,300/None			7,730/None		
Design (Style)	Traditional			Traditional			Traditional			Traditional		
Actual Age (Yrs.)	1951			1952			1955			1955		
Condition	Average			Average			Average			Average		
Above Grade	Total	Bedrooms	Bath	Total	Bedrooms	Bath	Total	Bedrooms	Bath	Total	Bedrooms	Bath
Room Count	5	2	1	5	3	1	5	3	2	5	3	2
Gross Living Area			1,148 Sq. Ft.			1,064 Sq. Ft.			1,175 Sq. Ft.			1,175 Sq. Ft.
Basement	None			None			None			None		
Air Conditioning	None			None			None			None		
Garage/Carport	Garage-2			Garage-1			Garage-2			Garage-2		
Porches, Patio, Pool	Cvrd. Porch/Cvrd. Patio			Cvrd. Porch/Cvrd. Patio			Cvrd. Porch/Cvrd. Patio			Cvrd. Porch/Cvrd. Patio		
Amenities/Upgrades	None			None			None			None		
Overall Comparison				☐ Sup. ☐ Similar ☒ Infer.			☒ Sup. ☐ Similar ☐ Infer.			☒ Sup. ☐ Similar ☐ Infer.		

EVALUATION SUMMARY

Comments: The subject sold 08/26/2003 for $595,0000. Property values have been increasing in this area since purchase in 2003. As of the appraisal date property values are stable. See sales #4-#6 for additional supportive data. Extensive research of the subject's immediate market area was conducted. The five sales and one active listing used were deemed excellent comparable properties and represent current market conditions in this area. There is a lack of 2 bedrooms-1 bathroom sales in this area, therefore mostly 3 bedroom sales were used. Overall comparison for each sale (Superior, Similar, Inferior) represent a total upward or downward or about the same unit of comparison for each sale.

This Restricted Use Appraisal was completed from the public record information from the desktop. No inspection was made of the subject or sales. The subject is assumed to be in a minimum of average conditon and generally conform the neighborhood, in terms of style, condition and construction. It sis assumed there are no adverse environmental conditions present in the improvements, on the site or in the immediate vicinity of the subject property. It is assumed there are no significant discrepancies between the public record information, multiple listing service, or other data sources used, and the existing site or improvements. Any photographs provided in this report were supplied by th client borrower, or above listed sources, with no warranties expressed or implied.

This is a Limited Restricted Use Appraisal and is intended for use by the client only. The function of this appraisal is to help the client analyze the risk associates with making a loan on the subject property.

Estimated Value for Loan Purposes: $ 660,000   as of   10/06/2004

CERTIFICATION AND LIMITING CONDITIONS

PURPOSE OF APPRAISAL: The purpose of this appraisal is to estimate the market value of the real property that is the subject of this report based upon a qualitative sales comparison analysis for use in the mortgage finance transaction.

DEFINITION OF MARKET VALUE: The most probable price which a property should bring in a competitive and open market under all conditions requisite to a fair sale, the buyer and seller each acting prudently and knowledgeably, and assuming the price is not affected by undue stimulus. Implicit in this definition is the consummation of a sale as of a specified date and the passing of title from seller to buyer under conditions whereby: (1) buyer and seller are typically motivated; (2) both parties are well informed or well advised, and acting in what they consider their best interests; (3) a reasonable time is allowed for exposure in the open market; (4) payment is made in terms of cash in United States dollars or in terms of financial arrangements comparable thereto; and (5) the price represents the normal consideration for the property sold unaffected by special or creative financing or sales concessions granted by anyone associated with the sale.

LIMITED APPRAISAL: This appraisal is a Limited Appraisal, subject to the Departure Provision of the USPAP that was adopted and promulgated by the Appraisal Standards Board of the Appraisal Foundation. This Limited Appraisal is intended to comply with Standards Rules (SR): 1-1, 1-2 and 1-5, and departs from SR 1-3 and 1-4, as allowed by USPAP.

RESTRICTED USE APPRAISAL REPORT: The Restricted Use Appraisal Report option limits the use of this report to the client. The appraiser's opinions and conclusions set forth in the report cannot be understood properly without additional information in the appraiser's workfile.

INTENDED USE: This appraisal is intended for use only by the client and/or its subsidiaries. The function of this appraisal is to help the client analyze the risk associated with making a loan on the subject property.

HIGHEST AND BEST USE: The Highest and Best Use of the subject property is assumed to be its present use; that is, one-four (1-4) family residential use.

Form DRA — "WinTOTAL" appraisal software by a la mode, inc. — 1-800-ALAMODE
A.S.A.P. Real Estate Appraisals (310) 937-6151

DESKTOP RESTRICTED USE APPRAISAL REPORT

File No.   Sample-Restricted
Loan No.

SCOPE OF THE APPRAISAL: The scope of this appraisal consists of identifying the characteristics of the subject property that are relevant to the purpose and intended use of the appraisal. This may be accomplished by reviewing public record data, prior appraisal or other documentation from a disinterested source and which is considered reliable from the appraiser's perspective. Unless otherwise noted in the appraisal, no interior or exterior inspection of the subject property has been made.

In developing this appraisal, the appraiser has incorporated only the Sales Comparison approach. The appraiser has excluded the Cost and Income approaches, in accordance with the Departure Provision. The appraiser has determined that this appraisal process is not so limited that the results of the assignment are no longer credible, and the client agrees that the limited service is appropriate given the intended use. The data sources for the comparable sales may include public record data services, multiple listing services, automated valuation models and/or other data sources that become available. The confirmation of comparable sale data, i.e. closed sale documentation and property characteristics, is via public data sources only. The appraiser has not viewed the sales in the field. The data is collected, verified and analyzed, in accordance with the scope of work identified and the intended use of the appraisal. The appraiser acknowledges that an estimate of a reasonable time for the exposure in the open market is a condition in the definition of market value. The subject's marketing time is assumed to be typical for the subject's market area unless otherwise stated.

In the absence of an inspection, the appraiser has made some basic assumptions, including the following:
- The subject property is assumed to be in average overall condition and generally conforms to the neighborhood in terms of style, condition and construction materials.
- There are no adverse environmental conditions (hazardous wastes, toxic substances, etc.) present in the improvements, on the site, or in the immediate vicinity of the subject property.
- There are no significant discrepancies between the public record information or other data source and the existing site or improvements.

ANALYSIS OF ANY CURRENT AGREEMENT OF SALE, PRIOR SALE WITHIN THREE YEARS AND RECONCILIATION: Unless otherwise noted, the appraiser has no knowledge of any current agreement of sale nor any current or past listing agreement. Prior sales of the subject property within three years of the effective date of this appraisal have been researched and reported on the appraisal report (in the subject column) if available from public record sources. The appraiser has reconciled the quality and quantity of data available into an indication of Market Value, in accordance with the intended use and scope of the appraisal.

STATEMENT OF CONTINGENT AND LIMITING CONDITIONS: The Appraiser's Certification that appears in this report is subject to the following conditions:
1. The appraiser will not be responsible for matters of a legal nature that affect the subject property.
2. The appraiser assumes the title is good and marketable and, therefore, will not render any opinions about the title. The property is appraised on the basis of it being under responsible ownership.
3. The appraiser will not give testimony or appear in court because he or she performed this appraisal unless specific arrangements to do so have been made beforehand.
4. Except as noted herein, the appraiser has not made an exterior or interior inspection of the subject property. The appraiser assumes that there are no adverse conditions associated with the improvements or the subject site. Unless otherwise stated in this report, the appraiser has no knowledge of any hidden or apparent conditions of the property or adverse environmental conditions (including the presence of hazardous wastes, toxic substances, etc.) present in the improvements, on the site or in the immediate vicinity that would make property more or less valuable, and has assumed that there are no such conditions. The appraiser makes no guarantees or warranties, express or implied, regarding the condition of the property. The appraiser assumes that the improvements are in average condition. The appraiser will not be responsible for any such conditions that do exist or for any engineering or testing that might be required to discover whether such conditions exist. Because the appraiser is not an expert in the field of environmental hazards, the appraisal report may not be considered an environmental assessment of the property.
5. The appraiser obtained the information, estimates, and opinions that were expressed in the appraisal report from sources that he or she considers reliable and believes them to be true and correct. The appraiser does not assume responsibility for the accuracy of such items that were furnished by other parties.
6. The appraiser will not disclose the content of the appraisal report except as provided for in the Uniform Standards of Professional Appraisal Practice.

APPRAISER'S CERTIFICATION: The appraiser certifies, to the best of my knowledge and belief:
1. The statements of fact contained in this report are true and correct.
2. The reported analyses, opinions and conclusions are limited only by the reported assumptions and limiting conditions, and are my personal, impartial, and unbiased professional analyses, opinions and conclusions.
3. I have no present or prospective interest in the property that is the subject of this report, and no personal interest with respect to the parties involved.
4. I have no bias with respect to the property that is the subject of this report or to the parties involved with this assignment.
5. My engagement in this assignment was not contingent upon the development or reporting of predetermined results.
6. My compensation for completing this assignment is not contingent upon the development or reporting of a predetermined value or direction in value that favors the cause of the client, the amount of the value opinion, the attainment of a stipulated result, or the occurrence of a subsequent event directly related to the intended use of this appraisal.
7. My analyses, opinions and conclusions were developed, and this report has been prepared, in conformity with the Uniform Standards of Professional Appraisal Practice.
8. I have not made a personal inspection of the property that is the subject of this report, nor did I make inspections of the comparable sales.
9. No one provided significant professional assistance to the person signing this report, unless otherwise noted and acknowledged within this report.

APPRAISER:

Signature: _____

Name: Daniel M Christian

Company Name: ASAP Appraisals

Company Address: PO Box 3097

Torrance, CA 90510

Date of Report/Signature: 10/05/2004

State Certification #: AR007122

or State License #: _____

State: California

Expiration Date of Certification or License: 11/26/2004

ADDRESS OF PROPERTY APPRAISED:

4822 Mindora Drive

Torrance, CA 90505

APPRAISED VALUE OF THE SUBJECT PROPERTY: $ 660,000

EFFECTIVE DATE OF APPRAISAL: 10/06/2004

LENDER/CLIENT:

Name: John Joseph

Company Name: Professional Enterprises

Company Address: 1234 Any Street, Any City, CA 98765

SUPERVISORY APPRAISER (ONLY IF REQUIRED):

Signature: _____

Name: _____

Company Name: _____

Company Address: _____

Date of Report/Signature: _____

State Certification #: _____

or State License #: _____

State: _____

Expiration Date of Certification or License: _____

SUPERVISORY APPRAISER:

SUBJECT PROPERTY
- ☐ Did not inspect subject property
- ☐ Did inspect exterior of subject property from street
- ☐ Did inspect interior and exterior of subject property

COMPARABLE SALES
- ☐ Did not inspect exterior of comparable sales from street
- ☐ Did inspect exterior of comparable sales from street

USPAP COMPLIANCE ADDENDUM

File No.: Sample-Restricted

Borrower Smith		Order #	
Property Address 4822 Mindora Drive			
City Torrance	County Los Angeles	State CA	Zip Code 90505
Lender/Client Professional Enterprises		Client Reference #	

Only those items checked X apply to this report.

PURPOSE, FUNCTION AND INTENDED USE OF THE APPRAISAL

☒ The purpose of the appraisal is to provide an opinion of market value of the subject property as defined in this report, on behalf of the appraisal company facilitating the assignment for the referenced client as the intended user of the report. The only function of the appraisal is to assist the client mentioned in this report in evaluating the subject property for lending purposes. The use of this appraisal by anyone other than the stated intended user, or for any other use than the stated intended use, is prohibited.

☐ The purpose of the appraisal is to provide an opinion of market value of the subject property as defined in this report, on behalf of the appraisal company facilitating the assignment for the referenced client as the intended user of the report. The only function of the appraisal is to assist the client mentioned in this report in evaluating the subject property for Real Estate Owned (REO) purposes. The use of this appraisal by anyone other than the stated intended user, or for any other use than the stated intended use, is prohibited.

☐ The purpose of the appraisal is to _____ , on behalf of the appraisal company facilitating the assignment for the referenced client as the intended user of this report. The only function of the appraisal is to assist the client mentioned in this report in evaluating the subject property for _____ . The use of this appraisal by anyone other than the stated intended user, or for any other use than the stated intended use is prohibited.

TYPE OF APPRAISAL AND APPRAISAL REPORT

☐ This is a _____ Appraisal written in a _____ Report format and the USPAP Departure Rule has not been invoked.
☒ This is a Limited Appraisal written in a **Restricted** Report format and the USPAP Departure Rule has been invoked as disclosed in the body or addenda of the report. The client has agreed that a Limited Appraisal is sufficient for its purposes.

SCOPE (EXTENT) OF REPORT

☑ the appraisal is based on the information gathered by the appraiser from public records, other identified sources, inspection of the subject property and neighborhood, and selection of comparable sales, listings, and/or rentals within the subject market area. The original source of the comparables is shown in the Data Source section of the market grid along with the source of confirmation, if available. The original source is presented first. The sources and data are considered reliable. When conflicting information was provided, the source deemed most reliable has been used. Data believed to be unreliable was not included in the report nor used as a basis for the value conclusion. The extent of analysis applied to this assignment may be further imparted within the report, the Appraiser's Certification below and/or any other Statement of Limiting Conditions and Appraiser's Certification such as may be utilized within the Freddie Mac form 439 or Fannie Mae form 1004b (dated 6/93), when applicable.

MARKETING TIME AND EXPOSURE TIME FOR THE SUBJECT PROPERTY

☒ A reasonable marketing time for the subject property is **30-45** day(s) utilizing market conditions pertinent to the appraisal assignment
☒ A reasonable exposure time for the subject property is **1-30** day(s) utilizing market conditions pertinent to the appraisal assignment

APPRAISER'S CERTIFICATION

I certify that, to the best of my knowledge and belief:

- The statements of fact contained in this report are true and correct.
- The report analyses, opinions, and conclusions are limited only by the reported assumptions and limiting conditions, and are my personal, impartial, and unbiased professional analyses, opinions, and conclusions.
- I have no present or prospective interest in the property that is the subject of this report, and nor personal interest with respect to the parties involved, unless otherwise stated within the report.
- I have no bias with respect to the property that is the subject of this report or to the parties involved with this assignment
- My engagement in this assignment was not contingent upon developing or reporting predetermined results.
- My compensation for completing this assignment is not contingent upon the development or reporting of a predetermined value or direction in value that favors the cause of the client, the amount of the value opinion, the attainment of a stipulated result, or the occurrence of a subsequent event directly related to the intended use of this appraisal.
- My analyses, opinions, and conclusions were developed, and this report has been prepared, in conformity with the Uniform Standards of Professional Appraisal Practice.
- I have ☐ or have not ☒ made a personal inspection of the property that is the subject of this report. (If more than one person signs this report, this certification must clearly specify which individuals did and which individuals did not make a personal inspection of the appraisal property.)
- No one provided significant professional assistance to the person signing this report. (If there are exceptions, the name of each individual providing significant professional assistance must be stated.)

   NOTE: In the case of any conflict with a client provided certification (i.e., Fannie Mae or Freddie Mac), this revised certification shall take precedence

APPRAISER'S AND SUPERVISORY APPRAISER'S SIGNATURE

APPRAISER	SUPERVISORY-APPRAISER (only if required)
Signature:	Signature:
Name: Daniel M Christian	Name:
Date of Report (Inspection): 10/06/2004	Date of Report (Inspection):
State License/Certification #: AR007122	State License/Certification #:
State of License/Certification: California	State of License/Certification:
Expiration Date of License/Certification: 11/26/2004	Expiration Date of License/Certification:
	☐ Did inspect subject property ☐ Inspected Comparables
	☐ Interior & Exterior ☐ Interior & Exterior
	☐ Exterior only ☐ Exterior only

USPAP Compliance Addendum - 4/99

A.S.A.P. Real Estate Appraisals (310) 937-6151
Form FAUCA — "WinTOTAL" appraisal software by a la mode, inc. —- 1-800-ALAMODE

DESKTOP RESTRICTED USE APPRAISAL REPORT

ADDITIONAL COMPARABLES

FEATURE	SUBJECT	COMPARABLE # 4	COMPARABLE # 5	COMPARABLE # 6
Address	4822 Mindora Drive Torrance, CA 90505	5101 Laurette Street Torrance, CA	4808 Avenue B Torrance, CA	22419 Susana Avenue Torrance, CA
Proximity to Subject		0.39 miles	0.14 miles	0.52 miles
Sale Price	$	$ 660,000	$ 660,000	$ 725,000
Price/Gross Living Area		576.99	528.00	580.93
Date of Sale	N/A	05/17/2004	08/17/2004	08/25/2004
Location	Average	Average	Average	Average
Site/View	8,999/None	5,830/None	6,110/None	5,203/NOne
Design (Style)	Traditional	Traditional	Traditional	Traditional
Acutal Age (Yrs.)	1951	1955	1952	1952
Condition	Average	Average	Average	Average

Above Grade	Total	Bedrooms	Bath	Total	Bedrooms	Bath	Total	Bedrooms	Bath	Total	Bedrooms	Bath
Room Count	5	2	1	5	3	2	5	2	1	5	2	1.5

FEATURE	SUBJECT	COMPARABLE # 4	COMPARABLE # 5	COMPARABLE # 6
Gross Living Area	1,148 Sq. Ft.	1,162 Sq. Ft.	1,250 Sq. Ft.	1,248 Sq. Ft.
Basement	None	None	None	None
Air Conditioning	None	None	None	None
Garage/Carport	Garage-2	Garage-2	Garage-2	Garage-1
Porches, Patio, Pool	Cvrd. Porch/Cvrd. Patio	Cvrd. Porch/Cvrd. Patio	Porch, Patio. Pool	Cvrd. Porch/Cvrd. Patio
Amenities/Upgrades	None	None	None	None
Overall Comparison		☐ Sup. ☒ Similar ☐ Infer.	☐ Sup. ☒ Similar ☐ Infer.	☐ Sup. ☐ Similar ☒ Infer.

EVALUATION SUMMARY

Comments: Comparable sales #4, #5, and comparable listing #6 was provided as additional supportive data.

Plat Map

Borrower/Client	Smith			
Property Address	4822 Mindora Drive			
City	Torrance	County Los Angeles	State CA	Zip Code 90505
Lender	Professional Enterprises			

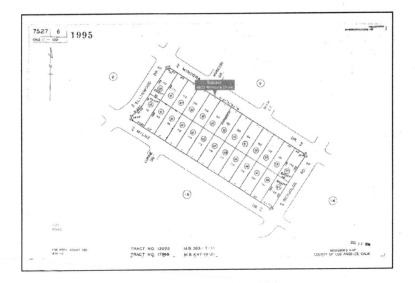

Location Map

Borrower/Client	Smith				
Property Address	4822 Mindora Drive				
City	Torrance	County Los Angeles		State CA	Zip Code 90505
Lender	Professional Enterprises				

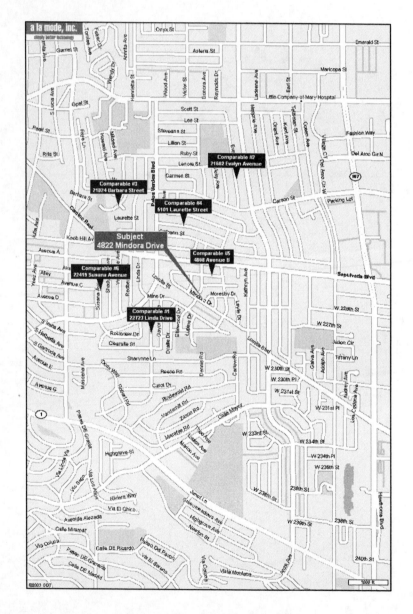

Form MAP.LOC — "WinTOTAL" appraisal software by a la mode, inc. — 1-800-ALAMODE

Subject Photos

Borrower/Client	Smith
Property Address	4822 Mindora Drive
City	Torrance
County	Los Angeles
State	CA
Zip Code	90505
Lender	Professional Enterprises

Subject Front
4822 Mindora Drive

Subject Rear

Subject Street

Comparable Photo Page

Borrower/Client	Smith			
Property Address	4822 Mindora Drive			
City	Torrance	County Los Angeles	State CA	Zip Code 90505
Lender	Professional Enterprises			

Comparable 1

22723 Linda Drive

Prox. to Subject	0.30 miles
Sale Price	652,000
Gross Living Area	1,064
Total Rooms	5
Total Bedrooms	3
Total Bathrooms	1
Location	Average
View	5,100/None
Site	
Quality	
Age	1952

Comparable 2

21602 Evalyn Avenue

Prox. to Subject	0.60 miles
Sale Price	679,000
Gross Living Area	1,175
Total Rooms	5
Total Bedrooms	3
Total Bathrooms	2
Location	Average
View	5,300/None
Site	
Quality	
Age	1955

Comparable 3

21824 Barbara Street

Prox. to Subject	0.63 miles
Sale Price	670,000
Gross Living Area	1,175
Total Rooms	5
Total Bedrooms	3
Total Bathrooms	2
Location	Average
View	7,730/None
Site	
Quality	
Age	1955

Comparable Photo Page

Borrower/Client	Smith						
Property Address	4822 Mindora Drive						
City	Torrance		County	Los Angeles	State	CA	Zip Code	90505
Lender	Professional Enterprises						

Comparable 4
5101 Laurette Street

Comparable 5
4808 Avenue B

NO PHOTO AVAILABLE

Comparable 6
22419 Susana Avenue

Form PIC3x5.BC — "WinTOTAL" appraisal software by a la mode, inc. — 1-800-ALAMODE

Reprinted with permission from:

Daniel M. Christian

State Certified Appraiser

ASAP Appraisals of Southern California

PO Box 3097

Torrance, CA 90510

Office: 310-937-6151

Fax: 310-937-6150

E-mail: daniel@asaprea.com

Website: www.asaprea.com

Appendix B: Calculations

SIMPLE INTEREST

Simple interest is calculated based only on the original principal amount.

The formula for calculating simple interest is:

$$\text{Interest} = \text{Principal} \times \text{Rate} \times \text{Time}$$

Be sure to state the rate and the time in the same way. In other words, if you are charging 14 percent per year, then you also have to list your time in years.

Here is an example:

You lend $100,000 at 14 percent interest per year for two years. To find out how much interest you will earn, plug the numbers into the formula:

$$\$100,000 \times 0.14 \times 2 = \$28,000$$

Now, look at the same $100,000 at 14 percent for six months. Remember, you will have to state the rate and time in the same terms so six months will become 0.5 years:

$$\$100,000 \times 0.14 \times 0.5 = \$7,000$$

COMPOUND INTEREST

How can you figure out how much money you will have (FV) in (n) years if you invest (x) dollars at (i) percent interest rate?

Here is the formula:

$$FV = x\,(1 + i)\,^{\wedge}n.$$

In other words, the future value (FV) of your money equals the initial amount invested times one plus the interest rate raised to the number of time periods invested.

For example, if you put $1,000 into a bond at 8 percent interest for 30 years, then the amount of money you would receive would be $1,000 times 1.08 to the 30th power. Mathematically, it looks like this:

$$FV = \$1,000 \times (1 + .08)\,^{\wedge}30$$

Thus, your bond would yield $10,062.66 in 30 years.

CASH FLOW

Cash flow is all of the property's money coming in minus all of the money going back out. It is like thinking about your property in terms of a checkbook. All the inflows are like deposits, and all the outflows are like checks or debits.

Inflows include rental income and other income plus vacancy and credit allowance.

Outflows include insurance, taxes, repairs and maintenance, supplies, utilities, and other debits.

Cash Flow	
Date:	
Prepared By:	
INCOME	
Gross Scheduled Rent Income	
Other Income	
TOTAL GROSS INCOME	
VACANCY & CREDIT ALLOWANCE	
GROSS OPERATING INCOME	
EXPENSES	
Insurance (Fire & Liability)	
Property Taxes	
Repairs & Maintenance	
Supplies & Miscellaneous	
Utilities	
Other	
TOTAL EXPENSES	
NET OPERATING INCOME	
Less Annual Debt Service, First Mortgage	
Less Annual Debt Service, Second Mortgage	
Less Capital Additions	
Plus Loan Proceeds	
Plus Interest Earned	
CASH FLOW BEFORE TAXES	
Less Income Tax Liability	
CASH FLOW AFTER TAXES	

LOAN-TO-VALUE RATIO

The loan-to-value ratio is the ratio between the financed amount and the property's value. It is expressed as a percentage.

Loan-to-Value Ratio = Loan Amount/Property's Appraised Value

Now, look at an example:

You loan $65,000 on a piece of property with an appraised value of $100,000. In this case, the LTV ratio is $65,000 divided by $100,000, or 65 percent.

Appendix C: Glossary

A

Abandonment - The relinquishing of a property by an owner or renter who leaves without passing ownership or tenancy rights to anyone else.

Abatement - A lowering of rent fees or another reduction benefiting the tenant, such as free rent, early move in, or removal of a harmful substance like asbestos.

Abnormal sale - A house or property sells for more or less than its current market value — for instance, 25 percent less than comparable homes nearby.

Absentee owner - Someone who owns a property without managing it or living on-site.

Absorption rate - How quickly homes sell or rental spaces gain occupants. Calculate this percentage by dividing the total number of homes or square feet of rental space in an area by the number purchased or filled during a given time.

Abstract of title - The summarized history of a piece of real estate that describes each time the property changed hands and notes all encumbrances that have lessened its value or use. This document is certified as complete and truthful by the abstractor.

Abut - To be adjacent. A property can abut — border — landmarks, such as roads and easements. When one property meets or joins another, the line between is an abutment.

Acceleration clause - Part of a rental contract saying a lender can insist that a borrower pay the balance of the loan right away under certain circumstances. A lender might invoke this clause if the renter defaults on the loan or seriously delays payments.

Acceptance - Completion of a sales contract, when someone offers to buy a property under specific terms and the owner accepts.

Accessory building - A building that serves a different function from the main building on a lot. Accessory buildings include garages, but they do not include separate structures for commercial use.

Accord and satisfaction - An agreement settling a debt where a creditor considers the debt repaid after accepting a different or smaller compensation than the debtor originally promised.

Accrued depreciation (accumulated depreciation) - The current sum of all depreciation expenses.

Accrued items, active - Expenses paid early for things in the next business year. For example, people can prepay rent for buildings they will occupy the following year.

Accrued items, passive - Expenses incurred that cannot be paid yet, such as taxes on real estate and interest on loans.

Acknowledgment - When someone formally declares they have signed a document before a notary public or another appropriately authorized person.

Acquisition appraisal - A government agency determines how much to pay a property owner after acquiring their property via negotiation or condemnation.

Acquisition cost - The total price someone pays for a property with all fees added in.

Acreage zoning (large-lot or "snob" zoning) - Zoning calling for large lots, meant to make commercial or residential areas less dense.

Act of God - In contracts, a natural disaster humans cannot control, such as an earthquake, severe storm, or flood. Contracts can include provisions relieving all those involved from obligation when such a disaster strikes a property.

Actual cash value - The cash value of an improvement for insurance purposes. It equals the cost of replacing something minus the wear and tear.

Actual damages (and special damages) - Actual damages are legally determined costs for repairing something wrongfully harmed or destroyed. Special damages include indirect effects of the property destruction, such as lessened income to a business in a damaged building.

Ad valor - Latin for "according to value." It is a tax based on the value of a property, particularly as determined by a local government.

ADC loan - The letters stand for acquisition, development, and construction. Developers use ADC loans to buy property, install utilities and roads, and erect buildings.

Addendum - An amendment or revision to a contract both parties consent to and sign.

Addition - Making a building larger through further construction; additions do not include improvements like finishing unfinished rooms.

Adjudication - A decision made in court.

Adjustable-Rate Mortgage (ARM) - Unlike a fixed-rate loan, this home loan has a changing interest rate, which fluctuates to stay current with rates of mortgage loans. It can also change with indexes of the government or financial market.

Adjustment date - The day in which the interest rate changes for an adjustable-rate mortgage.

Adjustment period - The time between changes in interest rates for an adjustable-rate mortgage.

Advance fee - Money clients pay before receiving services. Real estate agents can charge homeowners an advance fee to foot advertising bills while selling the property.

Adverse financial change condition - A provision that lets a lender cancel a loan agreement if the borrower loses his job or has other serious financial troubles.

Adverse possession - Blatantly and aggressively occupying another person's land and claiming entitlement without permission from the owner. Adverse possession does not include leasing property with an owner's consent or occupying property of unknown ownership.

Adviser - An investment banker or a broker representing a property owner during a real estate transaction. The adviser collects a fee when transaction or financing ends.

Aesthetic value - Value given to a property by its physical beauty.

Affidavit of title - A statement written under oath by a real estate grantor or seller and recognized by a notary public where the person gives his identity, confirms the title has not changed for the worse since last examined, and officially declares he possesses the property (if appropriate).

Affirmation - When someone has religious or other objections to giving oaths, an affirmation is a way to declare a statement is true without swearing an oath.

Affordability index - A measure designed by the National Association of Realtors® to describe how affordable houses are for residents buying in a given area.

Affordable housing - Public or private programs helping low-income people afford houses. These efforts can provide low-interest home loans, smaller down payments, and less demanding credit terms.

Agency - A relationship in which principal brokers — leaders of brokerage firms — allow agents to represent them in specific transactions.

Agency disclosure - An agreement required by most states where real estate agents who serve sellers and buyers must disclose who they represent.

Agent - Someone who acts on another's behalf under the law of agency. Property owners authorize licensed real estate brokers to be their agents.

Agreement of sale - A legal document giving the terms and price of a property sale, which both parties sign.

Alienation - Property going to a new owner by sale, gift, adverse possession, or eminent domain.

Alienation clause - Found in a deed of trust or a mortgage, this clause prevents the borrower from selling the property — and transferring the associated debt — to another person without the lender's permission. If the borrower sells, the lender can immediately demand full repayment of the debt.

Alluvion - Soil deposit that builds up on a property that is then considered the owner's possession.

Amenities - Advantages to owning a property not related to money or features that make it more desirable.

Americans with Disabilities Act (ADA) - Designed to ensure that disabled people have equal access to public accommodations and transportation, jobs, telecommunications, and government services. The ADA covers the design of public buildings.

Amortization - Paying off a debt and its interest in gradual installments.

Amortization schedule - A charted timetable for paying off a loan, showing how much of each payment goes toward interest and toward the debt itself.

Amortization term - Amount of time needed to pay off (amortize) a loan.

Anchor tenant - The person or business that draws the most visitors to a commercial property, for instance, a supermarket, among other stores.

Annexation - Occurs when a city expands its borders to encompass a certain area. Most states require public approval first, demonstrated by holding votes in the city and the area it will annex. Annexation also denotes personal property becoming part of real property.

Annual debt service - The yearly payments a person must make on a loan, comprising the principal and interest added over 12 months.

Annual percentage rate (APR) - The actual interest rate of a loan for a year, which might be higher than the rate advertised. It must be disclosed, in accordance with the Truth in Lending Act.

Appointments - Items in a building that may enhance or lessen how valuable or functional the property is. Examples include furniture, equipment, and fixtures.

Apportionment - Dividing yearly costs associated with a property between the seller and the buyer. Each party pays expenses like insurance or taxes for the portion of the year they owned the property.

Appraisal report - The report an appraiser writes while describing a property's value and summarizing how it was determined.

Appraised value - The monetary value of a property given in an appraisal report.

Appreciation - The process in which a home or property gains value, stemming from several factors, including additions to the building, changes in financial markets, and inflation.

Appropriation - Reserving land for public access, which might be required before development projects can progress.

Appurtenance - A privilege, right, or benefit tied to a piece of land without being physically part of the property. One example is the right to access someone else's land.

Appurtenant easement - The right, belonging to a parcel's owner, to use a neighbor's property.

Arbitration - When two parties use an impartial third entity to resolve a dispute instead of going to court. Real estate contracts can require arbitration, preventing lawsuits.

ARM (adjustable-rate mortgage) index - An openly published number that guides how adjustable-rate mortgages change.

Arm's length transaction - A deal in which each party protects its own interests above all.

Arrears - A payment made "in arrears" is given at the end of a month or other term. Late or defaulted payments can also be described as in arrears.

"As is" condition - A term in real estate contracts meaning the buyer or renter accepts the property and its flaws just as they are, giving up the right to insist on repairs or renovations.

Asbestos - A mineral, formerly common in insulation and other building materials, now prohibited because it is known to cause lung disease.

Asbestos-containing materials (ACM) - Materials made from asbestos that, since the early 1980s, have been prohibited because of their links to health hazards.

As-built drawings - Illustrations showing exactly how a building was constructed, including alterations to the original plans and the position of utilities and equipment.

Asking (advertised) price - The amount a property owner hopes a buyer will pay, which may change with negotiation.

Assessed value - The value a tax assessor determines a home to have, which can be used for computing a tax base.

Assessor - A public official responsible for valuing properties for tax purposes.

Asset - A valuable possession or property.

Assignment - Handing over the responsibilities and rights associated with a property to another, as a landlord does to a paying tenant. If that recipient fails to pay, the original party absorbs the debt.

Assignment of lease - Passing off the rights to use a leased property from one renter to another. For instance, a person who occupies an apartment for part of the year may recruit someone else to live there when they are gone.

Assignment of rents - A contract saying a tenant's rent payments will go to the owner's mortgage lender if the owner defaults.

Assignor - Someone who passes a property's interests and rights to a new recipient.

Associate broker (broker-associates, affiliate brokers, or broker-salespersons) - A real estate broker supervised by another broker. This manager holds the associate broker's license.

Association of unit owners - An organization of condominium owners who oversee the property where they live.

Assumable mortgage - A mortgage loan that can be shifted from one borrower to another.

Assumption - The purchase of another's mortgage.

Assumption clause - Part of the contract drawn when a mortgage changes hands — it makes the party buying the mortgage loan responsible for it.

Assumption fee - Money one must pay when buying another's mortgage to cover costs for processing the paperwork.

Attachment - A person's possessions that legal authorities seize when the person fails to pay a debt. For example, landlords attach items their tenants own to unpaid rent.

Attest - To observe an event and sign a document certifying that you witnessed it.

Attic - Space between the top story's ceiling and the roof that people can access. Conversely, a structural cavity is a similar space that people cannot enter.

Attorney-in-fact - Someone who can legally act on another's behalf, which can grant them the right to sell the other party's property.

Attorney's opinion of title - A summarized history of a piece of real estate that an attorney has scrutinized and declared valid, in his opinion.

Attornment - A legal agreement in which tenants formally accept a new landlord by signing a letter of attornment.

Auction - Selling personal property or land to the highest bidder, which states can do with foreclosed property. Bidders can make public or private offers, in writing or speech.

Auctioneer - A licensed person who carries out auctions of real estate or other property.

Authorization to sell - A contract licensing a real estate agent to sell one's property. The agent can advertise the property and collect a fee for selling it but cannot make the final agreement to sell.

Automated underwriting - Computer systems that allow lenders to approve loans faster and reduce the costs of lending.

Automatic extension - A clause found in a listing agreement saying that an agreement between a property owner and a real estate broker will persist after it expires, for a specified time.

Average occupancy - The percentage of time a property was occupied in the last year.

B

Backup offer - When a second buyer offers to purchase or lease property if the current buyer cannot follow through.

Balance - Unpaid debt. Appraisers also use balance to describe a situation when a property's improvements are proportional to the land and to each other, making the property's value peak.

Balance sheet - A list of someone's net worth, assets, and liabilities.

Balloon loan - A mortgage with monthly payments followed by a large final payment, which covers the remaining debt.

Balloon payment - The large, final payment in a balloon mortgage loan, which covers the debt not paid in earlier installments.

Bankruptcy - When someone cannot pay his or her debts on time. Declaring bankruptcy may lead to court decisions to ease or obliterate debts.

Bargain and sale deed - Gives the grantor the right to convey title without making warranties against encumbrances or liens, but the grantor can attach warranties if desired. *See definitions of "lien"* *and "encumbrance" for further information.*

Base loan amount - Sum of money forming the basic payments on a loan.

Base principal balance - Version of the original loan sum adjusted based on principal payments and later funding. It excludes other unsettled debts and accumulated interest.

Basis point - A term financial markets use to mean 1/100 of a percent.

Below grade - A building or part existing below the ground surface.

Benchmark - A permanent mark carefully measured to show height, which surveyors use to begin their surveys or measure the elevation of a site.

Beneficiary - Someone who gets or is entitled to benefits, such as a person receiving income from a trust fund. A beneficiary can also be the lender of a deed of trust loan.

Bequeath - To leave possessions to certain recipients in one's will. For passing on real estate in a will, use the term "devise."

Bill of sale - A document that legally transfers personal property — not real estate title — to a new owner.

Binder - An agreement signifying that a buyer wants to join a real estate contract. The buyer might also make a payment to show earnest desire and ability to purchase the property

Biweekly mortgage - A plan to make payments on a mortgage every two weeks. When debtors pay half the monthly fee every two weeks, they end up supplying 13 months' payment over a year, settling the debt faster.

Blanket loan - A mortgage that covers multiple pieces of real estate but partially frees each parcel from the mortgage lien when certain fractions of the debt are repaid.

Blighted areas - Part of a city or other area where the buildings are rundown or in need of repair.

Blueprint - Working set of thorough guidelines for a construction project.

Board of Realtors® - Licensed real estate professionals belonging to the state and National Association of Realtors®.

Bona fide - Considered free from fraud, such as a contract verified by a notary public.

Book value - A property's worth as determined by its purchase price and upgrades or additions minus any depreciation. Corporations use it to indicate their properties' values.

Boundary - The border around a property.

Branch office - An outlying arm of a real estate business, separate from the main office, where licensed brokers work on behalf of the headquarters.

Breach of contract - Breaking terms of a contract in a legally inexcusable way.

Bridge loan (gap loan, swing loan, or interim financing) - A short-term loan taken out between mortgages or used by those still looking for a more enduring loan. It can be useful for buildings under construction.

Broker - A person paid to liaise between sellers and buyers.

Brokerage - A group or corporation of brokers. Also means the broker industry.

Brownfield - A property where people once used hazardous substances, such as a vacant gas station or closed factory.

Brownstone - A row house adjoining other buildings that stands three to five stories tall.

Buffer zone - A piece of land separating two properties with different purposes. Buffer zones are parks or are used in similar ways.

Build-out - Upgrades made to real estate following a tenant's orders.

Build to suit - When a landowner pays to construct a building suited to a tenant's needs, and then the tenant leases it. Build to suit is used for tenants who want to do business in a specific type of building without owning the building.

Buildable acres - A proportion of land that buildings can occupy, which takes into consideration the amount of space that will go to roads, open areas, setbacks, or spots not suitable for construction.

Building code - Local laws describing how people can use a given property, including what types of construction, building materials, and improvements are legal.

Building line (setback) - A border set a certain distance from a lot's sides, showing where people may not construct buildings.

Building permit - A document giving permission to build, alter, or demolish improvements to buildings, while following zoning laws and building codes.

Building restrictions - Specifications as to sizes, locations, and appearances a building can legally have as part of a building code.

Building standards - Themes the developer or owner of a building uses in its construction, such as certain types of windows or doors.

Bulk sale - When a buyer purchases an entire group of real estate assets in different locations.

Buy-back agreement - A contract term stating that the seller will purchase a property back if certain events happen.

Buy-down mortgage - A home loan in which the seller or builder pays a lender to lower mortgage payments for the party who bought the property.

Buyer's agent - A real estate agent that acts on behalf of someone looking to purchase property and owes that party common-law or statutory agency duties.

Buyer's broker - A broker who represents someone looking to buy residential real estate and owes that party common-law or statutory agency duties, as a buyer's agent does.

Buyers' market - A situation where buyers can be choosy about real estate and shrewd about pricing because there are more properties than buyers. This can happen when economies are slow, when too many buildings are constructed, or when population numbers fall.

C

Cancellation clause - A contract term stating that, if certain things happen, the contract becomes void. For instance, if someone sells property he has been renting out, this clause cancels the lease.

Cap - Prevents the interest rate on an adjustable-rate mortgage from growing past a certain amount. It guards the borrower against skyrocketing monthly payments.

Capital - To a real estate agent, capital means cash or the capacity to exchange assets for money.

Capital appreciation - Growth in a property's value once partial sales and capital improvements are accounted for. It differs from a capital gain, which one receives by selling the property.

Capital gain - Extra money gained when someone sells a property for more than they paid to buy it.

Capital improvements - Bouts of spending that improve or preserve a property, such as adding useful buildings.

Carryback financing - A seller helps a buyer finance the purchase of a property.

Cash flow - How much income an investment pays minus expenses. Cash flow is negative if expenses are larger than the income.

Cashier's check - Preferable for real estate deals, a cashier's check guarantees the recipient gets paid, pulling money directly from the bank instead of someone's account.

Cash-out refinance - Refinancing a mortgage for more money than it originally covered to get extra money for personal use.

Caveat emptor - "Let the buyer beware" in Latin. The buyer purchases property at his own risk, shouldering the responsibility of examining it for defects.

Certificate of completion - Paperwork an engineer or architect issues saying a construction project is complete, meeting the terms in its blueprint. Signing this document can signal that a buyer must now make the final payment.

Certificate of insurance - A document issued by insurance companies that confirms a certain individual is covered.

Certificate of occupancy (CO) - A document stating that a structure complies with health requirements and building codes. These certificates come from building agencies or local governments.

Certificate of sale - A document one receives when purchasing a building foreclosed for tax reasons. It proves the buyer paid the necessary taxes for the redemption period and claimed the property title afterward.

Certificate of title - After an attorney scrutinizes public records, the certificate of title is the attorney's official opinion on who owns the title to a property or other aspects of its status.

Certified check - Draws on money in a bank customer's account, not the bank's own funds — unlike a cashier's check. These less-secure checks are prohibited in certain real estate transactions.

Chain of title - All the times a title has moved from owner to owner, until the present. Attorneys use this history to evaluate the title's status.

Chattel - Tangible, personal property, such as jewelry or clothes.

Circulation factor - Space allowing internal circulation in an office — not part of net square footage.

Class "A" - High-quality or nicely located property that will bring in a great deal of rent money.

Class "B" - Desirable property that falls short of bringing in the highest rent price possible.

Class "C" - Low-rent property with acceptable living conditions but sparse amenities.

Clear title - A title free from potential problems or hassles, such as legal encumbrances, defects, and liens.

Clearance letter - The written results of a termite inspection, provided by a licensed inspector. Mortgages backed by the Department of Veterans Affairs or Federal Housing Administration, along with certain other home loans, cannot progress without this letter.

Closing - The end of a sale, where a buyer pays the seller, when both parties or their representatives sign necessary documents, and the buyer receives the title and loan.

Closing costs - Money spent when closing a real estate deal, including fees for appraising property and for the loan and title but not the actual property.

Closing statement (HUD-1 Settlement Statement) - A thorough account of how people spent, gained, and loaned money or started loans when parties buy and sell real estate.

Cloud on title - Any circumstance or document making it uncertain who holds the title to real estate. Sometimes hard to remove, clouds on title may be cleared up by a suit to quiet title or a quitclaim deed, after a title search reveals the cloud.

Cluster housing - Closely grouped homes with tiny yards where residents share a common recreation spot.

Co-borrower - *See "co-signer."*

Collateral - Something a borrower stands to lose by not paying a debt. The property is collateral in the mortgage loan financing its purchase.

Collection - When a borrower does not repay a debt, the lender seeks payment and prepares for a possible foreclosure, sending notices to the borrower.

Commercial leasehold insurance - Insurance that pays rent if a tenant cannot — Lenders might require businesses in shopping centers to carry this insurance.

Commercial mortgage - Money loaned for businesses to buy their properties or buildings.

Commercial mortgage broker - A broker who specializes in brokering mortgages for businesses.

Commercial mortgage lender - A lender who specifically funds mortgage loans for commercial uses.

Commercial property - Property slated for businesses, not homes or residential buildings.

Commingling - A real estate agent who illegally mixes his or her own money and a client's in one account, instead of keeping the customer's funds in an escrow or trust account.

Commission - Money clients pay brokers for selling or buying property, consisting of a certain percent of the property's price.

Commitment fee - Those applying for loans pay this price to lenders, and the lenders agree to follow certain terms on a loan.

Common area assessments (homeowners association fees) - Money condominium owners or planned unit development (PUD) residents give their homeowners association, which then spends it to maintain the building or property.

Common area maintenance (CAM) - Fees tenants pay beyond their rent for the upkeep of common facilities, such as parking lots and halls.

Common areas - Used by all condominium residents or unit owners in planned unit developments (PUDs). These spaces are maintained by homeowners associations using residents' money.

Common (or party) wall - A wall that separates units in a duplex, condominium, or similar building.

Community property - Property purchased by a married couple and, in certain states, owned by both people.

Comparable sales (comparables or comps) - The price similar properties nearby sold for — sellers assume another such property in that area will fetch a comparable price.

Comparative unit method - A way to appraise properties by examining them in chunks of a certain size, such as square feet or acres.

Competent party - A person who can legally partake in a contract because the individual is old enough, mentally stable, and not influenced by drugs or alcohol.

Competitive market analysis (CMA) - Comparing the price on a seller's home to costs of other houses sold recently that have similar amenities, styles, and locations.

Completion bond - Legal guarantee that a project will be finished as specified.

Compound interest - Additional interest one pays for his or her mortgage besides the accrued interest.

Concessions - Money or other benefits landlords give tenants to encourage them to sign leases.

Condemnation - When the government seizes private property without permission from its owner and renders it public through eminent domain.

Conditional commitment - A lender's pledge to loan money if the borrower satisfies specific terms.

Conditional sale - A real estate contract stating the seller owns the property until the buyer fulfills all the contract's conditions.

Condominium - A building where the many residents jointly own common areas and hold titles to private living spaces called units.

Condominium conversion - When a rental property changes from one form of ownership to become a condominium.

Condominium hotel - A condominium that works as a commercial hotel, where people live for short periods, use a registration desk, and have cleaning, food, and telephone services, but tenants own their living units.

Condominium owners association - A group of people who own units in a condominium, manage its common spaces, and enforce its rules.

Conforming loan - A mortgage that Freddie Mac or Fannie Mae finds acceptable to purchase.

Construction documents - Illustrations and notes an engineer or architect makes to specify how a construction project will proceed and what materials it requires.

Construction to permanent loan - A loan to finance construction that can, in some instances, later transform into a mortgage.

Consumer price index (CPI) - A way to measure inflation based on the prices of things specific populations purchase over certain times.

Contiguous space - Divided spaces over one floor or connecting floors that can combine so a tenant in the building can rent them all simultaneously.

Contingency - Circumstances that must exist for a contract to bind the parties. If a contract is contingent on something that never happens, parties are free from it.

Contour map - Displays the physical features of a site — topography — using contour lines for different elevations.

Contract - Legal document binding one or both parties involved to fulfill their promises. If a party breaks its promise in the contract, there is a legal remedy.

Contract for deed/land contract - A contract in which a party pays for property in installments. The buyer can live on the property and use it but does not own the title before paying the full price in monthly fees.

Contract for sale - *See "purchase agreement."*

Controlled business arrangement - A situation where consumers are offered a bundle of services, such as real estate agents' aid, mortgage brokerage, and home inspection.

Conventional loan - A borrower uses this long-term loan from a non-government lender to buy a house. Conventional loans include fixed-term and fixed-rate mortgages but not loans backed by the Federal Housing Administration or Department of Veterans Affairs.

Conversion - Assigning property a new use or type of ownership — changing a large house into an apartment complex, for instance.

Conveyance - The document stating that a title passes to a new owner. Conveyance also means transference of titles between parties ("closing").

Cooling-off period - Time when parties can legally abandon a contract and not be bound.

According to the Truth in Lending Act, a cooling-off period is mandatory for contracts involving private residences.

Cooperative (co-op) - A complex made of residents who own shares in a corporation, which owns the property. Each resident has rights to one unit in the building.

Co-ownership - When two or more people own a title.

Corporation - Legally considered a single body, registered by the secretary of state. Some features of corporations include unending life, shares that can be traded, central leadership, and limits on their liabilities.

Co-signer - Someone who agrees to pay a debt if the borrower cannot. This party or person signs the loan agreement or promissory note alongside the borrower but does not own the title or appear on the deed.

Cost approach appraisal - Approximating a property's value by adding the land's worth to the cost an appraiser says one would pay to replace the building minus depreciation — this approach does not use prices of nearby homes to estimate a building's value.

Cost approach land value - The value basic interest in land would carry if the land could be developed to its ideal usage.

Cost of living index - Numbers showing how much certain basic commodities cost compared to their prices in a baseline year — how these goods and services have become cheaper or pricier.

Counteroffer - When someone makes an offer and the recipient makes a new offer back, refusing the original.

Courier fee - Cost for delivering documents to all those involved in a real estate deal, which they pay when the transaction closes.

Courtesy to brokers - Act of splitting pay between cooperating brokers and listing brokers.

Covenant - An agreement binding at least two parties that promise to act certain ways toward a property — a covenant appears in documents like leases, deed contracts, and mortgages.

Covenant not to compete
(noncompete clause or noncompete
covenant) - One party promises in
writing not to make or distribute
the same products as the other
party within a certain area.

Creative financing - A
non-traditional mortgage from
a third-party lender, such as a
balloon payment.

Credit - Borrowing money to
purchase something valuable
and agreeing to repay the lender
afterward.

Credit history - A record of
someone's debts, past and present,
and how reliably the person settled
them.

Credit rating - A number
describing how much someone
deserves a loan, determined from
their current finances and credit
history.

Credit report - A record of
someone's prior residences, jobs,
and credit — used to determine
if the person is worthy of further
credit.

Credit score (credit risk score
or FICO score) - A calculated
summary of the data on someone's
credit report.

Creditor - A party owed money.

Curb appeal - A property or
home's good looks, as noted by
viewers on its street.

D

Damages - Amount of money
someone gets through legal means
because someone harmed them
in any fashion — this includes
damaging an owner's building.

DBA - Abbreviation for "Doing
Business As." Used to note
someone's invented business name
or trade name but not meant to
deceive clients.

Debt service - Total money one
needs to pay all the principal and
interest of a loan for a certain
amount of time.

Debt-to-equity ratio - How much
unpaid mortgage a property has
compared with its equity. The
ratio would be 1:2 if a property
had $100,000 of unpaid debt and
$50,000 of equity.

Debt-to-income ratio - What percent of monthly income someone spends repaying a debt — to calculate, divide the monthly money paid toward the debt by that month's gross income.

Declaration of restrictions - Rules people must follow if they live in a given condominium or subdivision.

Decree - A government- or court-issued order.

Deed - A document that legally transfers property to a new owner who receives the deed after negotiating with and paying the seller.

Deed in lieu of foreclosure - Returning one's property to a lender without foreclosure proceedings to avoid their negative effects and costs.

Deed of trust – An agreement between a lender and a borrower that transfers ownership in the property being sold to a neutral third party until the loan has been paid off.

Deed restrictions - Restrictions given in a deed on how property can be used. They can limit what kind of new structures people can build there or what activities or objects are allowed on the property.

Default - When a borrower fails to pay their mortgage or perform some other obligatory duty.

Deferred maintenance - Appraisers using this term refer to property defects the owner has not repaired, such as chipped paint or broken windows.

Deferred payment method - A strategy of delaying the date when someone will begin repaying a loan.

Deficiency judgment - A borrower is charged with a deficiency judgment when his property is foreclosed but selling it does not produce enough money to cover the remaining unpaid mortgage.

Delayed exchange - A party trades property for a second piece of real estate but does not receive it right away. This delay lets that party defer all taxable gains on the first piece of property.

Delinquency - A situation when a borrower misses mortgage payments. If continued, it brings foreclosure.

Delivery - Passing possession of an individual's real estate or other property to a different person.

Demand loan - A loan where lenders can call for buyers to fully repay them for whatever reason, any time.

Demising wall - A wall that separates a tenant's unit from a hall, other common area, or another tenant's living space.

Density - How concentrated the buildings are in a certain spot — buildings per unit area.

Density zoning - Zoning ordinances that limit the number of houses each acre of land can contain, on average, for a certain area.

Department of Housing and Urban Development (HUD) - A government agency that works to provide clean and safe living spaces without discrimination — it executes plans for community development and federal housing.

Deposit (earnest money) - Money one pays when offering to buy a property.

Depreciation - Appraisers use this term to refer to the depreciating value of a property because it grows old, obsolete, or has other defects. For real estate investors, this term means a tax deduction taken while owning income property.

Description - *See "land description."*

Designated agent - A person who holds a real estate license and has authority to be another's agent, backed by a broker.

Design-build - Situation in which one person manages the construction and design of a building. *Also see "build to suit."*

Development loan (construction loan) - Borrowed funds to buy real estate, prepare it for construction, and erect buildings.

Devise - Act of awarding someone real estate through a will — the devisor, or donor, leaves the property to the devisee.

Direct sales comparisons approach (market comparison approach) - An appraiser places a value on property by examining the prices on recently purchased estates nearby with similar qualities.

Disbursement - Money someone loans, invests, or otherwise pays out.

Discharge in bankruptcy - Occurs when a bankrupt party is freed from the debts they were assigned during bankruptcy proceedings.

Disclosure - A document listing all the relevant positive and negative information about a piece of real estate.

Discount broker - A broker whose fees are lower than most — these costs might be a flat rate instead of a percentage of the sale.

Discount points - Fees the lender can charge in exchange for offering lower interest rates than typical loan payments. Discount points represent percentages of the loan, with one point equaling one percent of the loaned money.

Dry closing - Both parties have made their agreement but have not exchanged money or documents. The escrow will finish the closing.

Dry mortgage (nonrecourse loan) - A mortgage for which the borrower pledges property for collateral but stands to lose nothing else to the lender and is not personally liable.

Due diligence - Actions by someone looking to purchase real estate — checking the property for defects or hazards and verifying a seller represents it.

Due on sale clause - A mortgage provision stating that, if the borrower sells the property the loan covers, they must immediately pay the lender the rest of the mortgage debt.

Duress - Circumstance where someone is illegally coerced or threatened to act unwillingly. If someone joins a contract under duress, it can be canceled.

E

Earnest money - Money a buyer deposits under a contract and loses if he backs out of purchasing the property — but if he buys the real estate, the money goes toward that sale.

Easement - A party's right to use a portion of a property it does not own for defined purposes, such as accommodating telephone or power lines.

Easement in gross - An easement tied personally to its owner, not meant to benefit any of the owner's land. One example involves someone granting another person rights to access part of his property for life.

Economic life - The number of years an improvement will continue giving property value.

Economic obsolescence (environmental or external obsolescence) - Decrease in a property's value as changes to surrounding areas render it obsolete or less desirable.

Effective gross income - How much gross income a property can bring in after subtracting an allowance for vacancy and collection.

Effective age - An assessment of a building's condition an appraiser presents.

Effective date - The date when securities can initiate, once a registration statement takes effect.

Efficiency unit - A small, one-room living space in a building housing several families — these units might lack full bathroom and kitchen facilities.

Egress - A way to exit a property via a public road or another means.

Elevation drawing - An illustration showing property from the front, side, or back to demonstrate how it is situated without including perspective.

Eminent domain - The ability for the government to buy property at market price and render it public.

Encroachment - Part of a building or other structure illegally intruding on another's land, alley, or street — encroachment includes any upgrade or improvement extending onto someone else's lot unlawfully.

Encumbrance - Anything that diminishes a property's worth or makes it less useful or enjoyable. Examples include taxes, mortgages, easements, judgment liens, and rules restricting how the property is used.

Endorsement - Signing the back of a check one pays. Also, endorsement means supporting a statement or making it more credible.

Entitlement - Being owed something with legal backing.

Entity - A legally recognized corporation or person.

Environmental audit - Examination of a property for hazards.

Environmental Impact Statement - A document stating the negative effects of a major project on the environment, as required by law.

Environmental Protection Agency (EPA) - A federal agency that works to prevent pollution and enforces national laws against it.

Equalization factor - A number by which one multiplies a property's value to align it with state tax assessments. This adjusted value provides a basis for the ad valorem tax.

Equity - A property's value minus its liabilities, such as unpaid debts

Equity buildup - Equity that accumulates gradually as the borrower repays the loan.

Equity mortgage - *See "home equity line" and "home equity loan."*

Equity of redemption - The owner's right to recover property before the foreclosure sale, providing he comes up with enough money for loan payments and real estate taxes.

Errors and omissions insurance - Protects against errors made by a builder or architect.

Escalation clause - A lease term stating the landlord can increase rent if his own expenses grow.

Escalator clause - A lease term requiring tenants to pay a higher rent as costs increase.

Escape clause - Releases parties from the sale contract if something expected does not happen — for instance, if a buyer cannot secure a loan to purchase the property.

Escrow - Closing of a deal by an escrow agent — a neutral third party. Escrows are also sums of money or valuable possessions passed to a third party, who delivers them when certain conditions are met.

Escrow account (impound account) - Used by mortgage lenders and servicing businesses to store money that will pay real estate taxes, homeowners insurance, and other items.

Escrow agent (escrow company) - A third party who neutrally ensures that those having a real estate transaction meet the necessary conditions, such as putting valuables in an escrow account, before any money or property changes hands.

Escrow disbursement - Paying out the money from an escrow account for property expenses due, such as mortgage insurance or taxes.

Estate - An individual's property and all other assets after he dies.

Estate in land - Details on how much interest someone holds in real estate and the nature of that interest.

Estimated closing costs - Approximately how much it costs for a real estate sale to occur.

Ethics - Moral code that guides professional behavior.

Eviction - Removal of a property's occupant by law.

Evidence of title - A certificate of title or other proof that one owns a property. Examples include title insurance, a Torrens registration certificate, or an abstract of title, along with a lawyer's opinion.

Examination of title - An inquiry and report revealing who has owned a property through its history — performed by title companies.

Exception - Something an insurance policy does not cover.

Exchange - A swap of similar property. For example, trading two pieces of real estate.

Exclusive agency listing - An owner exclusively contracts and pays a real estate broker to sell a property during a certain time period under the owner's terms. The owner can still sell the property himself without paying the broker if he finds a buyer the broker has not claimed or approached.

Executed contract - An accord for which each party has completed its duty.

Executor (executrix for females) - The person a will names to manage an estate.

Exhibit - A secondary document used in support of a different, main document.

Expansion option - A lease provision allowing a tenant to lease bordering areas, expanding their rented space, after a certain amount of time — this provision shows up in commercial leases.

Express agreement - A written or verbal contract allowing parties to declare their intentions and contract terms in speech.

Extended coverage - Extra insurance against problems that homeowners policies do not typically cover, such as uncommon hazards a property faces.

Extender clause - A rarely used clause that makes a listing agreement renewable automatically

until involved parties decide to end it.

Extension - When both parties agree to lengthen a time period given by a contract.

F

Fair Credit Reporting Act (FCRA) - Federal laws governing the procedures credit reporting agencies use.

Fair Housing Act - Federal legislation stating that someone providing housing cannot discriminate against people because of religion, gender, disability, appearance, race, nationality, or familial status.

Fair market value - A price determined by how much a buyer will agree to pay and how little a seller will accept. In a competitive market, properties would sell at certain times for market value.

Fannie Mae - *See "Federal National Mortgage Association."*

Fannie Mae Community Home Buyers Program - In this type of community lending meant to help low- to medium-income families buy homes, Fannie Mae and mortgage insurers provide flexible guidelines for participating lenders to underwrite loans — it decides who has enough credit to receive them.

Farmer's Home Administration (FMHA) - An agency that gives farmers and people living in rural areas access to credit — part of the U.S. Department of Agriculture.

Feasibility study - Determines how well a proposed development will achieve an investor's goals — it appraises income, expenses, and how the property can be used or designed to the greatest effect.

Federal Deposit Insurance Corporation (FDIC) - An independent part of the U.S. government, this agency insures commercial banks' deposits.

Federal Emergency Management Agency (FEMA) - Provides flood insurance for property owners at risk and performs other functions.

Federal Housing Administration (FHA) - A government agency that works to make housing available by providing loan programs,

as well as guarantee and insure programs for loans.

Federal National Mortgage Association (FNMA) - Nicknamed Fannie Mae, a shareholder-owned company that is congressionally chartered and leads the nation in supplying mortgage funds. Fannie Mae purchases lenders' mortgages and sells them in another form — as securities — in secondary mortgage markets.

Federal Reserve System - Acting as the nation's primary banking system, the Federal Reserve System supplies the country with money and sets interest rates.

Federal tax lien - A debt set against a piece of real estate when someone neglects to pay federal taxes. The Internal Revenue Service (IRS) uses this lien to encourage the owner to pay income taxes.

Fee appraiser (independent fee appraiser or review appraiser) - An individual who is paid by the prospective property buyer to appraise real estate.

Fee for service - Money a consumer pays an individual

holding a real estate license for services.

Fee simple - The greatest interest in real estate that laws recognize — it entitles the interested party to all possible property rights.

FHA loan - A loan granted by a lender that is approved by the Federal Housing Administration — the FHA insures this loan.

Fiduciary relationship - A confident and trusting relationship between principal and agent or another two parties.

Filled land - Land artificially raised with piled rocks, gravel, or dirt — if a property has filled land, sellers disclose that fact to buyers.

Financing gap - Portion of a property's price the buyer cannot afford. For example, a buyer might have funds and loans covering 90 percent of a $100,000 real estate sale, leaving a $10,000 gap.

Fire insurance - Insurance that covers property lost or damaged in a fire — it can include related water or smoke damage.

Fire wall - A wall made of fire-resistant substances meant to slow spreading flames.

Firm commitment - A document where a lender agrees to loan a borrower money needed to buy property.

First mortgage - A property's original mortgage, which must be paid before any other mortgages. When a property has more than one lien, the first mortgage has priority, and it is the earliest debt settled for a foreclosed property.

Fiscal year - The 12-month calendar of financial reports, typically starting the first day of January.

Fixed costs and fixed expenses - Fees that do not change with productivity, sales success or a property's occupants.

Fixed-rate mortgage - A home loan with a constant, unchanging interest rate.

Fixture - A possession one fixes permanently to a property, making it part of the real estate.

Flag lot - Skirting a subdivision's rules by dividing property into distinct parcels.

Flat - An apartment on one story only.

Flex space - A structure with offices or showrooms that also contains space for factory work, laboratories, storage, and other purposes — the arrangement of these different spaces can change.

Flexible payment mortgage (adjustable-rate mortgage) - A home loan with a variable interest rate, which changes while allowing the borrower to repay the debt.

Flip - To profit from purchasing and quickly reselling property.

Flood certification - Determination of whether property falls within a designated flood zone.

Flood insurance - Required for properties in designated flood zones, a policy that protects against losses caused by floods.

Flood-prone area - A place with a 1 percent chance of one flood per century, where chances remain that high each year.

Floor plan - A drawing depicting how rooms are positioned in a home or other building.

Flue - The cavity that guides soot and smoke from a fireplace into the chimney.

Footing - A grounded concrete support beneath a foundation that bears another structure and distributes its weight evenly — footings are wider than the things they support.

For Sale By Owner (FSBO) - An owner sells property without using a real estate broker, which allows the owner to work directly with the buyer or the buyer's real estate agent.

Forbearance - Granting someone time to fix a problem — such as a loan default — before making any legal moves.

Force majeure - An unstoppable external force that causes parties to breach a contract.

Foreclosure - When an individual loses property in order to settle a mortgage debt they cannot pay. This legal procedure turns the property title over to the mortgage lender or it allows a third party to buy the property — without any encumbrances that would lessen its value — in a foreclosure sale.

Forfeiture - Losing valuable possessions or money by failing to follow a contract.

Foundation drain tile - A pipe that drains water from a foundation — it is sometimes made of clay.

Foundation walls - Underground walls providing a building's main support. These concrete or masonry walls can also define a basement.

Franchise - Agreement where a company lets offshoot offices use its name and services for a fee. Franchises in real estate include brokerages working for a national business.

Free and clear title - See "clear title."

Free-standing building - A structure separate from others, such as a shed in the backyard.

Front-end ratio - A lender's comparison of how much a person pays each month to finance his or her housing and how much money he or she earns.

Front footage - Length, in feet, of the front edge of a piece of land.

Front money - Money needed to buy land and prepare it for development.

Frontage - The foremost part of a lot, which can border a road or body of water.

Full disclosure - Keeping nothing secret that could influence a sale. For example, telling the buyer a property's defects.

Full recourse - If the borrower stops repaying the loan, full responsibility goes to its endorser — the person who backed the loan.

Functional obsolescence - A state of lowered value when an improvement is badly designed or loses function.

Funding fee - Payment for mortgage protections, for example, the fee to secure a loan backed by the Department of Veterans Affairs.

G

Gambrel roof - A roof with two sloping sides. From its top, the slopes descend gently, but for the lower part, each side takes a steeper angle.

Gap in title - A missing link in the history of titles held for the property, which reveals incomplete records.

Garden apartment - A building in which at least a portion of the tenants can use a common lawn yard.

Garnishment - Automatic deductions from a borrower's paycheck to repay the lender for outstanding debts resulting from a legal judgment.

Gazebo - A small structure found in gardens, backyards, and parks — gazebos are partially open but roofed.

General contractor - The primary person in charge of a construction project, who is contracted to oversee it and can hire subcontractors to handle the project.

General (or master) plan - A long-term program, used by governments to dictate how property will be developed and utilized as the communities expand.

General real estate tax - The sum of municipality and government taxes on a piece of property.

General warranty deed - The most common and safest deed used when people transfer real estate. The party granting it guarantees sure and clear title to the property.

Gift letter - States that money an individual will use for a down payment or other purpose came from a friend or relative's gift, creating no debt. People send gift letters to lenders and government agencies.

Ginnie Mae - See "Government National Mortgage Association."

Good Faith Estimate (GFE) - The total cost of getting a home loan as estimated by a broker or lender, summing up all the fees the borrower must pay.

Government loan - A mortgage loan insured or backed by the

Department of Veterans Affairs, the Rural Housing Service, or the Federal Housing Administration.

Government National Mortgage Association (GNMA or Ginnie Mae) - Like Freddie Mac and Fannie Mae, this federally owned corporation funds lenders who make home loans — it also buys loans but only if they are government backed.

Government survey method - A standard approach for describing land features — this method is used in most American states, especially in the west.

Grace period - A set amount of time that allows an individual to make an overdue loan payment before suffering any consequences.

Grade - The height of a hill or slope compared to level ground, including how steeply it angles. To calculate grade, divide the raised area's elevation (in feet) by the number of horizontal feet you would travel to get there on flat ground. If a slope reaches 30 feet high by the time one travels 100 horizontal feet, its grade is 30 percent.

Grandfather clause - An idea that something built or made under an old set of rules is allowed to stay as it is, even when new rules replace the old set of rules.

Granny flat (in-law apartment) - A small space rented out in a home zoned for a single family.

Grant - Passing property over to a new owner, which may be accomplished by using deeds.

Grant deed - Grantors of these deeds give recipients their word that they have not passed the real estate to anyone else before. They affirm the property has no encumbrances lessening its use or value except what the deed lists. These are commonly used in California.

Gratuitous agent - An agent who services clients free of charge.

GRI (Graduate, Realtors® Institute) - people trained in finance, investing, appraisal, law, and sales as prescribed by the Realtors® Institute.

Gross building area - The sum of all the area of the floors in a building, excluding projecting pieces of architecture or other things not part of the house's bulk. It includes penthouses, basements, and mezzanines that are part of an outer wall's main surface.

Gross income - A household's total income minus expenses and taxes.

Gross income multiplier - A number used to estimate a property's value. One multiplies the property's yearly gross income by this figure.

Gross leasable area - Total amount of space meant for rent-paying tenants and no one else.

Gross rent multiplier (GRM) - A number used in gauging a property's value. One multiplies the property's monthly gross income by this figure.

Ground lease - A lease in which a tenant only rents land and not a building. The tenant may own or construct a building on the land by following the lease's rules.

Guaranteed sale program - Brokers can offer this option, agreeing to give a property owner a set amount of money if that person's listed real estate does not sell within a certain time. The owner is free to buy another house because his or her previous building is guaranteed to sell.

Guarantor - An individual making a guarantee.

Guaranty - An interaction where an individual agrees to settle another's obligations or debt if the other cannot.

H

Habitable room - Living spaces, which one counts while summing up a home's number of rooms — corridors and bathrooms are excluded.

Handicap - A disability that hinders one's mental or physical functions, limiting at least one life activity described in the Fair Housing Act.

Hard cost - Money spent to build improvements on a property.

Hard-money mortgage - Secured by cash from a borrower rather than real estate. The borrower pays money or pledges the equity of property.

Hazard insurance (homeowners insurance or fire insurance) - Insurance that covers property damage by wind, fire, and other destructive forces.

Heirs and assigns - People designated to receive another's property by a deed or will. Assigns receive the interest to a piece of real estate and heirs inherit a deceased person's property.

Hiatus - Missing information in a property's ownership history. Also, a hiatus is a gap created between two pieces of land because of an inaccurate legal description.

High-rise - A structure that exceeds 25 stories in a business district or exceeds six stories in a suburb.

High-water mark - A property line that separates a public waterway and a land parcel. Also, a line showing how far a medium tide comes up a shore.

Highest and best use - Most legal and sensible way one can use property or land in order to give it peak value in a financially realistic, well-supported way.

Historic structure - A building given special status for tax purposes because it is officially deemed historically important.

Hold harmless clause - One party pledging in a contract to guard another against legal actions and claims. Rent contracts may include this term to protect a building owner from lawsuits by a tenant's customers.

Holdover tenant - A tenant who holds onto a property once the lease ends.

Holdback - A chunk of loaned money the lender withholds until a certain event happens.

Holding company - A company that owns or manages one or more other companies.

Holding escrow - A situation in which a third party (escrow agent) holds onto a deed's final documents of title.

Home equity conversion mortgage (HECM or reverse annuity mortgage) - Allows homeowners to turn their home's equity into monthly cash payments, which a lender provides.

Home equity line - Open-ended credit for loans that homeowners receive by building up their property's value (equity).

Home equity loan - A loan an individual takes out while using his house as collateral.

Home inspector - A person authorized to assess how operational and structurally sound a property is.

Homeowners Association (HOA) - A group that enforces rules or restrictions that the developer has set on a neighborhood, condominium, or community. The HOA collects payments each month for the community's expenses and upkeep.

Homeowners insurance policy - See *"hazard insurance."*

Homeowners warranty - Insures devices and systems for heating, cooling, and other purposes over a certain period, guaranteeing that they will be fixed if needed.

Homestead - Land that a family owns and lives on. Parts of this

land or its value are safe from legal action relating to debt, in certain states.

Hostile possession - See *"adverse possession."*

House rules - Rules that govern the behavior of condominium occupants. Members of the Condominium Owners Association create these rules to foster peaceful relations between owners and residents.

Housing expense ratio (HER) - The portion of gross monthly income someone spends on housing costs, expressed as a percent.

Housing for the elderly - Living space with common access areas designed to accommodate people 55 or older.

Housing starts - The approximate number of construction projects for housing units beginning during a certain period.

Department of Housing and Urban Development (HUD) - A U.S. government agency that manages the Federal Housing Administration and various programs for developing houses and communities.

HUD median income - An estimate, from the Department of Housing and Urban Development (HUD), on how much money families in a given area earn, on average.

HUD-1 Settlement Statement (settlement sheet or closing statement) - A detailed list of the funds parties pay when their transaction completes.

Hundred percent location - The spot in a city where land is most valuable, which can mean the rent is highest and vehicle and foot traffic is heaviest.

HVAC - Stands for heating, ventilating, and air conditioning.

Hypothecate - To back a loan by pledging property but not surrendering it.

I

Illiquidity - Difficulty converting something to cash. Real property is deemed illiquid because turning it into money is not easy.

Impact fee - A fee paid by private developers to the city for permission to start a project. The money helps the city build infrastructure, such as sewers, for the new development.

Implied agency - Formed when a party acts like another party's agent and both show they accept this relationship.

Implied listing - An agreement where parties show their concurrence by how they act.

Implied warranty of habitability - A legal theory where landlords imply that property for rent is fit to live on and use for its intended purpose.

Impound - A portion of a mortgage payment set apart and saved to cover private mortgage insurance, pay real estate taxes, and insure property against hazards.

Improved land - Land with some development or construction, whether people can live there or not.

Improvement - Any construction that boosts a property's value, including private structures like buildings and fences, as well as public structures like roads and water piping.

In-house sale - A kind of sale made solely by the broker in the listing agreement, with no other brokers involved. This kind of sale includes situations where the broker finds the buyer or where the buyer approaches someone working for the broker.

Income approach - A way to estimate how much a moneymaking property is worth. One predicts how much net income the property will make each year through its entire life and capitalizes that income, determining its present value.

Income property - A piece of real estate that the owner uses to earn money without residing there.

Income statement - A document reporting an individual's financial history, including the amounts of money made and expenses paid, where that money came from and went, and how much the subject profited or lost — it can report on cash or accruals.

Incorporation by reference - Adding terms to a given document by referencing the other documents where they appear.

Incurable obsolescence - A flaw on a property that cannot be fixed or that is too expensive to merit repairs.

Indemnify - Guard another against harm or loss.

Indenture - An agreement on paper between at least two people whose interests differ. An indenture can also be a deed with reciprocal commitments the parties agree to fulfill.

Independent contractor - An individual hired to achieve a result through means they choose and control. Independent contractors pay their own expenses and taxes, and they receive no employee benefits. Real estate brokers are known to operate this way.

Index - A table of financial information that lenders use to determine how much interest a borrower will pay on an adjustable-rate mortgage.

Index loan - A long-lasting loan for which payment amounts change in tune with a certain index.

Indicated value - How much a piece of real estate is worth, depending on its land value and its cost minus depreciation, the net income it makes during yearly operations, and how much similar properties currently sell for.

Indirect costs - Money spent on development for things besides the labor and materials going directly into structures on the lot.

Indoor air quality - Degree of pollution in a building from smoke, radon, or other gaseous contaminants.

Industrial park - A zone meant for manufacturing and for related projects and entities.

Informed consent - Choosing to permit something after learning enough details to inform one's decision.

Infrastructure - Utility lines, roads, sewers, and other public developments meant to meet peoples' basic needs in a subdivision or city.

Initial interest rate - The starting interest rate for an adjustable-rate mortgage. It can fluctuate over time, changing the borrower's monthly mortgage payments.

Initial rate duration - The length of time an adjustable-rate mortgage is set to keep the interest rate it started with.

Injunction - A court order compelling someone to do or not to do a certain act.

Innocent misrepresentation - When someone lies accidentally.

Innocent purchaser - A party that buys contaminated property without knowing it is tainted, despite having it investigated beforehand. This buyer bears no obligation to clean it up.

Inside lot - Surrounded on three sides by other lots and fronted by a road — unlike a corner lot with two sides bordering roads.

Inspection report - A document prepared by a licensed inspector that describes the condition of a property.

Installment contract (contract for deed or articles of agreement for warranty deed) - A contract that allows a buyer to make gradual payments for real estate while the buyer possesses the property and the title remains with the seller for a time, possibly until the buyer finishes paying.

Installment note - It calls for the buyer to pay for the property in specific amounts over time.

Institutional lenders - Entities that invest in loans and other securities as a business, using others' funds they manage or their own money.

Instrument - A legal statement in writing that establishes parties' rights, relationship, or required duties, such as a contract.

Insulation disclosure - Open sharing of details about the insulation in a house required of real estate brokers and anyone building or selling new homes. Insulation disclosures reveal the insulation's thickness, components, and effectiveness (R-value).

Insurable title - A title that can get coverage from title insurance companies.

Insurance binder - Provides coverage temporarily until one can set up a permanent policy.

Insured mortgage - A mortgage guaranteed through a private mortgage insurance or the Federal Housing Administration.

Interest - A fee that borrowers pay their lenders alongside loan repayments. Lenders charge debtors interest for using their loaned money.

Interest in property - A share owned in a property, by law.

Interest-only loan - A type of mortgage where the borrower pays the monthly interest on a loan, making no payments against the debt itself.

Interest-rate buy-down plans - See "buy-down."

Interim financing - See "bridge loan."

Interstate Land Sales Full Disclosure Act - A nationwide law governing how real estate transactions between states will work.

Interval ownership - *See "time-share ownership plan."*

Intestate - If the owner of a property dies without a functioning will, he is intestate. The state laws of descent determine who inherits the property.

Intrinsic value - The worth a piece of real estate has because it is a kind of property the buyer happens to favor.

Inventory - The amount of real estate on the market, not taking into account its quality or availability.

Investment property - Real estate used to earn money.

Investment structure - Strategic doling out of investment money to different entities that will manage it via loans, joint ventures, leveraged acquisitions, participating debt, triple-net leases, and convertible debt.

Involuntary conversion - When a property's status or ownership changes without the current owner's consent. A house destroyed by a flood or condemned is involuntarily converted.

Involuntary lien - A lien against a property made without the owner's consent. For instance, governments can lay involuntary liens on properties if owners fail to pay taxes.

Ironclad agreement - An agreement that is unbreakable by anyone taking part.

Irrevocable consent - Approval a party gives that it cannot take back or cancel.

J

Joint liability and joint several liability - Owners each bear total liability for all damages.

Joint tenancy (tenancy in common) - People equally sharing ownership of a property. If one of them dies, the others receive his share.

Judgment lien - A claim laid via legal judgment against property owned by someone in debt.

Judicial foreclosure - A civil lawsuit turning over real estate to a lender or third party because the property owner fails to pay debts. Using civil lawsuits for foreclosure is standard in certain states.

Jumbo loan - A massive mortgage that Freddie Mac and Fannie Mae cannot take on.

Junior lien - A second mortgage or other obligation that will not be the first claim a property owner addresses.

Just compensation - A fair price that the government pays a property owner when using eminent domain to render the land public.

K

Key lot - Property desired for its location, which can allow the owner to use adjacent lots to their full potential. Also, a key lot is a property with its front on a secondary street and one side bordering the rear of a corner lot.

Key tenant - An important renter who leases copious space in a shopping center or other complex.

Kicker - An additional fee a debtor pays beyond a mortgage's interest and principal.

Kitchenette - Measuring less than 60 square feet, an area used for handling and cooking food.

Knockdown - Unassembled, pre-made building materials sent to a construction site for assembly and installation.

L

Land banker - An entity that develops land for future construction and inventories improved pieces of land for later uses.

Land description - A legal account of what a piece of property is like.

Land grant - Land the government provides for colleges specializing in agriculture or for other developments, such as roads and railroads.

Land leaseback - A deal in which an owner sells land and becomes a renting tenant, leasing from the new owner. This lease covers the land but not construction upon it, and when the lease ends, any structures built on the property go back to the party who originally owned it.

Land trust - A trust a landowner creates, which recognizes only one asset: real estate.

Land use map - A map displaying different uses of land in a certain area, along with how much is used and to what degree.

Landlocked - A property bounded by other lots, not directly bordering a road.

Landlord - A person who leases property to someone else.

Landlord's warrant - Legal permission for a landlord to take a tenant's property and publicly sell it or to drive the tenant to pay late rent or other fees.

Late charge - Additional money a lender demands when the debtor misses due payments.

Late payment - Money a borrower pays a lender after it was due.

Latent defect - A structural flaw an inspection misses, which can

pose a hazard to residents. Certain states require licensees and sellers to check for latent defects and reveal any they find.

Lead poisoning - Dangerous illness from lead building up in body tissues.

Lease - A verbal or written agreement that a tenant will pay for exclusive access to a landlord's property over a certain time. State laws require long-term leases to be written out, such as agreements exceeding one year.

Lease option/purchase - Allows a person to rent a home and then apply part of their lease payments toward purchasing it later.

Leasehold improvements - Fixtures a tenant installs or buys for a property. The tenant can legally remove them when the lease ends, if doing so leaves no damage.

Leasehold state - A situation where an individual holds a real estate title by leasing the property long-term without owning it.

Legal age - The age an individual must be in order to bear legal responsibility for their actions.

One must be 18 to enter real estate agreements or contracts.

Legal description - An account of the appearance of a certain parcel that is detailed enough for an independent surveyor to find and recognize it.

Legal notice - Giving legal notice means making others aware of something in whatever fashion the law requires. A tenant gives a landlord written legal notice before ending a lease.

Legatee - An individual given property through a will.

Lessee - An individual who rents property through a lease.

Lessor - An individual who leases property to another person.

Let - To lease real estate to a tenant, unlike subletting, which involves the tenant renting the property to someone else.

Levy - To set the tax rate on a piece of property after assessing it. To levy is also to collect or take. Seizing property to settle a debt is called levying an execution.

Liabilities - Debts to repay or obligations to fulfill.

Liability insurance - Insurance that guards owners against claims of property damage, negligence, or personal injury.

LIBOR (London Interbank Offered Rate) - A kind of index lenders use to set and change interest rates on adjustable-rate mortgages, known for its use with interest-only mortgages.

License - The right to broker real estate, given by a state. A license can also mean any right a person holds and cannot sell, or permission — which can be withdrawn — to use land for a time.

Lien - A claim laid on property, which can encourage the owner to settle a debt or obligation. Liens allow lenders to sell property if owners do not repay their debts.

Lien statement (offset statement) - A statement describing how much debt remains to be paid against a lien on real estate, its due date, interest to be paid, and claims declared.

Lien waiver - A document contractors sign giving up the right to make claims on a property once they have been paid for their work.

Life-care facility - A home for senior citizens that provides medical care.

Light industry - A zoning name for manufacturing companies that are not loud, polluting, or otherwise disruptive.

Limitations of actions - The window of time to take a legal action before it becomes prohibited.

Limited liability company - Joint ownership in which individuals are protected because they do not bear full liability. The participants are considered partners for tax purposes.

Limited referral agent - A licensed real estate salesperson who refers sellers and buyers to brokerages and gets paid when a deal closes.

Limited warranty deed - A deed with warranties that only cover the period the last person held a title before passing it on — not the time with its previous owners. Any

problems that arose when those earlier owners had the property do not fall under warranty.

Line of credit - Credit a financial institution grants a borrower for a specific period, with a set maximum limit.

Line of sight easement - A right stating that one cannot block the view on an easement's land.

Line stakes - Stakes marking the edge of a piece of land.

Lineal foot - A horizontal line across the ground measuring one foot long.

Liquid asset - Any asset easily exchanged for money.

Listing agreement - A relationship in which the owner of a real estate pays or otherwise compensates a broker to lease or sell property under certain conditions and for a specific price.

Listing broker - The person whose office makes the listing agreement, who can also work directly with the buyer.

Loan application fee - A fee borrowers pay lenders to review their applications for loans.

Loan officer - An individual who officially represents a lending institution with limited power to act for it.

Loan servicing - The steps lending institutions take with each loan. They include managing borrowers' payments and issuing statements; collecting on loans past due; making sure owners pay their taxes and insurance on a property; handling escrow/impound accounts; and further tasks, such as managing assumptions and payoffs.

Loan-to-value ratio (LTV ratio) - Comparison between the sum loaned as a mortgage and the value of the collateral property securing the loan.

Lock box - Holds the key to property being sold, locked away. Only agents holding the code or key can open the box.

Lock in - A lender's promise to charge a borrower a certain interest rate for a specific time span.

Lock-in period - The time span for which a lender promises a borrower a certain interest rate.

Loft - An unfinished building space. A loft is also open area on the two lowest floors that accommodates retail or manufacturing.

Long-term lease - A rental contract lasting three or more years before ending or being renewed.

Lot and block (recorded plat) system - A way to identify plots of land in a subdivision, using numbers for lots and blocks as they appear on a map called a subdivision plat.

Low-documentation loan - A mortgage for which borrowers provide only fundamental proof of their assets and income.

Low-rise - A structure standing four stories or less above ground.

M

Maggie Mae (Mortgage Guarantee Insurance Corporation, MGIC) - Provides insurance for those investing in mortgage loans.

Maintenance fee - Monthly fee paid by people in homeowners associations to maintain and mend common parts of the property where they live.

Maps and plats - Surveys showing the features of land parcels, including area measures, landmarks, property lines, ownership, and more.

Margin - A number added to the index determining interest rates on an adjustable rate mortgage. It adjusts the numbers in the index to create the interest rate a borrower gets.

Market conditions - Marketplace traits, such as demographics and rates of interest, employment, vacancies, property sales, and leases.

Market data approach (Sales comparison approach) - Gauging a property's value by comparing it with similar real estate sold recently.

Market study - Estimation of future demand for particular real estate projects, including possible rental fees and square feet sold or leased.

Marketable title - Legitimate, clearly held title at low risk for lawsuits over flaws.

Master deed - Used by condominium developers to record development on the whole property, broken down into units people own.

Master lease - The main lease controlling all following leases. It may encompass more real estate than the entire group of subsequent leases.

Maturity - The date a loan becomes due or a contract ends.

Maturity date - The day by which a borrower must fully repay a loan.

Mechanic's lien - Used by contractors and others involved in building on property to ensure they get paid. This claim lasts until the workers are compensated for services and supplies rendered for construction, improvement, or repair.

Merged credit report - A report that combines data from Experian,

Equifax, and TransUnion—three major credit bureaus.

Merger - The uniting of at least two investments, companies, or other interests.

Mezzanine - A floor midway between a structure's major stories or between the ceiling and floor in a single-story building.

Mezzanine financing - A blend of equity and debt that takes second priority behind a primary loan and allows lenders to possess property if the borrower does not pay the debt.

Mid-rise - A structure four to eight stories tall, or as many as 25 stories in business districts.

Minimum lot area - The lowest lot size a subdivision permits.

Minimum property requirements - Conditions property must meet before the Federal Housing Administration will underwrite a mortgage. The home must be reliably built, habitable, and up to housing standards in its location.

Mixed use - A multi-purpose part of a property, such as space for business as well as residency.

Mobile home - A manufactured home delivered somewhere and capable of relocating.

Model home - A home exemplifying others being developed. Model homes are furnished and displayed for buyers as part of an effort to sell other homes in a development.

Modular housing - Housing manufactured off-site and delivered to a site in pieces.

Month-to-month tenancy - An individual who pays rent month by month, with no longer commitment. This is the default situation if the landlord and tenant make no rental agreement. Month-to-month tenancy can take over after a lease expires.

Monument - A natural or man made landmark used to create property lines for a surveyor's description of real estate.

Moratorium - Time during which payments are not required or certain acts are prohibited.

Mortgage - Borrowed money for buying real estate, with the purchased property for collateral.

Mortgage banker - An institution that uses its own funds to make home loans, which mortgage investors and insurance companies can buy.

Mortgage broker - an individual who pairs loan seekers with mortgage lenders. Brokers are approved to work with certain lenders.

Mortgage insurance (MI) - Protects lenders from particular consequences if borrowers fail to repay loans. Lenders can require mortgage insurance for certain loans.

Mortgage insurance premium (MIP) - The price of mortgage insurance paid to private companies or governments.

Mortgage interest deduction - A tax deduction homeowners receive for paying yearly interest on mortgages.

Mortgage preapproval - A lender determines that a borrower has the finances and credit to merit a particular loan with specified terms.

Mortgagor - One who borrows money from a mortgage lender.

Mud room - A small chamber opening to a play place or yard. Mudrooms can house laundry machines.

Mudsill - A building's lowest horizontal part — possibly laid in or on the ground.

Multi-dwelling units - Collected properties housing more than one family but covered by one mortgage.

Multiple listing - Sharing of information and profit between real estate brokers. They agree to give one another details about listings and to split commissions from the sales.

Multiple listing clause - A clause requiring and authorizing a broker to share a listing he manages with other brokers.

Multiple Listing Service (MLS) - A group of brokers who share listing agreements, hoping to find suitable buyers quickly. Acceptable listings include exclusive-agency and exclusive-right-to-sell types.

Municipal ordinances - Laws by local governments regarding standards for subdivisions and buildings.

N

Narrative report - An appraisal written in explanatory paragraphs, not a letter, table, or form.

National Association of Realtors® - A group of real estate agents working toward the best practice in their field.

Negative amortization - When a borrower makes monthly payments smaller than the interest rate on an adjustable-rate mortgage. The leftover interest builds up and adds to the unpaid balance.

Negative cash flow - Occurs when a property makes too little income to pay for its own operations.

Net after taxes - Income a property makes minus its operating costs and taxes.

Net lease - Requires a tenant to pay taxes, insurance, utilities, and upkeep expenses for a property, along with rent.

Net Operating Income (NOI) - A property's income before taxes, with expected vacancies and operating costs factored in.

Net sales proceeds - Money made by selling part or all of an asset minus costs from closing the sale, paying a broker, and marketing the property.

Net usable acres - Part of a plot appropriate for construction, minus land that cannot be built on because of building code restrictions, such as zoning or density rules.

Net worth - A company's value, determined using the worth of its total assets minus all liabilities.

No cash out refinance (rate-and-term refinance) - Refinancing of a mortgage designed to cover only its remaining debt and fees for getting a second loan.

No-cost loan - A loan with a higher interest rate but no associated fees.

No deal/no commission clause - A contract clause stating that a broker gets paid only if the property title changes hands as the contract specifies.

No-documentation loan - A loan given for a large down payment to people with good credit where applicants need not verify their assets or income.

Nominee - An individual who represents another, within limits. This can include buying real estate for someone else.

Noncompete clause - Part of a lease stating that only a certain tenant's company can do business on a property.

Nonconforming loan - A loan too large or otherwise unsuitable for Freddie Mac or Fannie Mae to buy.

Nonconforming use - A way of utilizing property prohibited by zoning laws but allowed because it began before those ordinances existed.

Nondisclosure - Keeping a fact hidden, whether purposefully or accidentally.

Non-judicial foreclosure - Selling property because its owner fails to pay the mortgage, but not working through a court of law. This form of foreclosure might deter title insurers from providing a policy later.

Nonrecourse loan - A loan that does not hold the borrower personally responsible if he fails to pay.

Normal wear and tear - Normal degradation of property with time and usage. It involves things like small scratches on countertops or tramping down of carpet.

Notary public - An individual legally approved to witness and certify that deeds, mortgages, and other contracts or agreements are carried out. A notary public can also give oaths, take affidavits, and perform other duties.

Notice of default - A document sent to notify people they have defaulted on their loans and are open to legal action.

Notice to quit - A document telling a tenant to leave rented property by a certain date or to remedy a problem, such as overdue rent — also called an eviction notice.

Nuisance - Actions on a property keeping others from using nearby land to the fullest. Examples include making loud noises, letting pets wander, or producing pollutants in subdivisions that do not allow these things.

O

Observed condition - A way to appraise how much value a property has lost by assessing how much it has degraded, lost function, or grown obsolete relative to surrounding areas.

Obsolescence - Lessened value in property because it is outdated, whether because its components functions less well or it cannot compare with surrounding property.

Occupancy agreement - An agreement that allows the buyer to use a piece of real estate before the escrow closes and where the buyer gives the seller money for rent.

Occupancy permit - A permit issued by local governments that signifies a property meets safety and health standards necessary for it to be habitable.

Occupancy rate - Percent of space in a building currently being rented.

Off-site management - The administration of property from a distance.

Off-street parking - Found on private land.

Offer - Stated wish to sell real estate or buy it at a certain cost. Also, a selling price for securities or loans.

Offer and acceptance - Needed for a successful real estate sale contract.

Offer to lease - A document meant to lead to an official lease. This offer is made to help the owner and renter agree on lease terms.

Office exclusive - A listing handled by one real estate office only or kept from a Multiple Listing Service by the seller.

Offset statement - *See "lien statement."*

On or before - An expression meaning that something is due by a specific date.

On-site management - Duties a property manager must perform while present at the property.

One hundred percent commission - An agreement between a salesperson and a broker in which the salesperson pays the broker administrative fees and then keeps all the commission from certain sales.

Open-end loan - A loan that can increase to a certain amount, keeping the original mortgage as its backing.

Open listing - A contract where the seller pays a broker only if the broker finds a suitable buyer before the seller or another broker does.

Open space - Area of water or land devoted to people's enjoyment or use, whether private or public.

Operating budget - A financial plan for moneymaking property, based on logically predicted spending and income.

Operating expense - Normal expenses of running operations on a piece of real estate.

Opinion of title - A certificate giving an attorney's opinion of whether someone has valid title to the property for sale.

Option ARM loan - An adjustable-rate mortgage that gives the borrower several alternative ways to make monthly payments.

Option listing - Listing a property for sale and allowing the listing broker the choice to buy it.

Option to renew - A provision in rental contracts stating that, under certain terms, the tenant can lengthen the lease.

Oral contract - A verbal agreement, which cannot be enforced in real estate matters.

Ordinance - Civic regulation of land uses.

Orientation - How a building is situated in relation to prevailing winds and sun angles. The right orientation can give the building a heating or cooling advantage.

Origination fee - The price a borrower pays a lender to prepare a loan.

Out parcel - A piece of land near another property that once included it. Out parcel can also mean a single retail property in a shopping center.

Outside of closing (paid outside closing, POC on settlements) - Directly paying closing fees without following normal procedures.

Outstanding balance - Unpaid debt, which is a borrower's duty to address.

Over-improvement - Using the land too intensively. This includes spending money excessively to improve the property.

Overage - Additional money beyond rent paid for leasing retail property, which is determined by a sales' success.

Overhang - Roof edge that sticks out past an outer wall.

Owner financing - Occurs when a seller lends the buyer needed money to purchase his property.

Owner occupant - One who owns and inhabits property.

Ownership in severalty - Possession of property by one person, who is considered "severed" from additional title-holders.

P

Pad - A spot for one mobile home among others. Also, a pad is a site or foundation suitable to be improved — built upon or used — in a certain way.

Paper - A deed ,contract, mortgage, or note someone retrieves from the buyer after selling property.

Parcel - A lot, part of a tract.

Parking ratio - A figure comparing the leasable square feet in a building to its number of parking spots.

Partial sale - Selling a portion of a property.

Participating broker - An individual who finds a buyer for property listed with a different brokerage firm. Participating brokers can split payment with listing brokers.

Parties - Central or primary entities in legal processes or transactions that buy and sell real estate.

Partition - Court procedure to divide real estate between co-tenants when they do not agree to end shared ownership.

Payment bond - Assures a building owner that construction costs will be covered, and no one will file a mechanic's lien.

Payoff statement - A document reporting how much money a debtor must repay, in total. This statement, which the lender signs, protects the interests of both parties.

Penthouse - A luxurious dwelling on a high-rise building's uppermost floor.

Per diem interest - Due or added to each day.

Percentage lease - A rental contract used for business properties to call tenants to pay a percentage of their profits to the owner when sales exceed a specific amount.

Percentage rent - Rent payments that grow or shrink depending on how financially successful a commercial property is.

Perfecting title - Clearing a real property title of claims or clouds.

Performance bond - Posted by a contractor, its proceeds go toward fulfilling the contract, and it ensures that the contractor will fulfill all contract duties or pay the owner for losses if not.

Periodic tenancy - Rental of a building one month or year at a time, which does not necessarily give the tenant any right to extend the rental period.

Permanent financing - A lasting loan not meant to fund construction or other short-term needs.

Personal property (chattel) - Possessions that people can carry with them — not real property.

Personal representative (executor, administrator) – An individual appointed to carry out the will of a person who dies. This representative is chosen by the will itself or by the probate court.

Phase I Audit - The first check for negative environmental effects on a property. Having this audit allows buyers to avoid responsibility for fixing problems they find after purchasing the real estate.

Physical life - Predicted period that buildings or other structures on real estate will last or remain livable.

Piggyback loan - A multi-lender mortgage with one lender in charge. Also, a pledged long-term loan combined with a construction loan.

Pipe stem lot (flag lot) - A slender lot forming a corridor for nearby residents to reach a road, used in places where lots fronting roads are not always available. The pipe stem lot fronts the road on its short side.

Pitch - Angle, such as a roof slope. Pitch is also a black, viscous material used to patch roofs or pavement.

PITI (Principal, Interest, Taxes, Insurance) - The parts of each payment on mortgage insurance or impounded loans.

Planned unit development (PUD) - Has common areas and living units owned by an association, unlike a condominium, in which people own their individual units and the association owns common spaces.

Planning commission (zoning commission, zoning board, or planning board) - Citizens who a local government authorizes to collectively create zoning laws and hold hearings.

Plat - An illustration mapping borders of roads, easements, and pieces of property.

Plans and specifications - Illustrations specifying all details of a development project, including its electrical and mechanical features, as well as orders for design and use of certain materials.

Plat book - A public record showing how tracts of land are broken down, providing the size and shape of each parcel.

Plat map - A map showing property lines in a given area, such as a subdivision.

Plaza - A central public gathering space or courtyard amid a shopping center or other area.

Plot plan - A map of how a parcel is used or will be used. It details where it is, how large it is, how it is shaped, and what parking spaces and landscaping it has.

Pocket listing - Kept private by the listing broker for a time, before entering the Multiple Listing Service. Delaying its entry gives that broker time to find a buyer before other brokers do.

Point - *See "discount points."*

Potable water - Water safe to drink.

Power of attorney - Written permission for an individual to act as another's agent, under specific terms. The agent is called an attorney-in-fact.

Pre-approval letter - Tells a buyer how much money a lender will loan.

Pre-qualified loan - A lender's opinion that a borrower is eligible for a given loan. Lenders interview possible borrowers and examine their credit histories to decide pre-qualification, but lenders must formally evaluate people's finances before loaning them money.

Preliminary report - A document given by a title insurer before the insurance itself to show the company is willing to insure a title.

Premium - Extra worth beyond the face value of a bond or mortgage or extra money paid beyond market price for something excellent or desirable. Premiums are also prices of insurance coverage.

Prepaid expenses - Money handed over early for scheduled payments, such as insurance and taxes.

Prepayment - Money repaid to a lender before it is required in order to shrink a debt.

Prepayment penalty - Fee borrowers must give lenders for repaying the entire debt prematurely. Lenders charge this penalty because a buyer who pays off a loan early pays less interest and other fees.

Presale - Allows people to buy homes or other structures that are planned but not yet built.

Preservation district - Areas zoned to conserve wildernesses and beaches, as well as managed forests, grazing sites, and historic or picturesque spots.

Prevailing rate - The average amount of interest borrowers pay on mortgages.

Price - An expression of value in money — how much cash something is worth — but not value itself.

Prime rate – The lowest interest rate offered by banks to their best customers.

Principal broker - An individual licensed and in charge of everything a brokerage firm does.

Principal residence - Where a person mainly resides.

Principle of conformity - States that properties are worth more if they resemble others nearby in their dimensions, appearance, functionality, and age.

Priority - Sequence of importance. High-priority liens are those made first and addressed first. Tax liens are ahead of all others in priority.

Private Mortgage Insurance (PMI) - Insurance from private companies that guards lenders against losing money if a borrower fails to repay a loan. When a borrower takes a loan for more than 80 percent of a home's price, the lender must have this insurance.

Pro forma statement - Describes financial outcomes predicted, not necessarily realized.

Pro rata - Amount of operating and upkeep costs each tenant pays, based on the proportions of the property they rent.

Probate - Court decision of who is heir of an estate and what assets are included.

Processing fee - Money borrowers pay lenders for collecting needed information to set up their loans.

Profit and loss statement - A document that describes the money a business earns and spends, along with ensuing losses or profits over a certain time.

Progress payments - Funds loaned to builders in installments as a construction project progresses.

Promissory note - A pledge on paper to pay off a debt by a certain date.

Property manager - An individual paid to oversee another's property by handling upkeep and accounting and taking rent payments.

Property reports - Government documents compiled by developers and subdividers that describe properties for prospective buyers.

Proration - Costs assigned proportionally to the seller and the buyer when a transaction closes. These expenses are prepaid or paid at the end of a term.

Prospect - An individual expected to purchase.

Public auction - A meeting where the public gathers to buy property seized from a borrower to pay off a defaulted mortgage.

Public land - Federally owned land that can be purchased if the government no longer needs it.

Punch list - A list of problems to fix or features to complete for a nearly finished construction project.

Purchase agreement - A contract giving the conditions and terms of a property sale, signed by both parties.

Purchaser's policy (owner's policy) - Insurance the seller provides the buyer as required by their contract. This policy guards against problems with the title.

Q

Quadraplex - A building with four private home units.

Qualification - A borrower's eligibility for a loan based on his or her credit history and ability to repay.

Qualified acceptance - Occurs when someone takes an offer under specific conditions, adjusting or changing its terms.

Qualifying ratio - A comparison between a borrower's income and the debt payments he or she would handle after getting a loan of a certain size. It helps lenders decide how much money to loan.

Quarter section - 160 acres.

Quitclaim deed - A document that erases someone's ownership of real property and transfers it to another without any obligations and without guaranteeing the person giving it up had certain ownership.

R

Radon - A natural gas implicated in lung cancer.

Range of value - The spectrum of prices a piece of real estate might be worth on the market.

Rate lock - Guarantee a lender makes not to change a borrower's interest rate for a certain time.

Raw land - Undeveloped, untouched property.

Ready, willing, and able buyer - An individual who can and will accept the sales terms a property owner gives and do what is needed to close the deal.

Real estate agent - An individual with a license to coordinate sales of real property.

Real estate fundamentals - Things that determine a property's value.

Real estate investment trust (REIT) - A group of people who share ownership in a trust that invests in real estate. They receive profits from the trust and get tax breaks on income from the property.

Real estate license law - A law that governs who can broker real estate in a given state, to guard buyers and sellers against scams and ineptitude.

Real estate owned (REO) - Real property a lender or savings institution receives because of a foreclosure.

Real Estate Settlement Procedures Act (RESPA) - A federal law stating that lenders must give borrowers a reasonable estimate of what costs they will incur before they get a loan. It forbids lenders from giving or getting kickbacks and certain fees for referrals to agents specializing in real estate settlements.

Real property - Real estate and the associated rights, benefits, owned land, and improvements upon it.

Realtist - An individual who is part of the National Association of Real Estate Brokers (NAREB).

Realtor® - Trademarked name for an active member of the National Association of Realtors®.

Reasonable time - Amount of time that can realistically be expected for something to occur, such as parties fulfilling duties for a contract. It does not include reasonable times in contracts that can leave them vulnerable to legal challenges.

Recapture clause - A contract term allowing a party to take back rights or interests previously granted to others.

Recapture rate - To an appraiser, this refers to the rate at which someone recovers invested money.

Reciprocal easements - Restrictions on how subdivision or development land is used in all the owners' best interests. Also, reciprocal easements are easements pertaining to everyone involved.

Reclamation - Altering land so it can support construction, natural resource use, or other operations, such as priming wetlands for agriculture by draining off water.

Reconveyance - Occurs when a borrower gets a title back from the lender or the lender's trustee after paying off the mortgage.

Record owner - An individual who owns a real estate title, noted in a public record.

Record title - A publicly recorded title.

Recording - An action necessary to render a deed effective as a public notice. Deeds and other documents are filed at the recorder's office for a given county. Also, a recording (noun) is information from correctly implemented legal papers, documented by the registrar's office.

Recording fee - A price one pays to a real estate agent for making a property sale part of public records.

Recreational lease - A lease allowing the tenant to use property for recreation which can be used, for example, in large subdivisions' pools or sports facilities.

Rectangular (government) survey system - Surveying that uses markers called base lines and principal meridians as references to describe land.

Redlining - A lender discriminating illegally against borrowers in specific areas, failing to grant loans even if the borrowers are eligible.

Re-entry - A landlord's legal prerogative to repossess property when a tenant's lease ends.

Referral agency - An agency that finds possible sellers and buyers and refers them to real estate agencies, which handle other tasks surrounding a sale. A referral agency is comprised of a group of licensed salespeople who earn money for each referral.

Refinance - To substitute a new loan for an old one. Refinancing also means using money gained from a loan to repay another loan.

Registered land - Property documented within the Torrens system.

Registrar - An official record keeper who works with documents like mortgages and deeds.

Regulation - A rule applying to procedures or management activities, which can function as a law.

Regulation Z - Obliges lenders to share all the terms and costs of a mortgage with borrowers to clarify the agreement they are undertaking. This federal legislation applies the contents of the Truth and Lending Act.

Rehab (Rehabilitation, Rehabilitate) - A major restoration to help a structure last, which includes steps to improve the condition of a building.

Rehabilitation mortgage - A mortgage loan that pays for repairs and restorations on a building.

Reinstate - Restore something to its previous status. A defaulted loan is back payments and penalties are paid off.

Reissue rate - A lowered fee from a title insurer for insurance on a property recently covered by another policy.

Release (release of lien) - Liberates real property from being collateral in a mortgage.

Relocation clause - A lease provision stating the landlord can transfer a tenant to a different part of the building.

Relocation company - A company that helps an employee move to a new city, performing services like buying the person's new home and selling the old one.

Remaining term - The term or payments remaining before a loan is paid off.

Remediation - Clearing a property of environmental contaminants or lowering them to a tolerable amount.

Rendering - An artistic illustration of how an undeveloped structure will look when finished.

Renegotiation of lease - Occurs when a tenant and the owner discuss new terms different from what is in their existing contract.

Renewal option - A rental contract clause giving a tenant the choice to make a lease last longer.

Rent control - Government regulated caps meant to control housing costs so people have access to affordable rent and regulate how much rent landlords can ask for.

Rent escalation - Changes in rental fees reflecting upkeep costs for the property or living expenses.

Rent roll - A list of each tenant, his or her rent, and the expiry date of each lease.

Rent schedule - Created by a landlord to give a tenant predictions of rent payments, as determined by market forces, expected expenses for the building, and the owner's future plans regarding the property.

Rental agency - Receives compensation to coordinate the dealings between potential tenants and landlords.

Rental agreement - A spoken or documented agreement that someone will inhabit and use a landlord's building under specific conditions and terms.

Rental growth rate - Expected changes over time in how high rental rates will be, based on market forces.

Repairs - Fixing up features of a property but not trying to lengthen its useful life as a capital improvement would.

Replacement cost - Expectation of how much money it will take to build a new structure equal to a current one.

Replacement reserve fund - Money saved by a Planned Unit Development, condominium, or cooperative project to replace shared parts of a building.

Reproduction cost - The current expense of building a precise double of an existing structure.

Request for proposal (RFP) - Document from potential clients formally asking investment managers to describe their business records, investing tactics, fees charged, current chances for investing, and other information.

Rescission - One party voiding a contract, leaving both parties situated as they were before making the agreement.

Reserve account - Paid into by a borrower for the lender's protection.

Reserve fund - A fund that holds money in escrow for a building's expected maintenance costs.

Resident manager - An individual living in an apartment building while managing it.

Resort property - Real estate that has the natural beauty or built structures for vacation and enjoyment. Examples include golf courses and resorts associated with beaches and theme parks.

Restriction - Legal constraints on how people can use a piece of land.

Restrictive covenant - A limitation on how an owner can use property, included in the deed by the party granting it.

Resubdivision - Further breaking down a subdivision to form more lots.

Retainage - Payment for a contractor's work, delayed until a certain time, such as when construction finishes.

Retaining wall - An upright barrier against moving soil or water.

Revenue stamp - Placed on a deed to show that parties have paid state taxes for transferring a title.

Reverse mortgage - A mortgage loan that allows people with valuable property to get payments from lenders, drawn from the equity of their real estate.

Review appraiser - An individual from the government, a bank, or another authority who examines the contents of appraisal reports.

Revolving debt - Situation in which the debtor pays back a loan and borrows against that loan while continuing to repay it.

Rider - Something added to a contract, such as an amendment.

Right of first refusal - Given in a lease, it states the tenant gets the first chance to purchase the rented property. It can also allow the tenant to rent more property if he matches reasonable terms someone else has offered the landlord for that space.

Right of way - Permission for another to build roads on an owner's land or pass through without owning the land.

Right to rescission - Allows borrowers to back out three days or fewer after signing for a loan.

Right to use - Prerogative given by the law to inhabit or use real estate.

Rollover risk - Chance that renters will leave once their current lease ends.

Roof inspection clause - Included in certain sales contracts, it requires the seller to disclose what kind of roofing a home has, any possible defects, and a promise to handle repairs.

Rooming house - A home where guests pay to occupy bedrooms — guests may also be allowed to use the kitchen.

Row house - Homes attached to others on either side, meant to support one family each.

Rules and regulations - Orders describing what real estate licensees can or cannot do.

Runs with the land - A rule or privilege that runs with the land stays connected to the property no matter who owns it.

Rural - Not part of the heavily populated areas in and around cities.

R-value - A measurement of how well something provides insulation — blocks or conducts heat.

S

Sale and leaseback - Involves an owner selling property then renting it from the new owner via a long-term lease.

Sales comparison approach (market data approach) - Gauging a property's worth by studying the values of similar properties sold recently.

Sales contract - A document the seller and buyer sign to agree on the details of a property purchase.

Salesperson - An individual working for or with a licensed broker on real estate business.

Satellite tenant - Other renters in a mall or similar complex besides the anchor tenant.

Schematics - Sketches of project plans, without final touches.

Seasoned loan - A partially paid off loan.

Second mortgage - Another home loan after the first one. It takes second priority for repayment.

Secondary financing - Another mortgage beyond the first one taken out to help purchase a house. Government lenders allow junior mortgages, within limits.

Section 8 housing - Private rental spaces subsidized by the Department of Housing and

Urban Development, allowing tenants to pay only part of the rent.

Security deposit - Money tenants give a landlord when the lease begins and have returned to them when it ends, unless they damage the property or fail to pay rent.

Seller carryback - A situation where the party selling the house lends the buyer money to purchase it.

Seller financing - See "seller carryback."

Seller's market - Occurs when demand for real estate rises or supply drops, allowing sellers to charge more.

Selling broker - Real estate licensee who locates a buyer.

Semi-detached dwelling - A home attached to another structure by a single, "party" wall.

Servicer - An individual who collects loan payments from borrowers and handles their escrow accounts, acting for a trustee.

Setback - Required space between the edge of a building and a landmark or property line in a given zone.

Settlement - See "closing."

Settlement fees - See "closing fees."

Shell lease - Allows a tenant to rent an incomplete building and finish construction.

Sherman Anti-Trust Act - Federal legislation restricting trade relationships between states or with foreign countries. It aims to prevent monopolies or focus points of economic force that might harm the economy or consumers.

Short sale - Occurs when an owner sells property but the proceeds do not pay off his mortgage. The lender lets the remaining debt go, opting for less money and avoiding a foreclosure.

Sick building syndrome - A problem of contaminated air in industrial or business buildings. People exposed may suffer from irritated skin and eyes, upset stomachs, and headaches.

Sight line - A direction or plane of vision.

Silent second - A second mortgage the borrower does not disclose to the lender of the first.

Site - The location for a piece of real estate is. A site is also land beneath a structure or ground ready for construction.

Site analysis - An assessment of a parcel's usefulness for a certain purpose.

Site development - Preparation of a site for construction.

Site plan - Describes precisely where a parcel is and where builders will make improvements.

Situs - Traits of a location driving the market value of a piece of real estate, including nearby properties and their effects on its worth.

Slab - The uncovered horizontal surface forming a floor, which rests atop support beams.

Slum clearance (urban renewal) - Removing dilapidated buildings to make space for more beneficial land uses.

Small-claims court - Handles minor disagreements involving claims less than $1,000.

Soft money - Tax-deductible contributions to development projects or money used for fees supporting construction but not the act of building. For instance, soft money might pay architects or cover legal expenses.

Solar heating - Harnessing sunlight energy to heat water or rooms in a house.

Sole proprietorship - A situation in which one person owns a business alone establishing no partnerships.

Space plan - A map of required room configurations for tenants. Space plans can describe the dimensions and layouts of rooms, including where doors are.

Spec (Speculative) home - Built by a contractor who has yet to find a buyer but expects to locate a single family to purchase the home.

Special assessment - A selective levy or tax relating to a road, sewer, or other public improvement. It applies only to people who the improvement helps.

Special conditions (contingencies) - Circumstances that must be fulfilled before the real estate contract containing them can bind parties involved.

Special damages - *See "actual damages."*

Special use permit (conditional use permit) - A permit that allows people to use land in ways a given zone normally would not permit.

Special warranty deed - A guarantee for buyers against flaws in a property that originated under the last owner but not other previous owners.

Specifications - Specific details on the construction materials, techniques, dimensions, and other elements workers must use in a project, accompanying blueprints and plans.

Split level - A house with floors staggered so rooms in one part sit about halfway between stories in an adjacent part.

Splitting fees - Dividing up money earned, which real estate brokers can do only with one another or with sellers and buyers.

Spot loan - Made to condominiums or other properties a lender has not funded before.

Spot zoning - Designating one parcel of land for different uses than other zoned property around it — an act courts might prohibit.

Square-foot method - Approximating the cost of improvements by counting the proposed square feet and multiplying by the price for one square foot of the type of construction planned.

Staging - A scaffold that supports construction materials and workers, removed when no longer needed. Staging is also an informal term for getting homes ready to impress potential buyers.

Staking - Using pins, stakes, or paint marks to show property boundaries but not encroachments.

Standard metropolitan statistical area - A county containing one or more major cities housing at least 50,000 people.

Standards of Practice - The ethical code licensed members of the

National Association of Realtors° are required to adopt.

Starts - *See "housing starts."*

State-certified appraiser - An individual authorized by a state government to appraise property.

Statute - A law the legislature enacts.

Statute of frauds - State law imparting certain contracts, deeds, and other agreements affecting title cannot be legally enforced unless they are written out and signed.

Statute of limitations - A law specifying how much time can pass before it becomes too late to bring an issue to court.

Stigmatized property - A property where something bad occurred, giving it a negative reputation. Certain states limit disclosure of these events, which include illness, violence, and other tragedies.

Straight lease (flat lease) - Tells a tenant how much rent is due each period during the entire lease. The rent will not change.

Strip center (strip mall) - A line of stores too small to house an anchor tenant, such as a major department store.

Structural alterations - Modification of the parts supporting a building.

Structural defects - Damage to or weaknesses in the parts of a house bearing its weight.

Structural density - Comparison between how much floor space a building has and the lot's area. A typical industrial building has a structural density of 1 to 3, meaning its land area is three times its floor space.

Studio - A living space built for efficiency, having a kitchenette, bathroom, and one main area.

Subagency - Found in Multiple Listing Service agreements, subagencies involve real estate salespeople trying to sell other agents' listed properties.

Subprime loan - A loan with elevated fees and interest, granted to an individual with a lower credit score.

Subagent - In real estate, a salesperson authorized to work for the broker in a listing agreement.

Subcontractor - A contractor hired to work on part of a construction project by the main contractor. Subcontractors often specialize in doing certain jobs.

Subdivision - Land broken down into sections following a plan called a plat, which meets local land use laws.

Subdivision and development ordinances - *See "municipal ordinances."*

Subjective value (personal value) - The price a particular person would be willing to pay for a piece of real estate.

Sublease, subleasing, subletting - A lease contract between someone renting a space and one who rents it from the original renter.

Subordinate financing - A loan second to another in priority, taken out after the first loan.

Subordinate loan - A subsequent mortgage using the same real estate for collateral as the original loan.

Subordination - Placing a right, security, or loan at a lower priority or status than the first mortgage.

Subordination clause - A clause that gives a mortgage priority over another mortgage recorded earlier.

Subpoena duces tecum - A court's command for someone to provide certain documents, such as records or books.

Subscribe - To sign a document at the bottom.

Subsidized housing - Living spaces partially paid for by the government, including single-family homes, apartments, and assisted-living facilities.

Substantial improvement - A modification that increases the building's value more than 25 percent within two years.

Subsurface rights - Authority to own water, oil, gas, and other materials in the ground below a parcel of real estate.

Summary possession (eviction) - Occurs when an owner takes back leased property because the tenant stays after the lease ends or breaks the rental contract.

Super jumbo mortgage - Depending on the lender, a super

jumbo mortgage exceeds $650,000 or $1,000,000.

Superfund - Refers to the strict federal law requiring entities to clean up environmental hazards on property they once owned.

Surcharge - An extra fee a tenant must pay for using more electricity or other utilities than a lease allows.

Surety - Someone who knowingly gets involved in another's debt or commitment, such as a co-signer.

Surety bond - A commitment by a bonding or insurance firm promising to bear responsibility for debts, defaults, or other burdens.

Surface water - Storm water in the ground, not channeled into streams.

Surrender - Voiding of a rental contract by agreement of the landlord and tenant.

Survey - The measurement of the area and borders of land. Surveys note a house's position and size, the boundaries of a lot, easements affecting property, and any structures intruding on a lot (encroachments).

Survivorship - The right for a person sharing home ownership to continue possessing the property if the second owner dies.

Sweat equity - A nickname for the labor an owner invests to improve property.

T

Takeout financing - Required by construction lenders, takeout financing is a pledge to finance a construction project permanently once it is complete. To receive it, the building must have a certain number of units bought or meet other requirements.

Tangible personal property - Any possession one can touch, move, and see, excluding real estate property.

Tangible property - Any possession one can touch and see, including immovable possessions like real estate.

Tax base - The summed worth of all the property a taxing authority manages.

Tax certificate - A legal document given to someone to prove he paid property taxes and to show his right to receive the deed, with proper timing and circumstances.

Tax deed - A legal document that transfers a property to a new buyer after the owner loses it for neglecting tax payments.

Tax deferred exchange (tax-free exchange or 1031 exchange) - The use of money from the sale of one investment property to buy another similar property so tax on any profits from the sale is deferred.

Tax lien - A claim the federal government makes against a piece of real estate to induce its owner to pay neglected taxes.

Tax map - A record kept by courthouses and tax offices that maps a parcel's size, shape, location, and other details relevant to taxation.

Tax rate - The proportion of something's value one must pay as tax.

Tax sale - Selling of real property because the owner fails to pay taxes.

Teaser rate - A temporary, cheap interest rate meant to entice people to take out mortgages.

Tenancy at sufferance - Occupancy of a property without permission after a lease ends.

Tenancy at will - Occupancy of an owner's property with permission, which can be revoked whenever the owner chooses. The tenant is also free to leave at will.

Tenancy by the entirety - Shared property ownership by married couples when they wed. One spouse gets full ownership if the other dies.

Tenancy in common - Ownership of property by a group of people, with each person having a separate — not shared — interest and the ability to leave it to an heir. Each person is the exclusive owner of one part of the property.

Tenant (lessee) - Someone with rights to buildings or land through renting or ownership.

Tenant at will - Someone a landowner permits to occupy the property.

Tenant contributions - Money or service a tenant provides beyond paying rent, mandatory under the lease.

Tenant improvement (TI) - Positive changes to property made by renters or people working for them.

Tenant improvement allowance - Money a landlord provides for tenants to repair and upgrade rented property.

Tender - To provide something — such as money or materials — or fulfill an obligation or contract requirement.

Tenement - Items permanently affixed to buildings or land. Tenements are also long-standing apartments.

Termite inspection - A professional inspection for signs of invading termites.

Termite shield - A metal barrier meant to bar termites from a house.

Testimonium - An ending clause in a contract stating that parties have officially transferred property by signing the contract on the date given.

Thin market (limited market) - A market in which sales rates are low and only a few people are buying and selling.

Third party - Someone indirectly involved in or related to a transaction, contract, or other interaction.

Time is of the essence - A contract expression meaning that something must be done as soon as possible.

Time value of money - Means that money brings more enjoyment and use in the present than the future and has more value now.

Time-share ownership plan - Involves tenants sharing property but using it at different times of year.

Title - Ownership of real estate or proof thereof.

Title company - A company that insures titles and resolves who owns them.

Title exam - An investigation verifying that a seller's ownership of property appears in public records. It reveals any encumbrances the property bears.

Title insurance - Insurance that protects property buyers against flaws or legal problems that come with their real estate, if the policy mentions them.

Title report - An early description of a title, not including its ownership history.

Title search - A search of public records to reveal any potential problems that might hinder passing property to a new owner.

Topography - The shape and elevation across a piece of land.

Torrens System - A way of resolving conflicts over land ownership. Only certain states require brokers to work using the Torrens System.

Total expense ratio - It compares the money one owes each month to one's earnings with expenses and taxes subtracted.

Total inventory - Entire area of useable space at a property.

Total lender fees - Payment a lender requires for putting together a loan.

Total monthly housing costs - Monthly mortgage payments plus home-related insurance, real estate taxes, and any other monthly expenses of owning a home.

Townhouse - A dwelling — not a condominium — joined to others.

Township - A square containing 36 square miles used for government surveying.

Township lines - East-west survey lines separated by six miles, running parallel to the edge of a piece of land.

Township tiers - Land strips between township lines, given numbers showing how far south or north they are.

Tract - A unit of land part of a larger unit.

Tract house - Has a similar layout and style to surrounding homes.

Trade fixture - A possession affixed to a commercial property that one can detach when the rental contract ends.

Transfer tax - Taken by state or federal officials when real estate changes hands.

Treasury Index - An index used as a basis for changing interest rates on adjustable-rate mortgages.

Treble damages - Damages tripled from their original amount by legal processes allowed in particular states.

Trespass - To take or come onto land illegally.

Triple net lease ("NN") - A lease that requires the renter to pay taxes, insurance, and utilities in addition to rent.

Triplex - A building containing three dwellings.

Truss - A frame supporting a roof with widely spaced beams.

Trust account - The same as an escrow account in certain states. It contains all the money that is collected and held for specific uses.

Trust deed (deed of trust) - A legal arrangement entrusting a title to a lender, who can sell the property if the borrower fails to repay the loan.

Truth in Lending Act - A U.S. government law stating that lenders must provide documents to borrowers that honestly describe the details of a mortgage.

Turnkey project - A building project entirely completed by someone other than the owner; a purchased property that is already fully furnished and ready to use.

Turnover - The rate at which properties sell or tenants leave their rental homes in a community.

U

Under contract - A commitment to carry out a transaction with a specified buyer.

Under-floor ducts - Passages for phone and electricity wires beneath a floor, allowing businesses or offices choices of how to arrange devices using these lines.

Underground storage tank - A tank that holds water, gasoline, unwanted substances, or other liquids underground.

Under-improvement - A construction that does not make

full use of the property where it is located.

Undersigned - One whose name appears at the end of a document he signed.

Underwriting - The determination by a lender of the terms and conditions to set on loans, based on the risks each borrower presents.

Underwriting fee - A fee that covers the expenses mortgage lenders pay to validate borrowers' personal information and evaluate eligibility for a loan.

Undisclosed agency - A transaction in which one real estate agent represents both parties in a transaction and does not reveal the double allegiance. (This is only allowed in certain states.)

Undivided interest - An arrangement in which ownership of a property is shared equally by several owners who cannot act independently.

Unencumbered - Free from anything that makes a property less useful or enjoyable, such as legal claims.

Unenforceable contract - A contract that is unsigned or is otherwise useless for starting a lawsuit.

Unfair and deceptive practices - Intentional lies, misleading statements, and other harmful or unethical acts.

Uniform Building Code (UBC) - A code that provides national building standards, used widely in the western U.S.

Uniform Commercial Code (UCC) - Set of legal rules about commerce that standardizes financial transactions, such as fulfilling warranties, doing business, selling property or entire businesses, and loaning money, between states. (Every state except Louisiana uses a version of UCC.)

Uniform Residential Appraisal Report (URAR) - A form used for presenting appraisal results for a building, which can be crucial for purchasing secondary mortgages.

Uniform Settlement Statement - A legal document given to the buyer and seller in transactions involving federal loans, showing the amounts both parties will pay in closing their deal.

Unmarketable title - A seriously flawed title.

Unrecorded deed - Undocumented transfer of property ownership.

Unsecured loan - A loan based on a borrower's good credit, not any collateral property.

Upgrades - Improvements or alterations made before a sale's closing date and paid for by the buyer.

Upside down - A nickname for the situation where a borrower owes more on a mortgage than his property is worth.

Up-zoning - Re-classifying property as having higher usage than it was considered to have before.

Urban renewal (slum clearance) - The demolition of dilapidated city buildings and construction of new ones in an urban area.

Urban sprawl - Development spreading out from a city; it is sparser than the urban center and it can house people who work in the city.

Usable square footage - All the area within a tenant's living unit.

Use tax - A tax taken from those who import or buy tangible possessions.

Useful life - The period before a building depreciates or stops making money.

Usury - The charging of illegally high interest payments for a loan.

Utility easement - A legal arrangement that allows water, sewage, electric, or other utility lines to pass through someone's property.

V

VA loan - A loan made through a lender authorized by the Department of Veterans Affairs.

Vacancy factor - The percentage of future gross income expected to be lost because living spaces remain empty.

Vacancy rate - The proportion of total rental spaces that is vacant.

Valid contract - A contract that can be legally enforced because it has all the necessary parts of a working contract.

Valuable consideration - A contract clause that allows someone receiving a promise to make claims on the money or time of a person who does not fulfill their pledge.

Value-added - The value a property is expected to gain after improvement or repair.

Variable payment plan - A schedule for repaying a mortgage with varying monthly payments.

Variable rate - *See "adjustable-rate mortgage."*

Variance - Like a special uses permit, variance allows someone to improve or use property in ways the current zoning rules forbid.

Vendor's lien - A claim on land held by the seller until the buyer has fully paid for the property.

Veneer - A layer of brick, wood, or other material covering or hiding a less desirable surface.

Verification - A clause in a legal document in which parties swear their contract or other document contains no lies. Verification requires a qualified witness.

Verification of deposit (VOD) - A statement of a borrower's account history and current status, given by banks.

Verification of employment (VOE) - A document, signed by an employer, confirming that a loan recipient works at a given job.

Vestibule - An entryway opening onto a larger room.

Villa - A living unit having one story, a yard, and parking spots. Villas can be grouped in twos and fours or can form condominiums.

Visual rights - The right to preserve pleasing views, keeping them free of large signs or other obstructions.

Voluntary lien - A claim on a piece of real estate the owner allows and recognizes.

W

Wainscoting - A surface along the bottom of an inner wall.

Walkthrough - A visit to a home by the buyer just before closing the deal to make sure the property is unoccupied and free from unexpected defects.

Walk-up - A multiple-story apartment complex where people must use the stairs for lack of an elevator.

Warehouse fee - A fee, paid at closing, charged by a lender for keeping a borrower's mortgage before selling it to secondary buyers.

Warranty deed - Guarantees the person giving the deed will guard the recipient against all possible claims.

Waste line - A pipeline that drains the water from sinks, showers, and other plumbing fixtures besides toilets.

Water rights - Legal rights defining how people living on bodies of water can and cannot use nearby water sources.

Water table - The higher levels where water rests in the ground over a certain area.

Way - A passage for vehicles or pedestrians, such as an alley or street.

Wear and tear - Weathering of property from the elements, its age, or from people using it.

Weep hole - Small drains in walls for extra water.

Weighted average rental rate - A calculation that averages and compares the different rental rates of at least two buildings.

Wetland - Swamps, marshes, and other water-filled lands protected from development by environmental laws.

Will - A document that transfers property to another (the testator) when the will's creator dies.

Without recourse - A phrase meaning a borrower cannot appeal to a lender after failing to pay debts; the lender can take the property.

Work letter - A letter given to a tenant by a landlord detailing which improvements the landlord will take care of and which ones the tenant must handle.

Workers' Compensation Act - A law that requires employers to insure their employees against injuries at work.

Working drawings - Exact illustrations and details of how a construction project will progress.

Wraparound debt - A specific agreement by the lender and borrower in which the borrower uses money loaned by the mortgage lender to pay amounts owed on a mortgage. The loan used to pay mortgage debt "wraps around" the mortgage itself. A promissory note and mortgage document are needed to secure this type of loan.

Writ of execution - Allows real estate to be sold based on a court decision.

Write off - In accounting, this refers to money lost because it cannot be collected.

X

X - Can replace a signature of an illiterate person, if witnessed and affirmed by a notary.

X bracing - Bracing across a panel or divider.

Y

Year-to-year tenancy - Involves renting property one year at a time, also called periodic tenancy.

Yield - Money gained from an investment through interest and dividends.

Yield spread - The difference between two interest rates; as compensation, mortgage brokers get to keep the difference between the wholesale rate and the rate at which they lend to their borrowers.

Z

Zone condemnation - The clearing out of areas by knocking down structures, leaving space for new buildings.

Zoning - Division of cities or towns into areas meant for different kinds of buildings or uses, dictated by laws and local regulations.

Zoning ordinance - Laws and regulations specifying how people can use or build upon land in a certain zone.

Bibliography

Ashby, Delbert M. *Making Money Trading Mortgages*. 2004

Cowgill, Allen. *Untapped Funds, Hidden Wealth*. 2005.

Downing, Neil. *The New IRAs and How to Make Them Work for You*. Chicago, Illonis: Dearborn Trade Publishing, 2002.

Gallinelli, Frank. *What Every Real Estate Investor Needs to Know About Cash Flow--and 36 Other Key Financial Measures*. New York: McGraw-Hill, 2004.

Guttentag, Jack. *The Mortgage Encyclopedia: The Authoritative Guide to Mortgage Programs, Practices, Prices, and Pitfalls*. New York: McGraw-Hill, 2010.

Konipol, Don H. *Investing in High Yield Private Mortgage Notes and Trust Deeds*, 2003.

Konipol, Don H. *Real Estate Investors Guide to Private Mortgage Financing*, 2003.

Partain, Richard B. and Childers, Barbara. *Dictionary of Real Estate Lending Terms*. Bakersfield, California: PF Publications, 1989.

Partain, Richard B. *Real Estate Loan Brokerage: How to Become a Successful Mortgage Broker*. Bakersfield, California: PF Publications, 1994.

The Note Holder's Handbook. Avalon Finance, Inc., 2003.

U.S. Department of Treasury, Internal Revenue Service. *Publication 590: Individual Retirement Arrangements (IRAs)*. **www.irs.gov/pub/irs-pdf/p590.pdf**, 2009.

Author
Biography

Martha Maeda is an economic historian who writes on politics, ethics, and modern philosophy. After graduating from Northwestern University, she lived and worked in Australia, Japan, Latin America, and several African countries before settling in the United States. She has a special interest in microeconomics and the effects of globalization on the lives and businesses of people all over the world. She is the author of several books on personal finance, including *The Complete Guide to Investing in Exchange Traded Funds; The Complete Guide to Investing in Bonds and Bond Funds; How to Wipe Out Your Student Loans and be Debt Free Fast; The Complete Guide to IRAs and IRA Investing;* and *The Complete Guide to Spotting Accounting Fraud and Cover-ups.*

Teri Clark's interest in the new and different has led to a successful online writing career collaborating on nearly 100 books as an editor, researcher, ghostwriter, and author. The North Carolina resident, along with her husband, homeschools their four children. She can be reached at ghostwriting@gmail.com.

Matthew Stewart Tabacchi, originally from Pittsburgh, Pennsylvania, holds an associate's degree from Pittsburgh Institute of Aeronautics and maintains several mortgage licenses. These include a Mortgage Broker license (MB), a Mortgage Broker Business license (MBB), as well as three Mortgage Broker Business Branch licenses (MBBB). Mr. Tabacchi worked for companies such as Aabco Mortgage and Accredited Mortgage and now has an Allstate Mortgage firm that maintains a state lenders license and is based in Ocala, Florida. There are currently four Allstate mortgage offices serving central Florida. Mr. Tabacchi entered the mortgage business in 1992 and has mastered all the secrets of private mortgage lending. Today, the majority of the loans his firm underwrites are private investor-backed mortgages. Of the hundreds of private investors and thousands of private mortgage contracts Mr. Tabacchi's firm has managed and orchestrated over the years, no investor has ever lost a nickel. Allstate Mortgage is a full-service mortgage firm providing services to private investors and mortgage clients. They can provide full loan servicing for the private investor, enabling the process to be highly profitable and virtually effortless—with no risk. You can reach Matt at 352-351-0200 or 866-351-0200, and he will be happy to answer any questions you may have and help guide you into the highly profitable world of private mortgage investing.

Matthew Tabacchi

ALLSTATE MORTGAGE

809 NE 25th Avenue

Ocala, FL 34470

Phone: 352-351-0200

Fax: 352-351-4557

Web: **www.allstateocala.com**

E-mail: matt@allstateocala.com

Index

T

U

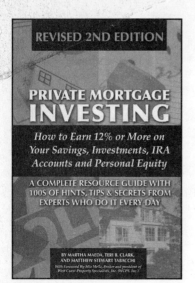

DID YOU BORROW THIS COPY?

Have you been borrowing a copy of *Private Mortgage Investing: How to Earn 12% or More on Your Savings, Investments, IRA Accounts, and Personal Equity REVISED 2nd EDITION* from a friend, colleague, or library? Wouldn't you like your own copy for quick and easy reference? To order, photocopy the form below and send to:

Atlantic Publishing Company
1405 SW 6th Avenue • Ocala, Florida 34471-0640